Final Cut Pro X Cookbook

Edit with style and ease using the latest editing technologies in Final Cut Pro X!

Jason Cox

BIRMINGHAM - MUMBAI

Final Cut Pro X Cookbook

First published: October 2012

Production Reference: 1250912

Published by Packt Publishing Ltd.
Livery Place
35 Livery Street
Birmingham B3 2PR, UK

ISBN 978-1-84969-296-0

www.packtpub.com

Cover Image by Artie Ng (artherng@yahoo.com.au)

Credits

Author
Jason Cox

Reviewers
Tyler Knowles

David J. Smolar

Acquisition Editor
Wilson D'souza

Lead Technical Editor
Arun Nadar

Technical Editors
Prasanna Joglekar

Devdutt Kulkarni

Project Coordinator
Yashodhan Dere

Proofreaders
Aaron Nash

Maria Gould

Indexer
Monica Ajmera

Production Coordinator
Prachali Bhiwandkar

Cover Work
Prachali Bhiwandkar

About the Author

Jason Cox has enjoyed capturing images since receiving his first Mickey-Matic film camera when he was four years old. Growing up in the Washington, D.C. area, he spent much of his youth wandering around with some form of a camera, still or video, in hand.

Jason graduated from Penn State with degrees in film production and English. After spending a couple of years as an entertainment journalist for a newspaper, Jason returned to D.C. to strike out on his own, eventually starting up his own L.L.C., *Some Might Say Media*. He currently juggles a mixed workload of freelance video production and editing, as well as teaching courses as a certified trainer for both Apple and Adobe software.

Outside of his working life, Jason enjoys traveling (he met his Scottish wife in New Zealand—long story!), playing old school Nintendo games, going to music and cultural events, and drinking chocolate milk.

Thanks to Luisa, Sean, Anthony, Katie, and the other certified trainers who have given me the support and inspiration to propel myself forward in the last couple of years.

And, of course, a huge thanks to my beautiful, amazing wife, Vikki, who spent months putting up with my constant reassurances of "I promise I'll have more time when the book is done!"

About the Reviewers

Tyler Knowles is a certified Final Cut Pro editor as well as an Apple certified trainer and technician. Tyler has over a dozen years of experience in digital video production and post-production. In six years as a professional living in Los Angeles, Tyler's editing work has been lent to five feature films, a children's television series, National commercial spots, music videos, student shorts, and numerous productions around California. Tyler is also noted as a Cinematographer, Sound Designer, Producer, and Director. Recently, Tyler directed an 87-minute mockumentary road trip movie about two guys hauling a horse trailer full of beer across the United States entitled *Go West Happy Cow*.

I'd like to thank my parents, Jack and Ellyn, for encouraging me to follow my dream of making movies.

David J. Smolar is an Apple-certified Final Cut Pro Editor and award-winning Producer with over 20 years' experience in digital media production, broadcasting, and production management. He has a B.A. from the University of Maryland and an M.A. in Digital Visual Media from American University. As a graduate student, David designed, opened, and managed American University's School of Communications' first Digital Video Editing Lab. He mastered his instructing skills by teaching nearly 50 undergraduate and graduate students Final Cut Pro. David's M.A. thesis documentary was the first in the school's history to be shot, edited, and output entirely in the digital realm.

David's early career began as an Engineer, Producer, and Assistant Editor for all-news WTOP while writing and reporting traffic and weather for Shadow Broadcasting. He spent over four years with Discovery Communications where, among other things, he supported executive producers on over 100 hours of programming, including the very popular series *I Shouldn't Be Alive*, *A Haunting*, and the history-making series of programs on the first tomb discovered in Egypt's Valley of the Kings since King Tut was unearthed. He supported, reviewed, and vetted programs for the Discovery, Science, Military, Times ID, and Discovery en Español channels.

Working for esteemed studios and from his home post-production studio, David crafted DVDs for industrial and government clients, wrote and produced a number of live musical performances, and trained non-technical clients in both Final Cut Studio and switching from a PC to a Mac. A member of AFTRA and the Screen Actors Guild, David appeared in the HBO series *The Wire* and *VEEP* along with a smattering of major studio films. In 2012, David designed the curriculum and lead classes for the DC-area MVI Media Academy, teaching anyone from any background everything about moviemaking. In May, he began work as a Quality Control Analyst for the new Verizon Digital Media Services group, helping create and maintain a fully-automated mass transform farm for major broadcasters, Hollywood studios, hotel chains, and international news conglomerates.

www.PacktPub.com

Support files, eBooks, discount offers and more

You might want to visit www.PacktPub.com for support files and downloads related to your book.

Did you know that Packt offers eBook versions of every book published, with PDF and ePub files available? You can upgrade to the eBook version at www.PacktPub.com and as a print book customer, you are entitled to a discount on the eBook copy. Get in touch with us at service@packtpub.com for more details.

At www.PacktPub.com, you can also read a collection of free technical articles, sign up for a range of free newsletters and receive exclusive discounts and offers on Packt books and eBooks.

http://PacktLib.PacktPub.com

Do you need instant solutions to your IT questions? PacktLib is Packt's online digital book library. Here, you can access, read and search across Packt's entire library of books.

Why Subscribe?

- ▶ Fully searchable across every book published by Packt
- ▶ Copy and paste, print and bookmark content
- ▶ On demand and accessible via web browser

Free Access for Packt account holders

If you have an account with Packt at www.PacktPub.com, you can use this to access PacktLib today and view nine entirely free books. Simply use your login credentials for immediate access.

Table of Contents

Preface   1

Chapter 1: Importing Your Media   5
  Introduction   5
  Importing from a tapeless video camera   6
  Importing MTS, M2TS, and M2T files   10
  Importing DSLR video   12
  Importing music from iTunes and GarageBand   14
  Importing still images   16
  Importing data from a tape-based camera   19
  Importing and working with layered Photoshop files   21
  Importing iMovie projects   24
  Importing Final Cut Pro 7 projects   26
  Working with your already organized media   31
  Relinking media files   33

Chapter 2: Customizing Your Workflow   37
  Introduction   38
  Getting acquainted with the Final Cut Pro X interface   38
  Customizing the keyboard   40
  Adding keywords to your clips   42
  Marking clips as favorites and rejected   45
  Creating a Smart Collection   49
  Working with a second computer monitor   52
  Working with a broadcast safe monitor   55
  Customizing the Event Library and Event Browser   57
  Batch changing clip names and other metadata   60
  Editing efficiently with optimized and proxy clips   64

Chapter 3: Basic Editing Mechanics   69

Introduction   69
Appending, inserting, and overwriting clips to a storyline   70
Working with (and without) the Magnetic Timeline   74
Creating connected clips   77
Replacing a clip   79
Splicing clips with the Blade tool   83
Using the Trim tool, part 1 – trimming and rippling   86
Using the Trim tool, part 2 – rolling   91
Using the Trim tool, part 3 – slipping and sliding   94
Creating and working with gap clips   101

Chapter 4: Enhancing Your Editing   105

Introduction   105
Making a three-point edit   106
Creating additional storylines   109
Trimming audio and video separately with a split edit
(also known as making a J or L cut)   112
Grouping clips together as a compound clip   114
Adding markers and to do items   118
Auditioning multiple shots or takes   120
Editing in beat to the music   123
Using the Precision Editor   127
Multicam part 1 – getting your media synced and prepped   131
Multicam part 2 – making the live cut   135
Multicam part 3 – fine-tuning your multicam edit   137

Chapter 5: Sweetening and Fixing Your Sound   141

Introduction   141
Reading and understanding the audio meters   142
Lowering your music during speakers   145
Lowering a loud, unexpected background sound with manual keyframes   148
Replacing bad audio with a cleaner recording   151
Sound effects, part 1 – browsing, connecting and panning   154
Sound effects, part 2 – animating with keyframes   157
Sound effects, part 3 – working in a surround sound space   160
Removing unwanted audio channels   165
Unlinking audio from video   166
Using FCPX's auto audio enhancements   169
Recording a voiceover   171

Chapter 6: Practical Magic a.k.a Useful Effects   175
Introduction   175
Adding an effect and changing its parameters   176
Animating parameters of an effect over time with keyframes   179
Adding a watermark or logo to your video   182
Downloading and installing more effects   186
Blurring out a face or logo   190
Disguising a voice   193
Copying and pasting effects onto multiple clips   194
Going green (screen) part 1 – the basics   196
Going green (screen) part 2 – improving your key   197
Going green (screen) addendum – using the mask effect
to cut out unwanted parts of an image   202

Chapter 7: Titles, Transitions, and Generators   205
Introduction   205
Adding transitions to clips   206
Adjusting the transition's parameters in the Viewer,
Inspector, and timeline   210
Creating counters and countdowns   214
Adding a timecode overlay   217
Inserting a placeholder clip   220
Creating a text style template   223
Creating a credit sequence   227
Creating a video-in-text effect   231
Creating a custom animated title   234
Creating and reusing show intro   237

Chapter 8: Get Your Movie to Move   243
Introduction   243
Making freeze frames and speed changes   244
Creating speed ramps   251
Showing an instant replay   254
Using the Transform tool   257
Cropping or trimming a clip   262
Panning and zooming over a photo or clip with the Ken Burns effect   267
Creating a video wall   271
Making your image move by keyframing in the Viewer   277
Moving clips in sync with compound clips   280
Changing keyframe timing in the timeline   285
Customizing motion paths with Bezier handles and modifying interpolation   287

Chapter 9: Altering the Aesthetics of Your Image   293

Introduction	293
Stabilizing a shaky shot	294
Automatically balancing color and/or match color to another shot	296
Manually color balancing with the Color Board	301
Picking a color look or creating your own	306
Fixing the exposure and adjusting the contrast with help from the Luma waveform monitor	311
Adding secondary color corrections, part 1 – shape masks	317
Adding secondary color corrections, part 2 – color masks	321
Adding secondary color corrections, part 3 – combining color and shape masks	325
Keeping only one color in your image	328
Spotlighting an object or text	333

Chapter 10: Getting Your Project Out of FCPX   339

Introduction	339
Exporting an archive-quality version of your film	340
Exporting for Apple devices and computers	343
Sharing your video on YouTube and other video sharing sites	347
Burning a Blu-ray or DVD	350
Roles, part 1 – labeling clips with Roles	354
Roles, part 2 – exporting selected Roles	359
Sharing large files over the web with Dropbox	363
Sharing your project with other applications using XML	367
Duplicating or moving projects from one drive to another	373
Archiving a project for possible future editing	376
Conclusion	379

Appendix: Working with Motion and Compressor   381

Introduction	381
Getting acquainted with the Motion interface	382
Enhancing title templates with Motion	385
Creating a custom Lower Third	392
Publishing a template to FCPX	400
Publishing parameters to a template	402
Getting acquainted with the Compressor interface	406
Adding chapter markers in Compressor	409
Burning a Blu-ray or DVD with chapter markers	412
Creating your own Compression preset	417
Creating a droplet based on a preset	421

Index   427

Preface

As technology becomes more and more accessible and easier to use, we are expected to do more in less time than ever before. Video editors are now expected to be able to not only edit, but create motion graphics, fix sound issues, enhance image quality and color, and more. And many workers in the PR and marketing world are finding the need to know how to get viral videos made from start to finish, as quickly as possible. Final Cut Pro X was built as a one-stop shop, with all the tools needed to produce a professional video from beginning to end.

Released in June 2011, FCPX's life got off to a bumpy start as many professionals were taken by surprise by Apple's dramatic shift in the user interface and feature set from Final Cut Pro 7. Some of these claims were merely a knee-jerk reaction and some were genuinely valid. At first glance, the interface resembled Final Cut's baby sibling, iMovie, leading to assumptions that Final Cut had been dumbed down. While the interface does indeed resemble iMovie, we must keep in mind that iMovie's current interface was designed in 2007 whereas Final Cut's interface was designed in the late 90s. So the reality of it is, on the surface, iMovie did have a superior, more modern interface to Final Cut's dated one.

As for the feature set, what pro features FCPX lacked when it was first released were quickly added via free software updates over the course of the next year. What started off as a bumpy ride has since smoothed out to a solid path and choice for both amateur and professional video editors. And with massive and extensive plug-in support found on Internet, FCPX's feature set continues to grow on nearly a daily basis. This isn't Final Cut Pro 8. This is a whole new generation of editing.

What this book covers

Chapter 1, Importing Your Media, focuses on making FCPX work for you the way you want it to, with advanced organizational tips as well as how to customize the interface.

Chapter 2, Customizing Your Workflow, focuses on getting your media ready for use in FCPX and provides tips on staying organized along the way.

Chapter 3, Basic Editing Mechanics, takes you through some of the fundamental editing tools, to get your video from a vision in your brain to a rough cut form as quickly as possible.

Chapter 4, Enhancing Your Editing, raises the bar a bit by introducing more advanced tools and techniques to accomplish more specialized tasks, such as editing music, creating a multicam edit, and more.

Chapter 5, Sweetening and Fixing Your Sound, teaches you how to read your audio meters and balance your audio, as well as recording voiceovers while working with surround sound, and more.

Chapter 6, Practical Magic: Also Known As Useful Effects, demonstrates some of the most useful and practical effects found in the Effects Browser, and how to install more and accomplish a green screen project.

Chapter 7, Titles, Transitions, and Generators, explores its namesake by revealing some of the deeper, hidden features to seemingly simple extras, which you can add to your project.

Chapter 8, Get Your Movie to Move, will teach users how to play with timing in FCPX, as well as how to animate your media on the screen with keyframes.

Chapter 9, Altering the Aesthetics of Your Image, introduces core color correction and grading concepts with FCPX's all-new Color Board, as well as how to isolate color changes using shape and color masks.

Chapter 10, Getting Your Project Out of FCPX, offers a plethora of options on what to do with your project once you've wrapped up the editing process, including burning optical media, uploading to social media sites, and archival tips and tricks.

Appendix, Working with Motion and Compressor, introduces you to Motion and Compressor interfaces, and also shows you how to publish templates to FCPX and get chapter markers to work for you.

What you need for this book

Honestly, you don't need much to get started with this cookbook. Hopefully, you've got some video files to work with; otherwise, why would you have purchased a video editing program in the first place? If you haven't imported any of your video from your camera yet, don't worry; the book covers that as well! It also wouldn't hurt to have a few photos and songs lying around your computer.

If you want to learn the basics of FCPX's companion programs, Motion and Compressor (which was covered in this book's Appendix), you can purchase both from the Mac App Store for $49.99 each.

Who this book is for

This book is for video editing enthusiasts looking to take their skills to the next level, and for Final Cut Pro 7 users who are ready to make the switch to a whole new editing paradigm. While the book is by no means highly advanced, it makes certain assumptions of your having a basic grasp on core video editing concepts and a familiarity with the Mac OS X environment.

Conventions

In this book, you will find a number of styles of text that distinguish between different kinds of information. Here are some examples of these styles, and an explanation of their meaning.

File types in text are shown as follows: " Deep inside you're likely to find files with the extension .mts, .m2ts, or .m2t (on some HDV cameras).."

New terms and **important words** are shown in bold. Words that you see on the screen, in menus or dialog boxes for example, appear in the text like this: "clicking on the **Next** button moves you to the next screen".

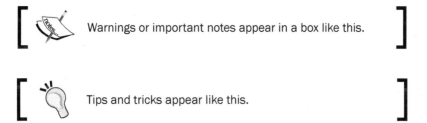

Warnings or important notes appear in a box like this.

Tips and tricks appear like this.

Reader feedback

Feedback from our readers is always welcome. Let us know what you think about this book—what you liked or may have disliked. Reader feedback is important for us to develop titles that you really get the most out of.

To send us general feedback, simply send an e-mail to feedback@packtpub.com, and mention the book title via the subject of your message.

If there is a topic that you have expertise in and you are interested in either writing or contributing to a book, see our author guide on www.packtpub.com/authors.

Customer support

Now that you are the proud owner of a Packt book, we have a number of things to help you to get the most from your purchase.

Downloading the color images of this book

We also provide you a PDF file that has color images of the screenshots used in this book. The color images will help you better understand the changes in the output. You can download this file from http://www.packtpub.com/sites/default/files/downloads/2960OT_Images.pdf.

Errata

Although we have taken every care to ensure the accuracy of our content, mistakes do happen. If you find a mistake in one of our books—maybe a mistake in the text or the code—we would be grateful if you would report this to us. By doing so, you can save other readers from frustration and help us improve subsequent versions of this book. If you find any errata, please report them by visiting http://www.packtpub.com/support, selecting your book, clicking on the **errata submission form** link, and entering the details of your errata. Once your errata are verified, your submission will be accepted and the errata will be uploaded on our website, or added to any list of existing errata, under the Errata section of that title. Any existing errata can be viewed by selecting your title from http://www.packtpub.com/support.

Piracy

Piracy of copyright material on the Internet is an ongoing problem across all media. At Packt, we take the protection of our copyright and licenses very seriously. If you come across any illegal copies of our works, in any form, on the Internet, please provide us with the location address or website name immediately so that we can pursue a remedy.

Please contact us at copyright@packtpub.com with a link to the suspected pirated material.

We appreciate your help in protecting our authors, and our ability to bring you valuable content.

Questions

You can contact us at questions@packtpub.com if you are having a problem with any aspect of the book, and we will do our best to address it.

1
Importing Your Media

In this chapter, we will cover:

- ▶ Importing from a tapeless video camera
- ▶ Importing MTS, M2TS, and M2T files
- ▶ Importing DSLR video
- ▶ Importing music from iTunes and GarageBand
- ▶ Importing still images
- ▶ Importing from a tape-based camera
- ▶ Importing and working with layered Photoshop files
- ▶ Importing iMovie projects
- ▶ Importing Final Cut Pro 7 projects
- ▶ Working with your already organized media
- ▶ Relinking media files

Introduction

Most artists have it easy—a painter grabs a brush, some paint and goes straight for the canvas. A writer grabs a pen and paper (or keyboard) and starts writing. A graphic artist grabs a tablet and starts drawing. If only it were that easy for video editors!

Well before an editor can start doing any actual work, we've got to spend a good amount of time getting organized and importing our media. The act of **importing** is simply the process of bringing our media inside FCPX and making the program aware of its existence. It's very similar to dragging a song file into iTunes—the song file already existed in some capacity, but by dropping it into iTunes, we're making iTunes aware that it exists. The same goes for FCPX in most cases.

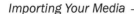

Unlike the digital music world, however, which only has a small handful of file formats, the digital video world has dozens, and the process for importing these different media types can vary greatly. And, to top it all off, we have many options to consider as to how we want FCPX to process and handle that media as it is imported!

FCPX can import many kinds of media, but there are many factors that must be considered before doing so to determine the best workflow for a project, and where there's a will there's a way—even if FCPX can't immediately import certain file types or projects from other programs, this chapter will help explain workarounds to do the impossible!

Importing from a tapeless video camera

Chances are, if you've bought a video camera in the last few years, it doesn't record to tape; it records to some form of tapeless media. In most consumer and prosumer cameras, this is typically an SD card, but could also be an internal drive, other various solid-state memory cards, or the thankfully short-lived trend of recordable mini DVDs. In the professional world, examples include Compact Flash, P2 cards (usually found in Panasonic models), SxS cards (many Sony and JVC models, Arri Alexa), or some other form of internal flash storage.

How to do it...

1. Plug your camera in to your Mac's USB port, or if you're using a higher-end setup with a capture box, plug the box into likely your FireWire or Thunderbolt box. If your camera uses an SD card as its storage medium, you can also simply stick the SD card into your Mac's card reader or external reader. If you are plugging the camera directly in, turn it on, and set it to the device's playback mode. If FCPX is running, it should automatically launch the **Import from Camera** window. If it does not, click on the **Import from Camera** icon in the left of the toolbar. You will see thumbnails of all of your camera's clips. You can easily scrub through them simply by passing your mouse over each one.

2. You can import clips one at a time by selecting a range and then clicking on **Import Selected...** or you can simply highlight them all and click on **Import All...** . To select a range, simply move your mouse over a clip until you find the point where you want to start and hit *I* on your keyboard. Then scrub ahead until you reach where you want the clip to end and hit *O*.

3. Whether you chose to select one, a few, or all your clips, once you click on the **Import** button you will arrive at the **Import options** screen. Choose what event you want your clips to live in, choose if you want to transcode the clips, and select any analyses you want FCPX to perform on the clips as it imports them. Click on **Import**. FCPX begins the import process. You can close the window and begin editing immediately!

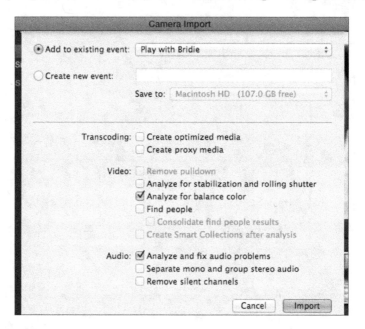

How it works...

The reason you can edit so quickly, even if you're importing a massive amount of footage, is thanks to some clever programming on Apple's part. While it might take a few minutes or even longer to import all the media off of your camera or memory card, FCPX will access the media directly on the original storage device, until it has finished its import process, and then switch over to the newly imported versions.

There's more...

Creating a camera archive

Creating a camera archive is the simplest and best way to make a backup of your raw footage. Tapeless cameras often store their media in really weird-looking ways with complex folder structures. In many cases, FCPX needs that exact folder structure in order to easily import the media.

A **camera archive** essentially takes a snapshot or image of your camera's currently stored media and saves it to one simple file that you can access in FCPX over and over again. This of course also frees you to delete the contents of the memory card or media drive and reuse it for another shoot.

In the **Camera Import** window, make sure your camera is selected in the left column and click on the **Create Archive** button in the bottom left corner. The resulting window will let you name the archive and pick a destination drive. Obviously, store your archive on an external drive if it's for backup purposes. If you were to keep it on the same drive as your FCPX system and the drive fails, you'd lose your backup as well!

The process creates a proprietary disk image with the original file structure of the memory card. FCPX needs the original file structure (not just the video files) in order to properly capture from the card. By default, it stores the archive in a folder called `Final Cut Camera Archives` on whatever drive you selected.

Later when you need to reimport from a camera archive, simply open the **Camera Import** window again, and if you don't see your needed archive under **Camera Archives** on the left, click on **Open Archive...** and find it in the resulting window.

To import all or not to import all

If you've got the time, there's nothing to stop you from looking at each and every clip one at a time in the **Import from Camera** window, selecting a range, and then importing that one clip. However, that's going to take you a while as you'll have to deal with the settings window every time you click on the **Import** button. If you've got the storage space (and most of us do today), just import everything and worry about weeding out the trash later.

But what about XYZ format?

There are two web pages you should bookmark to keep up to date.

One is `www.apple.com/finalcutpro/specs/`. This web page lists most of the formats FCPX can work with. Expect this list to grow with future versions.

The second site is `help.apple.com/finalcutpro/cameras/en/index.html`. This web site lets you search camera models for compatibility with FCPX.

Just because a format isn't listed on Apple's specs page, doesn't mean it's impossible to work with. Many camera manufacturers release plugins which enhance a program's capabilities. One great example is Canon (`www.canon.com`), who released a plugin for FCPX allowing users to import MXF files from a wide variety of their cameras.

Importing MTS, M2TS, and M2T files

If you've ever browsed the file structure of a memory card pulled from an AVCHD camera, you'll have seen a somewhat complex system of files and folders and almost nothing resembling a normal video file. Deep inside you're likely to find files with the extension .mts, .m2ts, or .m2t (on some HDV cameras). By themselves, these files are sitting ducks, unable to be read by most basic video playback software or imported directly by FCPX. But somehow, once you open up the **Import from Camera** window in FCPX, FCPX is able to translate all that apparent gobbledygook from the memory card into movie files. FCPX needs that gobbledygook to import the footage. But what if someone has given you a hard drive full of nothing but these standalone files? You'll need to convert or rewrap (explained in the following section) the clips before heading in to FCPX.

Getting ready

There are a number of programs out there that can tackle this task, but a highly recommended one is ClipWrap (http://www.divergentmedia.com/clipwrap). There is a trial, but you'll probably want to go ahead and buy the full version.

How to do it...

1. Open ClipWrap. Drag-and-drop your video files (ending in .mts, .m2ts, or .m2t) into the main interface.

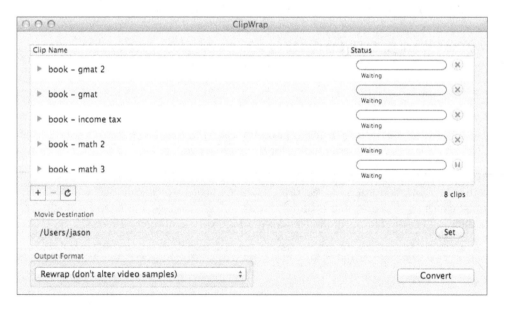

2. Set a destination for your new files under **Movie Destination**.

3. Click on the drop-down menu titled **Output Format**. You can choose to convert the files to a number of formats including ProRes 422 (the same format that is created when you select the **Create optimized media** option in FCPX). A faster, space-saving option, however, is to leave the default setting, **Rewrap (don't alter video samples)**:

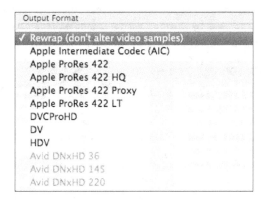

4. Click on **Convert**. When the process is done, you will have new video files that end in .mov and can be directly imported into FCPX via **File | Import | Files**.

How it works...

In the previous exercise, we chose not to transcode/convert the video files into another format. What we did was take the video and audio stream out of one container (.mts, .m2ts, or .m2t) and put it into another (QuickTime, seen as .mov). It may sound crazy at first, but we basically took the birthday present (the video and audio) out of an ugly gift box that FCPX won't even open and put it into a prettier one that FCPX likes.

There's more...

Other alternatives

ClipWrap is far from the only solution out there, but it is definitely one of the best. The appendix of this book covers the basics of Compressor, Apple's compression software which can't convert raw AVCHD files in most cases, but can convert just about any file that QuickTime can play. The software company, iSkySoft, (www.iskysoft.com) makes a large number of video conversion tools for a reasonable price. If you're looking for a fully featured video encoding software package, look no further than Telestream Episode (www.telestream.net) or Sorenson Squeeze (www.sorensonmedia.com). These two applications are expensive, but can take just about any video file format out there and transcode it to almost anything else, with a wide variety of customizable settings.

Rewrapping or transcoding

As mentioned in step 3 in the previous section, we could have chosen to transcode to ProRes 422 instead of rewrapping. This is a totally fine option, just know the differences: transcoding, takes much longer, it takes up much more file space, but on the plus side, it is Final Cut Pro X's favorite format (because it's native to FCPX, made by Apple for Apple) and you may save time in the actual editing process by working with a faster more efficient codec once inside FCPX. If you chose to rewrap, you still have the option to transcode when you import into FCPX.

Importing DSLR video

With each passing day, more and more advanced enthusiasts, prosumers, and even some professionals are turning toward **digital single-lens reflex** (**DSLR**) still cameras for their video-making needs. DSLRs offer a few unique features at a reasonable price range that typically cost thousands more in dedicated video cameras. Two of these most prominent features include interchangeable lenses, as well as much greater control over depth-of-field than most low-to-mid-range video cameras offer. DSLR video does come with its own set of drawbacks, however. Many models offer vastly inferior on-board microphones, limited non-stop recording time, and little to no stabilization options. If you go the DSLR route, FCPX is perfectly suited to work with your camera's media as the majority of DSLRs create ready-to-edit H.264 files. And as your DSLR is NOT an actual video camera, we bypass the **Import from Camera** window entirely!

How to do it...

1. Connect your DSLR to your Mac via USB or simply insert the camera's card into a memory card reader.

2. Select **File | Import | Files...** .

3. Locate your storage device for your camera's media, likely located in the **DEVICES** list in the left side column of the **Import Files** window.

4. Once selected, find the folder with the media. This is usually a folder labeled **DCIM**. Select your following import settings to your liking and click on **Import**:

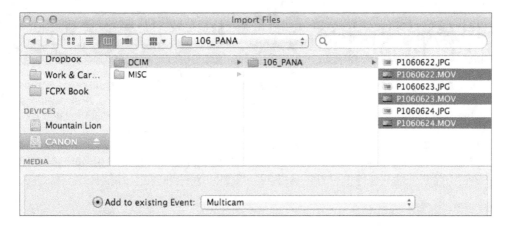

How it works...

As you can see, the process is very straightforward, and even easier than importing from a regular video camera! The part that often confuses new FCPX users is why we don't go to the **Import from Camera** window. A DSLR is a camera, right? Well, the **Import from Camera** window is strictly used for dedicated video cameras. A DSLR is a still camera that happens to also be able to record video. The individual files it creates (H.264) are immediately ready for import into FCPX and do not require being processed/transcoded.

There's more...

Transcoding H.264

As always, when you import files into FCPX, you have the option of transcoding. If H.264 is readily accepted by FCPX, why transcode to ProRes? Well, while H.264 is a space-efficient video codec, it's not particularly edit-friendly. It takes a lot more processing power to modify and render H.264 files as they are heavily compressed. If you're creating a very simple or short project with H.264 files that is simply a series of cuts with maybe a few transitions and a title or two, you're probably fine to save time and skip the transcoding process. However, if your project is going to become more involved with lots of extras, including effects and color correction, take the time to transcode upfront. You'll save yourself a lot of time in the editing process and your computer will thank you for not stressing it out!

See also

To better understand transcoding options in FCPX, read the *Creating optimized and proxy media* recipe.

Importing music from iTunes and GarageBand

A movie is nothing without its soundtrack. Can you imagine the plastic bag scene in American Beauty without Thomas Newman's haunting piano in the background? Or Luke Skywalker's epic lightsaber battle with Darth Vader in Return of the Jedi without John Williams' score?

Many of us have hundreds or thousands of tunes in our iTunes libraries today and a few of us, with the gift to craft music, probably have a number of projects in progress in GarageBand. Final Cut Pro X makes it simple to import either into your videos.

How to do it...

1. Click on the **Show/Hide Sound Browser** button on the right of the tool bar. The Sound Browser appears split into two sections. The first lists what sources we have to select from. GarageBand and iTunes should be listed:

2. Click on **iTunes**. Your entire music library appears in the bottom half of the window. You can narrow down the list by either clicking on the disclosure triangle to the left of the **iTunes** label and selecting a playlist, or by typing in the search box at the bottom of the browser window:

3. When you have found the song you want, you can click on the song title and drag it into your open project, dropping it wherever you choose. If you drag it to the end of a project, it will add it to the primary storyline. If you drag it below any clips along your timeline, it will connect itself to that clip as a **connected clip** (read more about the connected clip in the _Creating connected clips_ recipe).

4. Click on **GarageBand** in the Sound Browser. Just like clicking on **iTunes**, you will see a list of any **GarageBand** projects you have been working on. The only pre-requisite is that you have saved an `iLife Preview` of the file (you are prompted to do this when saving and closing a new **GarageBand** project for the first time). Just like with an iTunes track, click-and-drag the music file you want into your project.

How it works...

When you drag an audio file directly into a project, a duplicate of the file is added to the project's default event (set when you originally created the project). That means, even if you delete the song from iTunes or GarageBand, it will still work fine in your project. In addition, any compressed audio files you import from iTunes automatically get converted into uncompressed WAV files, which FCPX handles more smoothly than typically compressed MP3 and AAC files.

There's more...

Import now, use later

If your project hasn't really taken shape yet, but you know you want to import music from the Sound Browser to use later, you don't have to drag a song or sound effects directly into the timeline. Instead, simply click-and-drag them from the Sound Browser to the event of your choice in your **Event Library**. They will copy into the event and stay there until you are ready to use them. You can also apply keywords and make them favorites as well!

Tons of sound effects

If you haven't done so already, run your Mac's Software Update. A download titled **Final Cut Pro X Supplemental Content** should appear that will install more than 1,300 high-quality sound effects that can be accessed in the Sound Browser. Additionally, it will download extra presets for the Space Designer plugin, covered in the *Creating a surround sound space* recipe.

See also

Clicking and dragging is easy, but not always the fastest or most accurate way to add a file to a project's timeline. Read the *Creating connected clips, Appending, inserting, and overwriting clips to a storyline* recipes in *Chapter 3, Basic Editing Mechanics* to learn about the different types of edits in FCPX and how to use keyboard shortcuts to quickly add clips (both video and audio) to your timeline in different ways.

Importing still images

Making a movie isn't always about using moving images. There are plenty of instances where you need to use still images, whether for a slideshow, b-roll, documentary, or some other purpose.

How to do it...

1. With a project of your choosing open, click on the **Show/hide the Photos Browser** button in the toolbar, indicated by the camera icon:

2. The window, shown in the following screenshot, is broken down into two pieces. The top half shows what sources of photos you have to select from and the bottom half displays the photos in the source selection. Depending on what photo software you use, you may see **iPhoto**, **Aperture**, and/or **Photo Booth** listed in the source window. To easily dig deeper into the **iPhoto** or **Aperture** libraries (which are likely to have hundreds or even thousands of images), click on the disclosure triangle next to each to display a list of your albums, events, projects, and so on. You may also use the search box at the bottom of the window to narrow down your images:

3. Find the image you are seeking, and click-and-drag it into your project's timeline. If you drag it to the end of a project, it will add it to the primary storyline. If you drag it above any clips along your timeline, it will connect itself to that clip as a connected clip. In the following screenshot, the image was added as a connected clip over two other clips:

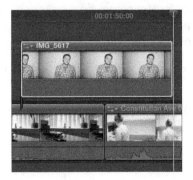

How it works...

When you drag an image file directly into a project, a duplicate of the file is added to the project's default event (set when you originally created the project). That means, even if you deleted the song from **iPhoto**, **Aperture**, or **Photo Booth**, it will still work fine in your project (assuming you have set FCPX to copy all imported media into **Events**).

There's more...

Import now, use later

If your project hasn't really taken shape yet, but you know you want to import photos from the Photos browser to use later, you don't have to drag a photo or photos directly into the timeline. Instead, simply click-and-drag them from the Photos browser to the event of your choosing. They will copy into the event in the Events browser and stay there until you are ready to use them. You can also apply keywords and make them favorites as well!

Selecting more than one image at once

If you were creating a slideshow, this would seem like a pretty painful process if you had to drag 117 images into your timeline! Luckily, you can easily drag two or more images into the project by one of two methods. Once you've selected an event or album in the Photos browser, you can do any of the following:

- ▶ Use the command key to select multiple images at once and drag them into your project
- ▶ If you simply want the entire event or album, click-and-drag the icon of the event/album itself into your project (or FCPX Event of your choosing) to add every item at once

Even if you're not going to use every image, sometimes this is a faster workflow so you can just easily delete the few images you don't want in your timeline as you go.

Importing images not in Apple photo software

Some Mac users don't use Apple's various photo offerings, which is fine. Perhaps your photos are simply residing in a series of folders somewhere on your computer. You can import images using the **File | Import** command and choose an event to place them in. You can even drag images directly from their folder in **Finder** into the FCPX interface and drop them on top of the event of your choice as well!

See also

So, what can you do with photos once you've got them imported? Try reading some of the recipes in the *Chapter 8, Get Your Movie to Move* such as *Panning and zooming over a photo or clip with the Ken Burns effect*, *Creating a video wall*, and *Cropping or trimming a clip*.

Clicking and dragging is easy, but not always the fastest or more accurate way to add a file to a project's timeline. Read the *Creating connected clips, Appending, inserting, and overwriting clips to a storyline* recipes in *Chapter 3, Basic Editing Mechanics* to learn about the different types of edits in FCPX and how to use keyboard shortcuts to quickly add clips (both video and audio) to your timeline in different ways.

Importing data from a tape-based camera

Today, it's hard to find a video camera in a store that still records to tape. The camera world has virtually completed its slow and painful transition from tape-based to tapeless media. However, for those of us who are clinging onto our old, yet trusted equipment, or who work in a professional environment that is forced to use their technology till the day it dies, we still need FCPX to be able to import from these cameras.

Luckily, FCPX can still import from most tape-based camera formats, including HDV, DV, DVCAM, DVCPRO, DVCPRO 50, and DVCPRO HD. However, support for the process has been severely deprecated. It's still an easy task, but there aren't nearly as many bells and whistles to import from tape as there used to be in FCP7.

How to do it...

1. Turn on your camera and set it to playback mode (this differs from camera to camera). Attach it via FireWire to your Mac or capture device.

2. If FCPX is open, it should automatically open the **Import from Camera** window. If not, click on the **Import From Camera** icon in the left of the toolbar:

3. Queue your tape to the point you want to import from either by using the camera's controls, or by using the *J*, *K*, and *L* keys on your keyboard to rewind, pause, or play, respectively. Click on **Import**:

4. In the next window, pick your settings such as what event you want the video saved to and if you want any analysis or transcoding done. When you're done, click on **Import** again.

5. FCPX begins importing right away. It will continue to do so until it either reaches the end of the tape, your disk fills up (don't let this happen!), or you click on **Stop Import**. Remember that tape-based capture happens in real time. If you have 57 minutes of footage, it will take 57 minutes to capture!

There's more...

If you're lucky...

Depending on your camera, FCPX may be able to detect starts and stops (when you click on Record and Pause) on your tape automatically. If it can, FCPX will split up your imported footage into individual clips!

If you run into problems, try a camera archive

Reports of tape capture problems in FCPX have been widely reported (such as dropped frames, missing video, and so on). As Apple pushes technology farther and faster, they tend to leave behind what they believe to be dying technologies (in this case, tape). Users who have run into various issues capturing from tape have also found better success by creating a camera archive of their footage first, then importing from that, rather than doing an immediate and direct import. Read the *Creating a camera archive* section for more info. When all else fails, try importing your footage into iMovie first, then import that project into FCPX!

Importing and working with layered Photoshop files

Importing a standard photograph or image file is a very straightforward process, covered in the *Importing a still image* recipe. But what about when you've created a complex Photoshop file with multiple layers? Luckily, it's just as easy to import .psd files into FCPX as any other media file, but FCPX has to handle such a file a bit differently in order to accommodate the multiple levels of a layered file.

Getting ready

Layering in Photoshop has been around for many, many years so you don't need any specific version of the program to create one of these files. In this exercise, we created a very simple layered file of a slightly overlapping red, green, and blue circle. You can create a similar file as well, or use your own creation. When you've created your layered image, simply save the file in the standard .psd format. Do not export it as a JPEG, TIFF, or any other image format or it will flatten your image!

You don't need to have Photoshop installed on your machine in order for FCPX to import and handle .psd files, so if a client sends you a .psd via email, you're still able to work with it in FCPX!

How to do it...

1. As always, highlight the Event you want to import the file into, and choose **File | Import | Files...**. Find your .psd file or files wherever they may be and choose **Import**.

2. The files appear in your event. In this case, we have imported two identical looking .psd files of a simple red, blue, and green circle. One file contains layers and the other was flattened. Note that the flattened .psd file appears with a standard image icon while the layered version has an icon indicating that the file has been turned into a compound clip:

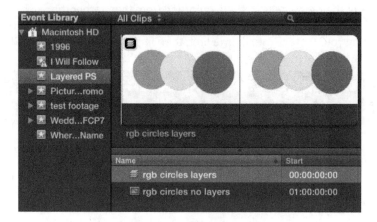

3. Edit the layered file/compound clip into a timeline of your choosing. In this case we will place it in an empty timeline. It still looks like one clip, but that's the trick to get compound clips—it appears as one, but secretly houses numerous media clips inside:

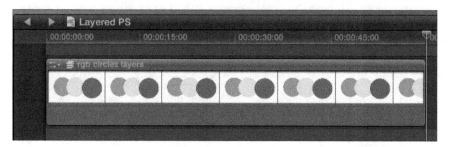

4. Double-click on the clip. Voila! We have loaded the compound clip into its own timeline and now see all the layers as individual clips stacked on top of one another. We can treat each layer as a regular clip and tweak it however we like!

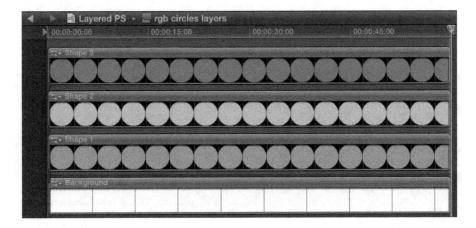

5. Let's make the red circle larger. Click on the red circle clip in the timeline. Then click on the **Transform** button under the Unified Viewer. Resizable corner handles appear on the red circle.

6. Click and hold on one of the blue corner handles and drag away from the circle. The circle will get larger:

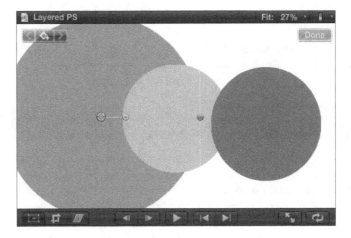

7. Maybe we want to delete a layer entirely. Click on the green circle clip in the timeline and hit *Delete*. The green circle disappears. Click on the back arrow **Timeline History** button to return to your main timeline:

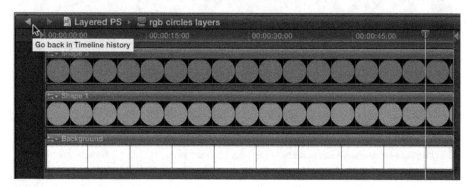

There's more...

Background layers

Unless you consciously deleted it or changed settings in Photoshop before saving, chances are your `.psd` file will have a white background. When you import it into FCPX, that white background will still be there, but luckily, it's just a layer and can be deleted easily.

See also

For more detail on the **Transform** tool mentioned in this recipe, read the *Using the Transform tool* recipe in the *Chapter 8, Get Your Movie to Move*. To learn more about compound clips, read the recipe Grouping clips together as a compound clip in *Chapter 4, Enhance Your Editing*.

Importing iMovie projects

We all have to get our feet wet somewhere when it comes to learning how to edit video, and rarely do people start right off the bat in something as grandiose as FCPX. Many of us get our hands dirty in a simpler program such as iMovie before making the leap into more professional editing. Even if you've got a bunch of projects sitting in iMovie, you can easily import them into FCPX to take advantage of its far wider range of features and capabilities. The process is incredibly easy, but there are a few things you should know about when going through the process.

Getting ready

All this requires is an active project in iMovie '11 or later:

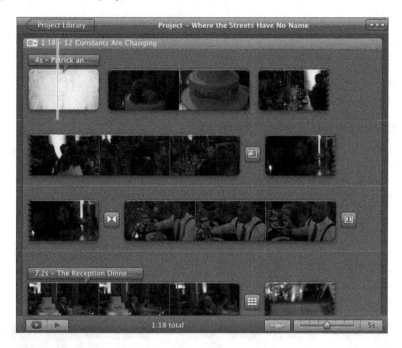

How to do it...

1. In FCPX, select **File | Import | iMovie Project**.

2. Select your iMovie project file and select **Import**.

3. FCPX will take a few moments to copy over the necessary media, creating both a new event and a new project. Double-click on the project and begin editing!

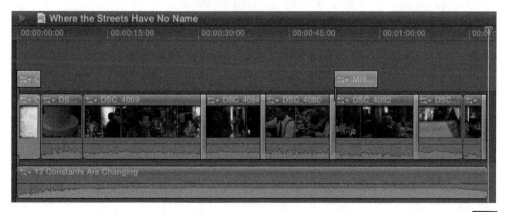

How it works...

The transition from iMovie to FCPX is very smooth. Not only are the interfaces very similar, but FCPX has every title, effect, and transition that iMovie possesses (and obviously many more). One of the only caveats is with the **Movie Trailers** feature of iMovie. These will not import into FCPX properly unless you go to **File | Convert to Project** in iMovie before you try and import the project into FCPX.

There's more...

Importing just your iMovie events

If you didn't have an active project you wanted to import from iMovie into FCPX, but simply wanted to take all of the media from your iMovie events, you can do this as well. In FCPX, just go to **File | Import | iMovie Event Library**. This will import every event you have in iMovie. It's an all or nothing deal!

Analyzing iMovie footage

Even if you have your preferences set to analyze all imported footage for people, stabilization, and so on, FCPX skips over this when importing iMovie projects. If you want to override this, you can have FCPX review your footage after the fact by selecting your clips, right-clicking, and choosing **Analyze and Fix....**

Importing Final Cut Pro 7 projects

One of the biggest complaints about FCPX when it was released, was that it had zero capability to import projects that had been created in Final Cut Pro 7. This obviously irked many long time FCP users who had vast amount of archived projects that would never be able to be opened unless they kept FCP7 on their machine. Apple chose not to directly rectify this problem, but thanks to the release of version 10.0.3 and its stronger XML capabilities, a company called Intelligent Assistance released **7toX for Final Cut Pro**. This program acts as a middleman to get your FCP7 project files converted for FCPX.

Getting ready

First off, you obviously must own Final Cut Pro 7 and have an active project to work with. Secondly, you must download 7toX for Final Cut Pro from the Mac App Store (Snow Leopard or above required). At the time of publishing, the application costs $9.99.

How to do it...

1. We start in Final Cut Pro 7. Make sure your browser window is active and nothing inside is currently selected:

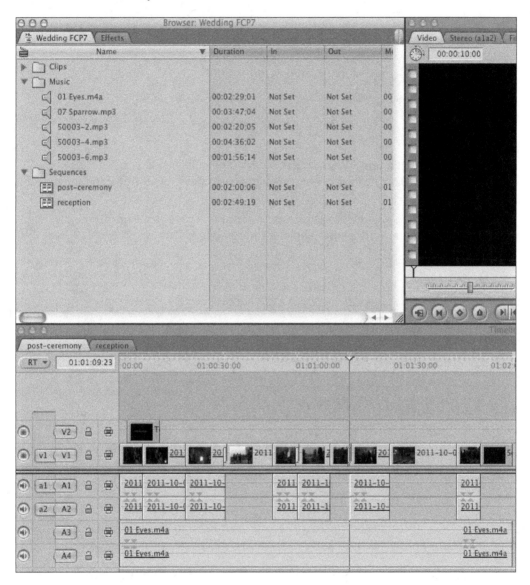

2. Go to **File** | **Export** | **XML....** In the XML export window, make sure Apple **XML Interchange Format, version 5** is selected, and then click on **OK**:

3. If you are on the same Mac or partition as FCPX, quit FCP7. If not, copy the newly created XML file to a flash drive or hard drive and bring it to the Mac/partition with FCPX.

4. Open 7toX. It will immediately prompt you for a FCP7 XML file. Locate your XML file (not the original FCP7 project file) and click on **Open**:

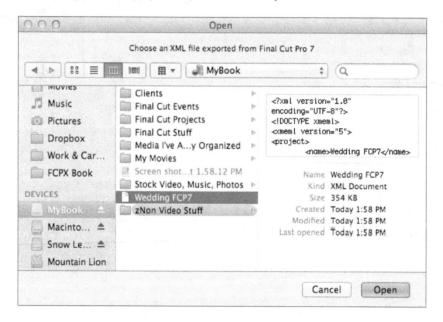

5. 7toX will ask if you want to send it to FCPX or save an XML. Click on **Send to Final Cut Pro X**.

How it works...

The team behind 7toX has done an incredible job translating projects from FCP7 to FCPX. When you send a project to FCPX using 7toX, the first thing that happens is that a new event is created with the name of your original project. All clips that had been imported into that project in FCP7 are imported into the new event.

> FCPX does not copy any of the media into the `Final Cut Events` folder, even if you normally have the option on by default! It merely references the original media from whatever original location FCP7 had referenced it from. This means you better have all your media in the exact same place as it was when you worked with it in FCP7.

Additionally, any bins (what FCP7 calls **folders**) you had in FCP7 are converted into **keyword collections**! And last, but certainly not least, any sequences are converted into **compound clips**. These compound clips can be placed as a whole entity into a new FCPX project's timeline OR you can double-click on them to reveal a near-perfectly translated version of your original sequence—clips, transitions, filters, and more! Read on for exceptions.

There's more...

What does and doesn't translate

While 7toX does a Herculean feat of translating from FCP7 to FCPX, it isn't perfect, although not necessarily from a lack of effort on the part of the programmers. There are simply some things that cannot translate between the two programs given their radically different interfaces and features. This happens often when translating between two major programs (such as FCP7 to Adobe Premiere or vice versa).

All basic mechanics of editing from a FCP7 timeline translate—your clips and timing, many transitions, audio levels, and even some titles. However, a few things do not translate such as Motion 4 project files, offline media, sequence markers, travel mattes, and a few more.

The list of what does and doesn't translate is quite long and the makers of 7toX are committed to updating the program, so the best thing to do is read about the program in greater detail at www.assistedediting.intelligentassistance.com/7toX.

Xto7

Intelligent Assistance also makes Xto7, which, as you can probably infer from the name, does the exact opposite as 7toX and will take a FCPX project and convert it so it can be imported into FCP7. Perhaps you've done a rough cut of your project quickly in FCPX, but really want to send your project to Color, Soundtrack Pro, or DVD Studio Pro. This is the answer. Read more about it at www.assistedediting.intelligentassistance.com/Xto7.

See also

As stated in the previous section, FCPX will import your old FCP7 sequences as compound clips. If you don't know what a compound clip is or does, read the *Grouping clips together as a compound clip* recipe in *Chapter 4, Enhancing Your Editing*. Also, as stated before, when FCPX imports FCP7 projects via 7toX, all media is referenced from the original media location, it is not imported into the Final Cut Events folder. If you're unsure of how this process works, continue to the following, *Working with your already organized media* section.

Working with your already organized media

By default, when you import media into FCPX, it is set to actually copy the files into the `Final Cut Pro Events` folder (located either in your user's `Movies` folder or on the root of an external hard drive). This is often the safest way to work, but not always the most efficient. On one hand, it makes sure all your media is consolidated into one location and therefore, makes it less likely that you will accidentally move, delete, or rename your original media. This also makes it easy to move projects from one drive to another. But, on the other hand, it also means that you have now duplicated all of your clips and eaten up a lot of potentially valuable hard drive space. Additionally, if you plan on re-importing the same media into multiple events, FCPX will copy the file each and every time. So it's really a game of pros and cons and is ultimately up to you.

How to do it...

1. Right-click on an event and choose **Import Files...** (by pressing *Command + Shift + I*).

2. Find the files you want to import in the new window. Select multiple files by holding down the *Command* key. Also, select the event you want to add the media to.

3. Before hitting **Import**, deselect the checkmark next to **Copy Files to Final Cut Events** folder. It is your choice whether or not you want to create optimized or proxy media. Then click on **Import**. FCPX will go through the normal import process—or so it seems. It may seem to take less time than normal. This is because it didn't have to duplicate the files.

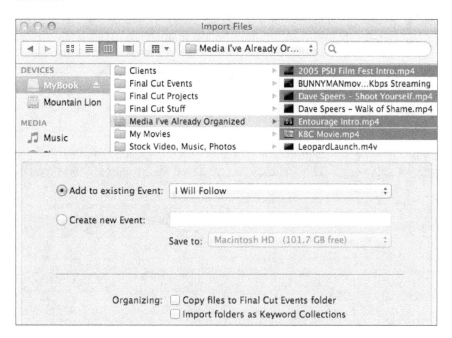

4. Minimize or hide (by pressing *Command + H*) FCPX. Go to the `Final Cut Events` folder where your event resides (either in your user's home folder or on the root level of your external drive). Open the folder, then open the folder named `Original Media`. Instead of seeing the full clips you imported, there are only alias files. Double-clicking on one will take you to the actual location of the file, where you originally imported it from.

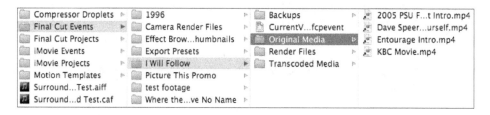

There's more...

Be organized!

If you're the type of editor who knows in advance that they want to turn off auto-copy in FCPX upon import feature, then hopefully you're a pretty organized person. If not, be warned! Once you've imported media into FCPX manually without copying into the `Final Cut Events` folder, be careful not to move, rename, or delete any of your original media files or they will appear offline in FCPX!

Optimized and proxy media

If you choose to create optimized and/or proxy media upon import, FCPX does create and place the additional media files in the `Final Cut Events` folder even if you deselected **Copy Files to Final Cut Events.** That command only applies to the original media. Any transcoded clips must live in the `Final Cut Events` folder.

See also

If you were being very careful with your media organization, but still somehow managed to get your media offline and need to relink it, read the next *Relinking media files* recipe.

Relinking media files

Occasionally, Final Cut Pro X may lose track of files. We hate to say it, but most of the time it's due to user error (no offense!). It happens to the best of us. Perhaps you imported some media into FCPX and a few days later, you moved, deleted, or renamed the original files. This is most likely to happen if you chose not to have FCPX automatically copy files into the `Final Cut Events` folder upon import, but really, there are many other scenarios where this can occur. Here's how to fix it.

Getting ready

This isn't something you usually want to get ready for because you'd have to purposely mess things up! But, if you want to experiment, shut down FCPX, open your `Final Cut Events` folder, find an inconsequential event (we're going to fix the problem we're creating, but better safe than sorry) and remove a few files from the `Original Media` folder.

How to do it...

1. To identify if you need to relink media, look for this symbol in your Event Browser. It's hard to miss if most or all of your clips have been replaced by this big red icon! You will also see a little alert triangle over the event icon:

2. With the problematic event selected, choose **File | Relink Event Files...** (you can also right-click on the event to choose the same option).

3. The **Relink Files** window appears. You are given the option to relink only the missing files or all files. We're just going to relink the missing files, but read the following *There's more...* section for a more advanced use of this window.

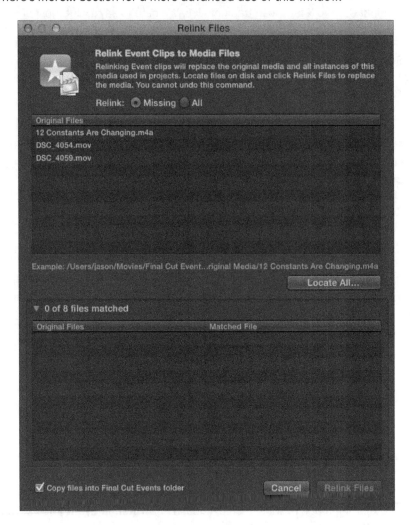

4. Click the **Locate All...** button. A box appears that will allow you to browse your hard drives. From here, you're on your own! Where did you move your media? Or did you rename it? Somehow, you must track down the lost media. In the following screenshot, we found our lost media in a folder on our desktop:

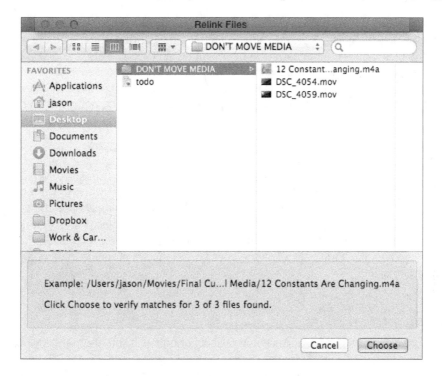

5. Once you've found at least one of your files (hopefully, they're all together in one place), click on the one FCPX has chosen to search for first (listed after **Example**) and click on **Choose**. The **Relink Files** window shows the files successfully matched. Click on **Relink Files** and the files are successfully relinked.

How it works...

When an event clip is relinked, it is relinked in every instance of that clip in all projects as well. Meaning, if you used a piece of media four times across different projects, it is immediately relinked in all four of those projects.

There's more...

Relinking online clips

The previous exercise assumed you needed to relink media because of a mistake (losing track of your files). However, there are cases where you would purposely want to relink perfectly working, online clips to a different set of clips.

The simplest example is, if you happened to take your original media files into a different program for a task such as advanced color correction and you want to replace the modified files with the old, uncorrected ones you've been editing in FCPX. The process starts off the same as the exercise. Highlight the Event you want to relink and choose **Relink Event Files...**. This time, click on the **All** button, then click on **Locate All...**, and then find the folder with the new, modified media. This will allow you to relink all files in the Event, not just the ones that have gone missing.

Relinking in the timeline

As mentioned in step four in the previous section, relinking event files relinks every instance of an Event clip across all projects where that clip was referenced. If you only want to relink a clip (or clips) to one instance in one particular project, you can. Simply open the project of your choosing, highlight the clip(s) you want to relink, and finally, select **File | Relink Project Clips**. You will be brought to the same **Relink Files** window as in the exercise, only this time, when you relink media, it will only relink the specific instance(s) of media in this project and not across all projects.

See also

You are more likely to experience files going missing or offline, if you are manually managing your media as described in the *Manually organizing your media outside of FCPX* recipe. Read this recipe to make sure you understand the pros and cons of ignoring the default setting in FCPX to copy all your media into one location.

2
Customizing Your Workflow

In this chapter, we will cover the following:

- ► Getting acquainted with the Final Cut Pro X interface
- ► Customizing the keyboard
- ► Creating a camera archive
- ► Adding keywords to your clips
- ► Marking clips as favorites and rejected
- ► Creating a Smart Collection
- ► Working with a second computer monitor
- ► Working with a broadcast safe monitor
- ► Customizing the Event Library and Event Browser
- ► Batch changing clip names and other metadata
- ► Editing efficiently with optimized and proxy clips

Introduction

As video editors, we need to be flexible. Changing deadlines, various video file formats, backseat editors (a.k.a. directors and producers); they all make us have to constantly adapt our workflow. In turn, we need flexibility in our editing software. Luckily, **Final Cut Pro X** (**FCPX**) has plenty of tools to adjust to our needs and different working environments.

For Final Cut Pro 7 users, FCPX's one-window interface seems restrictive at first compared to FCP7's multiwindowed layout. This is misleading, however, as almost all the different areas of the interface can be hidden or resized easily based on our needs. Keyboard shortcuts have also changed, but we can alter those as well. And thanks to the 10.0.3 update that arrived in early 2012, we have much more flexibility in connecting to additional broadcast-quality hardware.

In addition, FCPX vastly exceeds FCP7's media management capabilities. Cross-referencing media is a piece of cake, thanks to the introduction of keywords and favorites.

Although none of the recipes in this chapter are essential to use FCPX, taking the time to go through them and make the program work the way you want it to can save countless hours of work in the long run.

Getting acquainted with the Final Cut Pro X interface

Before we truly get underway with learning the ins and outs of FCPX, we've got to learn to walk before we can run. FCPX is a very deep program with a huge palette of tools and features, and every user should have a basic idea of what's what and what's where before trying to edit their masterpiece. This recipe is not so much an exercise, as it is an overview that will walk you through the most commonly used pieces of the interface.

How to do it...

1. Open up Final Cut Pro X. There are several parts to the FCPX interface, which are shown in the following screenshot. Your interface may not show every part in our screenshot, but as we'll see, you can easily show and hide many of the components according to your needs.

2. Go through the following list to know more about the sections marked in the preceding screenshot:

   ❑ **Section 1**: This is the **Event Library** section. All media you import into FCPX will be contained in an event inside the **Event Library** section. The **Event Library** section can easily be hidden and shown at any time with the keyboard shortcut *Command + Shift + 1*.

   ❑ **Section 2**: This is the **Event Browser** section. Once you select an event from the **Event Library** section, you will see all of the clips displayed in the Event Browser section. We'll learn later on how to customize the view of the Event Browser section to meet your project's needs.

   ❑ **Section 3**: This is the **Viewer** section. It displays the currently active clip whether it be in your Event Browser or in your timeline, so pay attention to the mouse pointer or the clip you've selected, because that will control what appears in the Viewer.

   ❑ **Section 4**: This is the **Inspector** section. The Inspector section is where all the good stuff is hidden. When you want to manipulate a clip in any number of ways (adjust color, shape, size, volume, and so on), the Inspector section has all the tools you need in one place. The Inspector window can be easily hidden and shown with *Command + 4*.

- ❑ **Section 5**: This is the **Toolbar** section. It primarily consists of numerous buttons, which we'll learn about as we go along in this book. Each one performs a different function or hides/reveals different parts of the interface. For example, the button on the far right of the toolbar (the circle with the letter **i** in it) is a button that will hide and show the Inspector section.

- ❑ **Section 6**: This is the the **Timeline** section. This is the main edit area for your project. You will add your media here along with titles, music, generators, and more.

- ❑ **Section 7**: This is the **Effects Browser**, containing the list of all available effects in FCPX. It is one of seven different browsers that can occupy this portion of the interface, along with the photos, music, transitions, titles, generators, and themes. They are all hidden and revealed by clicking on their respective icons, located right above the browser in the Toolbar section.

There's more...

That's not all, folks!

As mentioned previously, the main interface components covered in this recipe are not the whole show—there are others! In later recipes, we'll learn to display video scopes, the **Timeline Index** section, the **Project Library** section, and more.

Customizing the keyboard

Final Cut Pro X's keyboard shortcuts are greatly revamped and remapped from Final Cut Pro 7. Or, if you're coming from a different editing suite, keyboard shortcuts are going to be very different anyway. Luckily, FCPX has an easy-to-use keyboard shortcut editor.

How to do it...

1. Click on **Final Cut Pro** in the menu bar and select **Commands | Customize**, or hit *Command + Option + K* on the keyboard.

2. The **Command Editor** window pops up. To learn what each key is capable of in FCPX, click on it and look below the digital keyboard in the **Key Detail** box. Every possible command with every possible modifier key is listed! Additionally, the command list at the bottom provides you with a list of every possible command in FCPX and which, if any, keyboard shortcut has been applied to it.

3. FCPX doesn't let you modify the default layout, so we must create our own copy first. Click on **Default** in the upper-left corner of the window and choose **Duplicate...** Enter in a name for your shortcuts and click on **OK**.

4. Not every command has a keyboard shortcut. Let's say we wanted to make one for **Analyze and Fix...**, which displays the window where we can tell FCPX to check clips for people, color, sound issues, and so on. A keyboard shortcut using the letter **A** would make sense.

5. Click on the letter **A** on the virtual keyboard. Notice in the **Key Detail** box that *Option + A* has no command assigned to it.

6. Use the search box in the upper-right corner to find the **Analyze and Fix...** command (type the word `analyze`). Drag the command from the command list into the **Key Detail** window right on top of the **Option** symbol. Click on **Save**, as shown in the following screenshot:

There's more...

Multiuser environments

This is a great way for multiple editors sharing one FCPX rig to customize the program for themselves. Each time an editor opens up FCPX, all he/she has to do is click on **Final Cut Pro** in the the menu bar, scroll down to **Customize**, and choose the keyboard layout of his/her choice!

Accessories to help

If you're happy with the default layout and just want an easy reminder of what keys do what, a few companies produce rubber keyboard covers for FCPX that place the major single key shortcut labels right on top of the keys! Two such companies are ProVantage (`http://www.provantage.com`) and KB Covers (`http://www.kbcovers.com`). You can also find physical keyboards with printed shortcuts on them at `www.editorskeys.com` and `www.logickeyboard.com`.

Adding keywords to your clips

New to FCPX is a handy keyword system that allows for great cross-referencing and makes clips easy to find, even if you've got hundreds of them or more! Perhaps you are organizing footage you shot at a fair. You have a clip that is a crowd shot, but also features a performance artist. In FCP7, you would have to pick one **bin** or a folder for a clip to reside. Now, you can apply the keywords **crowd** and **artist** to a clip and make it show up in each keyword collection (more information on that in a moment).

How to do it...

1. Select your event in the **Event Library** section. You can select either filmstrip view or list view for this process, but usually the more visual filmstrip view works better as you can see many clips at once.

2. Click on the **Keyword Editor** button (key icon) in the menu bar, or press *Command + K*. This brings up the floating **Keyword Editor** window. Click on the disclosure triangle next to **Keyword Shortcuts**, as shown in the following screenshot:

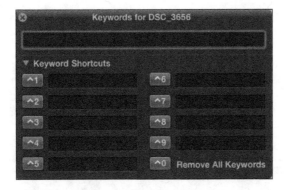

3. Nine empty spaces are now displayed where you can create temporary keyboard shortcuts for often-used keywords.

4. Highlight one or more clips in your event that you want to add a keyword to. In the following screenshots, images of kids have been selected:

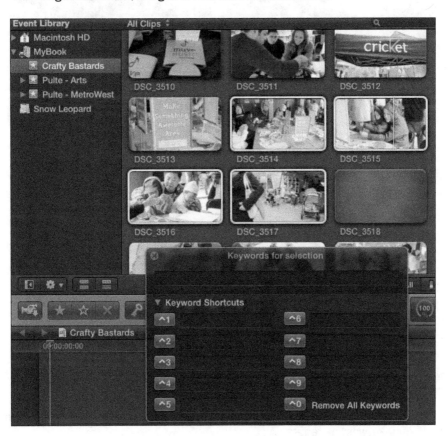

5. In the text box at the top of **Keyword Editor**, type in your keyword (in this case, `Kids`). Hit *Return*. The keyword has been applied to the selected clips. Take note of a few visual cues on screen—first, the blue line over each clip, which tells us a keyword has been applied to that clip. Second, an indented blue key icon with the name of the keyword appearing underneath our event name in **Event Library**. By adding a keyword to one or more clips, FCPX automatically creates this keyword collection. Selecting the collection will narrow down your event to only those clips that match that keyword.

6. To apply an additional keyword to a clip (or clips), simply select the desired clip(s) and repeat step 5 with a new keyword. A new keyword collection will appear underneath your event with the tagged clip(s). Don't worry, adding multiple keywords to a clip doesn't duplicate the clip!

How it works...

Keywords are simply metadata stored by FCPX in the project file itself. The clips themselves do not contain their keyword metadata.

There's more...

Using keyboard shortcuts

Notice that the keyword(s) you apply will also appear in the **Keyword Shortcuts** spaces **^1**, **^2**, and so on (those funny caret symbols represent the Control keyboard modifier key). You can now zip through clips, highlighting additional ones and simply hit the appropriate keyboard shortcut to apply the keyword, even if the clips are in a different event! Removing a keyword shortcut from the **Keyword Editor** window does *not* delete the keyword from tagged clips.

Applying keywords to ranges of clips

Keywords don't have to be applied to whole clips, they can be applied to only ranges of clips as well! Simply select a clip from your Event Browser, select a range (either by dragging across the portion you want or by using **I** and **O** to mark a range), and then add your keyword. The blue keyword line will only appear across the range of the clip you have selected, and only that portion of the clip will appear in the keyword collection. While this is great, don't let it confuse you! If you're reviewing a clip and if you find part of the clip seems to be missing, you are probably looking at a selection from the clip in a keyword collection, favorite, or Smart Collection (coming up in future recipes).

Removing keywords from clips

Lastly, to remove a keyword from a clip or clip range, simply select the clip or clips in the **Event Library** section, open the **Keyword Editor** window, click on the keyword you want to remove from the clip, and hit *Delete*. This does *not* delete the original clip; it only removes the selected clip(s) from the keyword collection! It's just like removing a song from an iTunes playlist or a photo from an iPhoto or Aperture album—the original files still exist! To permanently delete a clip, you would have to delete it from the original event heading.

See also

Similar to keywording is the ability to mark a clip or part of a clip as a favorite. Read ahead to the *Marking clips as favorites and rejected* recipe for more information on the difference. Also, for the organizational junkies out there, the crème de la crème of organizational tools is the Smart Collection, explained in the *Creating a smart collection* recipe.

Marking clips as favorites and rejected

In addition to keywording, you can mark clips simply as a Favorite or Rejected in order to further organize and reference your footage. The process for marking a clip or part of a clip is very similar to keywording. iMovie users will be very familiar with this process, as the feature was pulled straight from FCPX's little sibling.

How to do it...

1. Select a range of a clip that contains the portion of the clip you will likely use in your project. You can select the entire clip if you desire, but using the Favorite feature is most useful when selecting just a range within a clip.

2. Click on the green star on the left of the menu bar, or hit *F* on the keyboard:

3. A green line appears over the selected range of the clip, indicating it is now a Favorite. Repeat this process with as many clips as you like.

4. Once you have marked your clips as Favorites, click on the **Filter** pop-up menu in the upper-left corner of Event Browser. Select **Favorites** from the drop-down menu or hit *Command + F*:

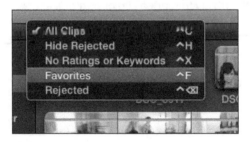

5. Now you are looking at only the clip ranges that you have marked as **Favorites**, as shown in the following screenshot:

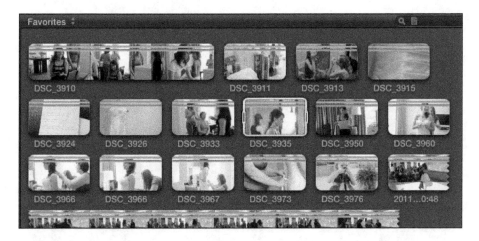

6. Click on the **Filter** pop-up menu again and change it back to **All Clips**.

7. Select a whole clip or clip range that contains a portion of the clip you will be unlikely to use in your project.

8. Click on the red star on the left of the menu bar, or hit *Delete* on the keyboard:

9. A red line appears over the selected range of the clip, indicating it is now rejected. Repeat this process with as many clips as you like.

10. Once you have marked your clips as Rejected, click on the **Filter** pop-up menu again. Select **Hide Rejected** from the menu. Any clip(s) marked as rejected would disappear! If you have marked a middle portion of a clip, it will look as though that clip has been duplicated, but in reality, this view just splits the clip into pieces as it's hiding a chunk of video in the middle. Take note of the two clips in the following screenshot labeled **DSC_3517**—it's one clip, but we have rejected the middle portion and selected **Hide Rejected**, so we see the beginning and end of the clip as individual clips!

11. Click on the **Filter** pop-up menu once again and choose **Rejected**. You will now see just the clips you marked as Rejected. If you want to delete the clips, go to **Edit | Select All** (*Command + A*), then **Edit | Move to Trash** (*Command + Delete*).

There's more...

Where'd my clips go!?

Don't forget which Event Browser view you're in! Just like we mentioned in the *Adding keywords to your clips* recipe, if you're skimming through a clip and you find that part of the clip is missing, double-check the **Filter** pop-up menu at the top of the Event Browser window.

Be careful when deleting rejected clips

Warning! If you delete a rejected range of a clip, it will reject the entire original source clip. As long as you've got the hard drive space, it's usually safer to simply leave clips as rejected and leave your **Filter** view set to **Hide Rejected**.

Creating a Smart Collection

Keywords, favorites, rejected clips, oh my! But wait, there's more—**Smart Collections**. This tool will satiate even the most organized editors out there. Perhaps you want to simply be able to click on one button and see all clips with the keywords **exterior**, **interview**, and **actor** simultaneously applied. Or perhaps you want to be able to see all clips marked as Favorites with the **interior** keyword applied. It gets much deeper than that, but let's take it easy at first and decide that we want to find the clips marked as Favorites with a particular set of keywords applied to them.

How to do it...

1. With the **Event Library** or Event Browser window active, choose **Edit | Find...** or hit *Command + F*. The **Filter** window will appear. This window allows us to create a list of rules or search criteria to find the clips we want and view them together in a Smart Collection.

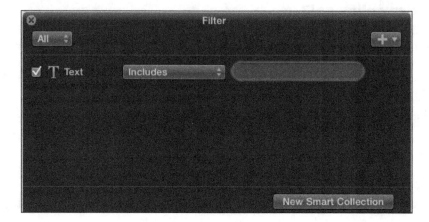

2. The first default option is to filter by **Text**. You can simply type in the empty field to narrow down your clips in real time by the clip names shown in the **Name** column in the browser, as well as in the **Notes** field.

3. As we've decided not to search by text, deselect the checkbox next to the big orange **T**. Then click on the **Add Rule** pop-up menu, indicated by the **+** button in the upper-right corner.

4. Select **Ratings**. This will now only show us clips we have marked as Favorites:

5. Click on the **Add Rule** pop-up menu again and select **Keywords**. We now have the option to select or deselect whichever keyword combinations we choose. In the following screenshot, the **Getting Ready**, **Pre-Ceremony**, and **XA10** keywords have been checked. We have now created a filter where a wedding videographer can see his/her favorite clips he/she shot with a particular camera (the Canon XA-10) before the ceremony began!

6. Click on **New Smart Collection** in the lower-right corner. This creates a Smart Collection underneath the heading of the event you were browsing with the **Filter** window. Now, any time you want to look for clips that meet your criteria, you can!

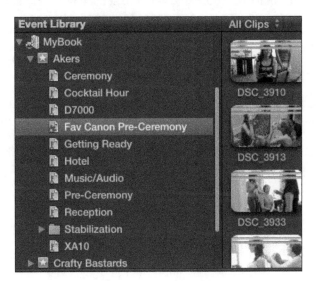

How it works...

Once more, it's all about the metadata. Smart Collections have not moved your media anywhere different; they just provide an instant search every time you click on them based upon the criteria you set in the Filter window.

There's more...

Scratching the metadata surface

Smart Collections can get much deeper and more complicated than what this recipe has illustrated. Do you want to see all clips that are 1920x1080 shot on Canon cameras with one person framed in a medium shot with the keyword **Fred**? You can do it. How about all clips shot in the last 14 days that are from Scene 30 of your movie? Done! Play around with all the options to see how deep the rabbit hole goes.

Working with a second computer monitor

As the world continues its inevitable shift away from desktop computers to more portable options such as laptops and tablets, one repercussion is sometimes having to work with smaller monitors or displays. For many tasks, such as checking e-mail or browsing the Web, this isn't much of an issue. But for video editors, trying to edit or color correct high-definition material on a 15-inch MacBook Pro is far from ideal! Luckily, not only we can plug our laptops into larger displays, but Final Cut Pro X can use entire second screen to display your Viewer window on a full screen, which also frees up space to expand other windows such as Event Browser, Inspector, and more.

Getting ready

First off, you've got to have a second display! The most common displays use VGA, DVI, and Mini DisplayPort and HDMI for their connections, although hooking up via HDMI to HDTVs is possible as well with an adapter. You very well may need an adapter depending on your combination of Mac and external monitor. After learning what ports your Mac has, check www.apple.com/store for an appropriate adapter.

Secondly, if you want to be efficient with your space use, you'll want to make sure that **Mirror Displays** is turned off. If you plug your monitor into your Mac and see exactly the same image on both screens, it's been turned on. Go to **System Preferences**, click on the **Displays** icon, and finally, click on the **Arrangement** tab. Deselect the **Mirror Displays** checkbox. You are now working in an extended desktop environment. Windows can be dragged between the monitors for additional workspace.

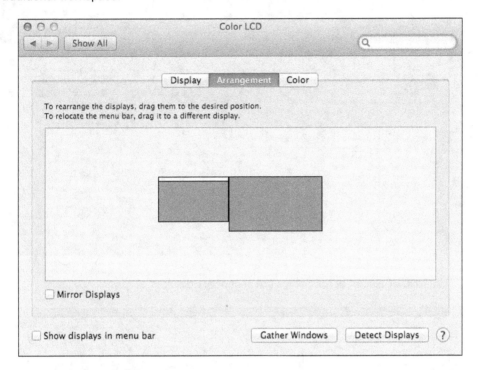

How to do it...

1. Open any project you like.

2. Go to **Window | Show Viewer in Second Display**. Your Viewer will disappear from your primary display and appear full screen on your second monitor! You still have access to the buttons from the Viewer window such as **Transform**, **Crop**, and **Trim**, and the ability to bring up your video scopes, too. Additionally, you have much more room on your primary monitor for your Event Browser. It's a real win-win strategy!

The following screenshot shows the primary display:

The following screenshot shows the secondary display:

3. When you want to return to the standard window layout, just go back to the **Window** menu and select **Show Viewer in the Main Window**.

There's more...

Alternate second display options

Optionally, instead of sending your Viewer to your second monitor, you can choose to send your Event Library and Event Browser to the second monitor. Simply go to **Window | Show Events on Second Display**. This view isn't very handy when you're deep into the editing process, but is great when you're first getting started and skimming through your media, tagging keywords, marking favorites, and so forth.

See also

If you are working with professional broadcasting equipment and want to work with a broadcast safe monitor, read the *Working with a broadcast safe monitor* recipe.

Working with a broadcast safe monitor

Regular computer displays and HDTVs aren't usually the most trustworthy devices when it comes to getting an accurate idea of the color of your image and how it will appear once broadcast out to the world. Industry pros and production houses almost always have broadcast monitors, which are hyper-accurate displays with numerous configurations and settings to make sure you're seeing the most accurate color possible. FCPX can connect to these monitors if the stars align and if you've got the right equipment to hand.

Getting ready

For this to work, you need three major pieces—a Thunderbolt-enabled Mac, a broadcast monitor, and a compatible third-party interface to act as the middle man between your Mac and the monitor. Black Magic Design (`www.blackmagic-design.com`) and AJA (`www.aja.com`) are two of the biggest manufacturers of such products. You will then need to install the appropriate drivers from the manufacturers as well.

How to do it...

1. Connect the video monitor to the third-party interface and ensure it is turned on.

2. In FCPX, choose **Final Cut Pro | Preferences**. Click on the **Playback** tab, click on the pop-up menu for **A/V Output**, and select your device, as shown in the following screenshot:

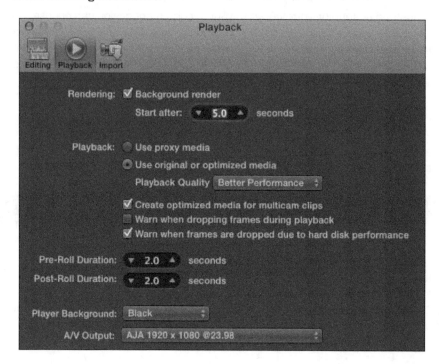

3. Close the **Preferences** window, and then go to the **Window** menu and select **A/V Output**. The content from the **Viewer** window is now displayed on the external monitor. The normal Viewer controls can only be seen inside FCPX.

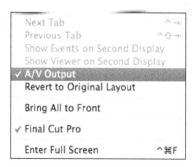

There's more...

What's a broadcast monitor, anyway?

A lot of people wonder what makes a broadcast monitor so special. Why not just hook up your Mac to an HDTV, as described in the recipe *Working with second computer displays*? The truth is, you can if you wish, but monitors made specifically for broadcast have far greater color fidelity, calibration tools, and more inputs than normal computer monitors or consumer HDTVs. They're also much more expensive; it's not uncommon to pay a few thousand dollars for a 20-inch broadcast monitor!

See also

If you don't have access to a broadcast monitor, try hooking your Mac up on a second computer monitor or HDTV in the *Working with second computer displays* recipe.

Customizing the Event Library and Event Browser

When people got a first look at FCPX when it arrived on the market, many quickly lamented that it looked too much like Apple's consumer-oriented counterpart, iMovie. Beyond FCPX's powerful feature set, its interface is also much more customizable than how it appears at first glance. The Event Library and Event Browser windows are a great example of this, giving users many different ways to view and organize their content.

How to do it...

1. Choose any one of your events in the **Event Library** section (your list of events on the far left of the screen), ideally one with a range of different media types. Then click on the **Show clips in filmstrip view** button below the library list if it is not already selected. Your clips appear as virtual filmstrips that you can skim over with your mouse. We will return to the alternate option, **Show clips in list view**, later.

2. Click on the **Action** pop-up menu (the cog wheel icon) underneath the **Event Library** section, as shown in the following screenshot:

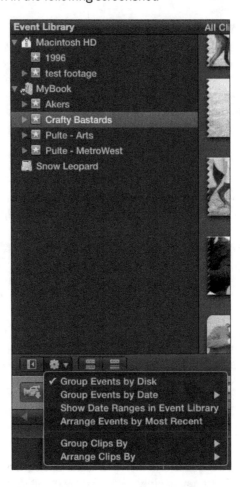

3. **Group Events by Disk** is checked. This will show you your events by which disk they reside on. This is usually handy to keep on, although it can be deselected. The other options are fairly straightforward. You can choose to show date ranges for your events, group them by date, or arrange them by date (normally, they are listed alphabetically).

4. The more interesting are the two bottom options, which relate to how clips will be organized in the Event Browser window. Hover over **Group Clips By** and look at the options available to you (**Date Imported**, **Duration**, and so on). Select file type. Your browser window rearranges clips so that they are organized by media type—**JPEG image**, **QuickTime movie**, **MP3 audio**, and so on. You can easily hide and show whatever file type(s) you like by clicking the disclosure triangle next to the file type heading.

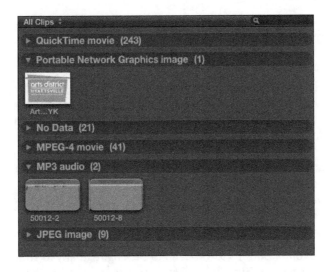

5. Now, click on **Show clips in list view**. Instead of the more visual filmstrip view, we get a more compact, list-oriented view of our media, with whatever media is selected at the moment in a filmstrip view above the list, as shown in the following screenshot:

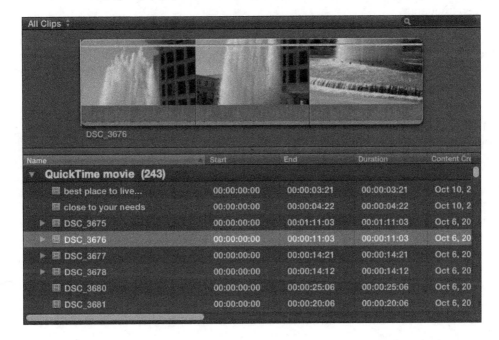

6. Scroll horizontally to see many column headings such as **Start**, **End**, **Duration**, **Codecs**, and so on. Click on any column heading to order your media by the selected heading. Remember, if you want to turn off the grouping we created in step 4, simply click on the **Action** pop-up menu again and choose **Group Clips By | None**.

There's more...

List view versus filmstrip view – pros and cons

What is better for viewing your clips, list view or filmstrip view? It's a good question with no right answer. Longtime editors will most likely be more used to the list view, as it is most akin to the user interface of other professional editing programs. The filmstrip view may appeal more to newer editors or those coming up from iMovie, as it is a little more visual and less technical. Both have their pros and cons. I like the filmstrip view when I'm first reviewing my newly imported footage and applying keywords to clips, as I can see thumbnails from literally a couple of dozen clips at once. Once my media is organized and I'm getting underway with my editing, however, I find the list view a more consolidated, efficient way to look at things.

Knowing your buttons

There are a couple of other buttons to get used to clicking regularly to streamline your workflow. The first is the **Show/Hide the Event Library** (*Command + Shift + 1*) button located right next to the **Action** pop-up menu. Once you've selected the event, you're going to be working on it for a while, so hide the **Event Library** window to gain valuable screen real estate back. I only keep this up if I have a lot of keyword collections that I am hopping back and forth between frequently.

Also, take note of the **i** button on the far right of the menu bar. This is the **Inspector** button. Although we haven't delved into this very important button yet, for now just know that it shows and hides the **Inspector** window and should be closed when not in use, as it takes up a lot of space as well.

Batch changing clip names and other metadata

We've all been there—you import 287 clips from your camera and the filenames show up as something cumbersome DSC_0042, or perhaps 2011-06-15 05:45:40 or ZOOM004. For our sanity, we need to label them better, and of course, it can help us speed up our workflow when skimming through hundreds or even thousands of clips.

How to do it...

1. Highlight the group of clips you want to rename. Usually, they will be together, but this is not a requirement. You can select items that are not next to each other by selecting one, then holding down the *Command* key and clicking on any other clips you want to select, as shown in the following screenshot:

2. Click on the blue **Inspector** button on the far-right side of the menu bar, as shown in the following screenshot:

3. Click on the **Info** tab at the top of the **Inspector** window, as shown in the following screenshot:

4. Click on the **Action** pop-up menu that appears right above the **Inspector** button. Scroll to **Apply Custom Name** and we will see a number of options available to us. In this case, we don't want to see the original clip names or the embedded dates on the clips; we just want to choose **Custom Name with Counter**. But before we can, we have to set a custom name! So click on **Edit...** for now, as shown in the following screenshot:

5. The **Naming Presets** window opens. This window may first appear daunting, but we're going to keep things simple right now. Click on the **Custom Name with Counter** preset in the left list, as shown in the following screenshot:

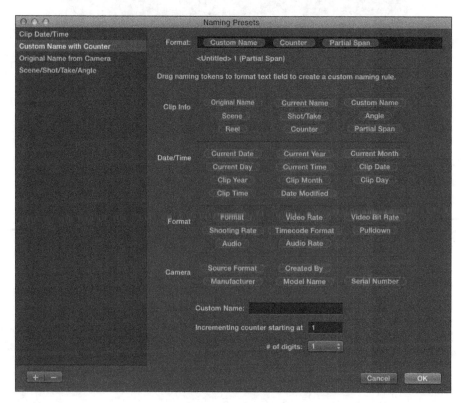

6. Near the bottom of the screen, fill in the box that is labeled **Custom Name**. In this exercise, we will write `Constitution Ave`. You can also change which number the counter starts at and how many digits are used in the counter as well. When you are content, click on **OK**:

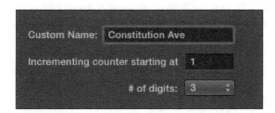

7. Finally, click on the **Action** pop-up menu one more time, select **Apply Custom Name** and lastly, **Custom Name with Counter**. Voila, all your selected clips have been renamed, as shown in the following screenshot:

There's more...

Creating custom naming presets

You have probably realized that you can create your own totally custom naming convention in the **Naming Presets** window. For example, if you want to select a batch of clips and have all of them renamed to display the clips' camera format, frame rate, and finally end with a custom name and counter, you can do it. Simply select your batch of clips, reopen the **Naming Presets** window, and click on the **+** button in the lower-left corner, which allows you to custom create your own preset. Just drag-and-drop the "naming tokens" into the naming format box at the top of the window.

Altering a clip's metadata for more powerful organization

In the **Naming Presets** window, you probably saw a ton of metadata options that you may want to use to rename clips. But you're wondering, "How do I see and/or modify these fields in the first place?" After you've selected one or more clips and opened the **Info** tab in the **Inspector** window (steps 1, 2, and 3), look at the left of the **Action** pop-up menu and you will see a pop-up window labeled **Basic View** (yours might say something slightly different if you've ever clicked here before). Click on the pop-up window and you will see a list of different categories of metadata views. Click through each one to get an idea of what they display. In a number of cases you can type in your own information for the values! If you see **Multiple Values**, it means you have selected two or more clips that have differing values. You can even customize these metadata views by clicking on **Edit Metadata View...** under the metadata view pop-up menu. Once you've entered in the information you want, you can create your own batch rename command using steps 1 to 4 in this recipe and then the instructions in the previous *There's more...* section.

Editing efficiently with optimized and proxy clips

It seems that there are almost as many video codecs and containers as there are actual spoken languages in the world—H.264, MPEG-2, AVCHD, and so on. Some are made for editing and some for delivery. Final Cut Pro works with some like a knife through butter, and with others like hammering through steel. Worse yet, sometimes as an editor you are handed a project that deals with multiple formats at once. While the multilingual Final Cut can handle such a task and mix formats in one project, it's far more efficient if it only has to focus on one, easy-to-understand language at a time. In turn, Apple has made it very simple to streamline this cumbersome issue and create edit-efficient versions of our media upon import (or after).

How to do it...

1. You have two possible routes here to start. If you are importing files directly from your hard drive, open the **Import** window by going to **File | Import | Files...** (*Command + Shift + I*). If you are importing from a camera, go to **File | Import from Camera** (*Command + I*), select your clips, and click on **Import Selected** or **Import All**.

2. Take a look at the options in the resulting window. If they are not selected already, select the checkboxes marked **Create optimized media** and **Create proxy media**. Then click on **Import**, as shown in the following screenshot:

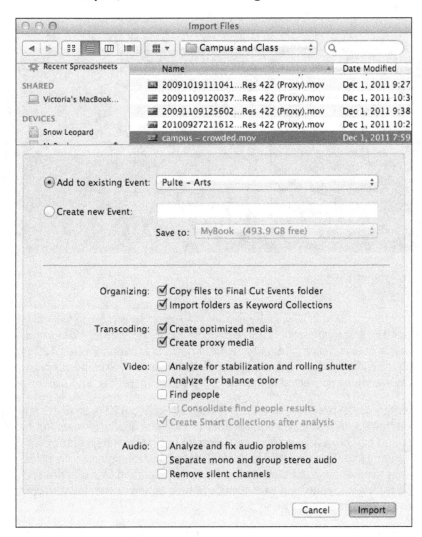

3. Depending on how many clips you have chosen to import, this process may take a while. Click on the **Background Tasks** (*Command + 9*) manager in the toolbar to check on the progress. Even if the process hasn't completed, you can still begin editing!

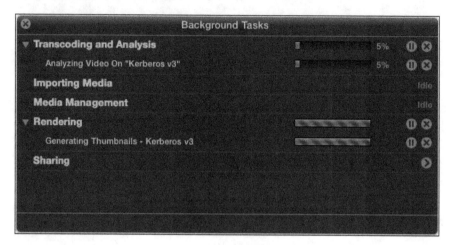

How it works...

When you create optimized and/or proxy media, FCPX is actually making two new versions of your media. The first (optimized) is full resolution and in the ProRes 422 format and the second (proxy) is quarter resolution and in a lower data rate format, ProRes 422 Proxy. Perhaps, you have imported some footage from a DSLR, an AVCHD camera, and an HDV camera. With everything converted to ProRes, FCPX will skim, render, and export faster.

What's the difference between the two ProRes flavors? ProRes 422 is an extremely high-quality codec that's sufficient for all but the absolute highest quality formats (for example, RED footage and other raw camera formats). Despite having such high quality, it's also very efficient for editing use. The only drawback of it is that it creates massive file sizes. ProRes 422 Proxy, on the other hand, creates smaller, quarter-resolution files that are also efficient. Using the Proxy format is especially useful if you're on a laptop or working with complex projects with multiple streams of video playing at once.

When working with ProRes 422 (and other high-bitrate formats), it's usually recommended to have a striped RAID array as your media drive, as these drives have a higher bandwidth/throughput than single drives, which is a necessity with large video files. This is changing a bit, however, with the advent of solid-state drives and the newer Thunderbolt bus. But, if you don't have the latest and greatest tech on hand, make sure you are using a FireWire 800 drive at the bare minimum.

So how do you use one or the other? Go to **Final Cut Pro | Preferences** and click on the **Playback** tab. There you will see the options **Use proxy media** and **Use original or optimized media**. You can flip back and forth at will and in the background, FCPX just flips a little switch and will start working with whichever type of media you've selected.

One good workflow would be to work with the proxy clips for most of your early rough cutting and effect applying, as FCPX will do this very quickly with the smaller-resolution files. When you need to take a closer look at your footage for tasks such as color correction and ultimately exporting, flip the switch to use the optimized, full-resolution media. Of course, if you're lucky enough to be working on a high-end machine with a solid-state drive, 16 GB of RAM, and a Thunderbolt external drive, working with proxy media is probably unnecessary and a waste of time!

There's more...

Oops, I forgot to convert at import...

You don't have to create the optimized and/or proxy clips at import. You can do it after the fact by simply right-clicking on any clip(s) in the Event Browser window and choosing **Transcode Media...**

Why do I see all these red boxes where my clips should be?

If you ever go to **Go to Preferences** and choose **Use proxy media**, and some or all your clips seem to go offline (all your clips turn red), do not be alarmed! You have (hopefully) not lost your media; it just means that you never created proxy media for those clips in the first place. At this point, either click back to work with your original or optimized media, or simply highlight your media in Event Browser, right-click, select **Transcode Media...**, and then create the proxy clips.

3
Basic Editing Mechanics

In this chapter, we will cover the following:

- ▶ Appending, inserting, and overwriting clips to a storyline
- ▶ Working with (and without) the Magnetic Timeline
- ▶ Creating connected clips
- ▶ Replacing a clip
- ▶ Splicing clips with the Blade tool
- ▶ Using the Trim tool, part 1 – trimming and rippling
- ▶ Using the Trim tool, part 2 – rolling
- ▶ Using the Trim tool, part 3 – slipping and sliding
- ▶ Creating and working with gap clips

Introduction

Consider this as the walk before you run chapter. Before you can really start having a ball in FCPX and making flashy movies, you must understand the basic techniques of how FCPX handles the editing of clips into a timeline. There are many differences in how FCPX edits in contrast to FCP7 or other video editing software. As Apple put it, they built FCPX with the next decade in mind, not the last one. All new tools and features such as Magnetic Timeline, Precision Editor, Range Selection tool, and many others, can seriously speed up your workflow once you have a good grasp of how they work.

Appending, inserting, and overwriting clips to a storyline

The safest and simplest way to add a clip to a project is to **append** it. No matter where your playhead is currently located in a project, appending a clip from your browser will always throw it to the end of the project, ensuring you don't accidentally overwrite a clip or split a clip into two.

In other scenarios, however, we may realize we need to go back to an earlier stage in a project and stick a new clip in the middle somewhere. Maybe we want to add some short filler clip between two interview sound bites. We can accomplish this by **inserting**. If we don't mind being a bit more destructive, we can also **overwrite**, which plows over anything in its path.

Getting ready

Simply have an open, empty project ready to add some test clips to.

How to do it...

1. Select a clip or range of a clip in your Event Browser.

2. Click on the **Append** button in the toolbar, or press *E* on your keyboard. The clip is added to the timeline, as shown in the following screenshot:

3. Move your playhead back to the beginning of the project. There are multiple ways to accomplish this. You can do it in any of the following ways:

   ❑ Drag the playhead back to the beginning of the timeline

   ❑ Hover your cursor over the timeline to make it the active pane of the interface, then hit the up arrow to move to the previous edit point

   ❑ Hit *Command + 2* to make the timeline active, then hit the up arrow

   ❑ Hit *Command + 2* followed by the Home key (or *fn* + left arrow) to move to the start of a project

4. Select another clip from your Event Browser and again hit *E* on your keyboard. Even though your playhead was before the first clip, it still added the second clip after the first, as shown in the following screenshot:

5. Position your playhead between the two clips. Try a different method than the one you used in step 3 to move the playhead.

6. Select a clip from your browser and then click on the **Insert** button in the toolbar or hit *W* on your keyboard:

The clip will place itself between the two original clips and "push" (better known as rippling) the second clip further down the storyline. No media is lost, but your project is now longer.

7. Select **Edit | Undo** or hit *Command + Z*. The timeline resets to right before the place where we inserted the clip and your playhead should return to right between the two original clips.

8. Select **Edit | Overwrite** or hit *D* on your keyboard. The new clip has been overwritten into the storyline. Depending on the length of the clip you have chosen to overwrite, it has overwritten either some or all of the clip that followed. In the following example, the clip we used in the overwrite edit (**Clip 3**) was shorter than the clip we overwrote (**Clip 2**), so part of **Clip 2** was overwritten.

How it works...

Appending a clip always takes your selected clip and adds it to the end of your project timeline. Your playhead or skimmer location is totally irrelevant.

Inserting a clip will place a clip exactly where the playhead (or skimmer, if it appears in the timeline) is located. Be careful—if you accidentally place your playhead or skimmer in the middle of a clip and then insert a new clip, it will split the original clip into two! There may be rare scenarios where you want to do this, but more often than not, you want to avoid this by making sure your playhead is between two clips.

When you overwrite a clip, it plows over anything in its path. Depending on the length of the clip, you will overwrite some or all of the media at the playhead's location!

Editing in secondary storylines

You can use all of these editing commands to add clips to secondary storylines as well. Simply click on the black banner above the connected storyline, place your playhead at the required location (if inserting or overwriting), and hit the appropriate keyboard shortcut. As long as the entire connected storyline is properly selected, it will edit the clip to the end of it rather than the primary storyline.

Editing only video or only audio

If you know that you only want to edit the audio or video from a clip into your timeline, but not both, you can do this with one setting change. Click on the triangle in the toolbar attached to the **Append**, **Connect**, and **Insert** buttons. There you will see the option to select **All**, **Audio Only**, or **Video Only**. Select one of the latter two and FCPX will only edit that element of a clip into your timeline.

Make sure your playhead is precisely between two clips

As we have described previously, when you insert a clip, you usually want to have your playhead or skimmer between two clips. To be more precise, in order to properly insert or overwrite, you want to be parked on the first frame of the incoming clip. This will prevent any flash frames, or single-frame clips from being created.

How do you know you're in the right spot, however? Here are a couple tips—first, zoom in closer to your timeline if necessary (*Command* + =). If you're too far zoomed out, it can be hard to drag your playhead to the right spot. Next, make sure **Snapping** is turned on. Hover over the button in the upper-right corner of your timeline and make sure it is illuminated blue. If not, click on it:

Start dragging your playhead toward an edit point between clips and it should "snap" into place when it gets close. Finally, you can verify that your playhead is at the appropriate location by looking for the on-screen indicator in the viewer shaped like the letter "L", which lets you know you have parked your playhead on the first frame of the incoming clip.

See also

Make sure that you read the *Creating additional storylines* recipe in *Chapter 4, Enhancing Your Editing* to learn more about connected storylines.

Working with (and without) the Magnetic Timeline

One of the biggest paradigm shifts in all of FCPX is the Magnetic Timeline. In most other video editing software, if you drag a clip around in the timeline, you have to be careful where and how you drop it, because it will likely overwrite or insert itself, potentially damaging your timeline or messing with the timing of your project. So Apple said, "No more!" Aiming to make your basic edits as nondestructive as possible, Apple created the Magnetic Timeline, allowing editors to swap clips to and fro in their timeline all day long without any chance of overwriting clips or messing with timing.

Getting ready

Append at least five clips into a test project. Also, ensure that the **Select** tool is active. Either press A on your keyboard or select it from the tool palette in the toolbar:

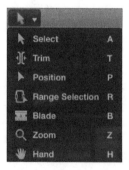

How to do it...

1. Click-and-drag the second clip in your project to the right, between your fourth and fifth clips. Don't let go yet. Notice a few things as follows:

    -   The space where the second clip was has disappeared

    -   The third and fourth clips have rippled to the left to fill that void

    -   A hollow blue box has appeared between the fourth and fifth clip indicating where the second clip will be placed if you let go

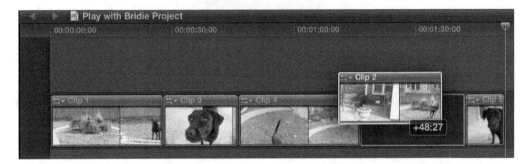

2. Let go. The second clip has been placed between the fourth and fifth clips. Nothing has been overwritten and the timing of your project is unchanged, as shown in the following screenshot:

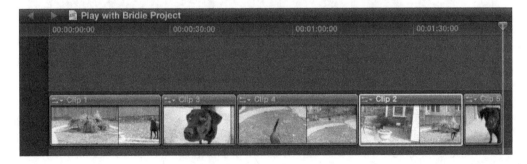

If you are a longtime video editor, this behavior might throw you off a bit. Perhaps it's just a muscle memory, but you might prefer your editing software to not automatically rearrange when you drag clips around. Luckily, Apple thought of this and gave us a workflow more akin to FCP7. It's called the **Position Tool** (nicknamed by many editors as the **Final Cut Pro 7 Tool**).

3. Click on **Edit** | **Undo** or hit *Command + Z* on your keyboard. The clips should jump back to their original order.

4. Go back to your tool palette and select the **Position** tool, or hit *P* on your keyboard:

5. Go back to the second clip in your timeline, and click-and-drag it to the right again. Don't let go yet! Take a note of the differences as follows:

   ❑ A gap has been left behind where the second clip was

   ❑ The third clip did not ripple back to the left to fill any gap

   ❑ It looks as if the second clip is covering part of the third and fourth clips; in fact, it is, as shown in the following screenshot:

6. Let go of the mouse. A gap is left behind where the second clip was and the second clip has overwritten part of both the third and fourth clips (depending on exactly where you have dropped the clip, it may only overwrite part of just one clip or the other).

There's more...

When to use the Position tool

If you're new to video editing, the Magnetic Timeline might seem great for editing, and it is, most of the time. However, there's a reason that the **Position** tool exists. If you're not careful, the Magnetic Timeline can mess up the sync and timing of your project. Perhaps halfway through your project, you have a song where you've cut a series of clips to the beat. If you moved one clip out to an earlier portion of your project before the song starts, it could throw the whole pacing of the edit off! You might want to turn on the **Position** tool (that is turn the Magnetic Timeline off) to prevent this sort of issue.

Deleting clips and the Magnetic Timeline

When you delete clips using the Magnetic Timeline, all clips following the deleted clip ripple back to fill the gap. This may seem great at first, but be careful! Depending on the complexity of your sequence, this can push certain elements you may have carefully lined up out of sync, such as narration or clips cut in beat with music. To delete a clip, but leave behind a gap clip, highlight the clip you want to remove and hit *Shift + Delete* (also known as the "big" *Delete* key on full external keyboards—you can simply hit the small *Delete* key on full-size keyboards). This ensures nothing is accidentally moved out of sync later in your project.

See also

For more information on gaps in your project, read the *Creating and working with gap clips* recipe.

Creating connected clips

Rearranging clips is a fact of life for an editor. As we've seen, the Magnetic Timeline can take a lot of the pain out of the process. But, what if your clips have b-roll and cutaways? Making sure these shots moved along with clips you were trying to rearrange used to take a lot of focus, but no longer. In their quest to reinvent the way you edit, Apple came up with the idea of **Connected Clips**, a feature that automatically tethers clips outside of the primary storyline to clips inside.

Getting ready

Have a project with a few clips laid down in the timeline.

How to do it...

1. Place your playhead anywhere over the first clip in the timeline, as shown in the following screenshot:

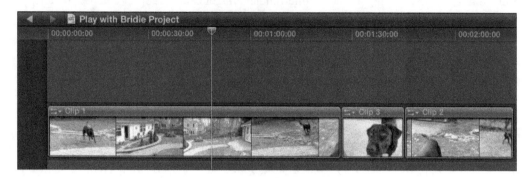

2. Up in your Event Browser, find the clip you want to use as b-roll or a cutaway and select a range or the entire clip.

3. Click on the **Connect the selected clip to the primary storyline** button in the toolbar or hit *Q* on your keyboard:

4. The clip appears above the clip in the primary storyline. Notice the tiny handle attaching the two clips, as shown in the following screenshot:

5. Click and hold on the clip in the primary storyline, drag it all the way to the end, and let go. Notice that the connected clip came along for the ride, as shown in the following screenshot:

There's more...

Repositioning connected clips

You don't always get the placement of your connected clips right at the first time. Luckily, they can be adjusted very easily. Simply click on the clip and drag it to left or right. Independent connected clips aren't bound by the same rules as clips in the primary timeline. Of course, this changes if you add a connected clip to a secondary storyline, so make sure to read the *Creating Additional Storylines* recipe in *Chapter 4, Enhancing Your Editing*.

See also

If you're unsure of how we rearranged clips so easily, read the *Working with (and without) the Magnetic Timeline* recipe. Also, to take connected clips to the next level, read the *Creating additional storylines* recipe in *Chapter 4, Enhancing Your Editing*.

Replacing a clip

There are a billion reasons why you might want or need to replace a clip—perhaps you need to swap out one logo for an updated one, maybe you need to pop in a different take or angle in a film, or maybe your montage is almost perfect if you just use a slightly different shot of a cute puppy. The reasons are endless. Final Cut Pro X gives you a few major ways to drop in replacement clips depending on the needs of your project.

Getting ready

Have a project ready to go where you want to replace one clip in your timeline with another from your Event Browser. In the following exercise, we're going to replace a relatively mundane shot from an arts and crafts fair (highlighted next) with a more exciting one:

How to do it...

1. In your Event Browser, select the range of the clip you want to use to replace the clip in the project. This is your source clip, as shown in the following screenshot:

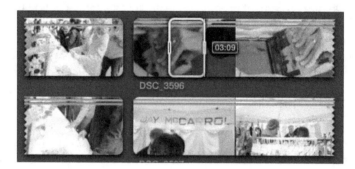

2. Drag the source clip you want to use down to your project and drop it directly on top of the clip you want to replace. A window pops up, giving you a list of options as follows:

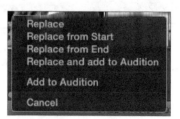

3. Choose **Replace**. The source clip replaces the old one. If the clip was longer than the original, the rest of the project would have been rippled to the right. If it was shorter, the project would have been rippled to the left. In the example used, the source clip was longer, so everything after was pushed farther down the timeline, as shown in the following screenshot:

Perhaps you didn't want to mess up the timing of your project, however. This is very important in projects needing to be of a very specific length, for example commercials or music videos.

4. Hit *Command + Z* to undo. Repeat step 2 by dragging the source clip again onto the clip you want to replace. But this time, select **Replace from Start**. The timing of your project remains unchanged, as shown in the following screenshot:

How it works...

When you select **Replace from Start**, FCPX prevents your project length from changing. It does this by lining up the selection starts of each clip (the source start in your Event Browser and the start of the clip in your project you're trying to replace) and overwriting the old clip with the source clip only for the duration of the old clip. It ignores the selection end of your source clip. Let's say you have a 2-second clip in your timeline. Next, you select a 4-second range of a clip in your Event Browser. If you select **Replace from Start**, FCPX only takes the first 2 seconds of your source clip to perfectly fit the duration of the replaced clip.

Replace from End works exactly the opposite. It ignores the selection start and works backwards, pulling as much media as it needs to from the end of your selected range to replace your clip in the timeline. This is useful if you want your clip to end on a specific moment or action, but you don't want to keep toying with the timing when the clip starts to end on the right moment.

There's more...

Transform properties and effects don't transfer, but here's a workaround

When you replace clips in any fashion, know that the properties and effects of the old, replaced clip are not applied to the new source clip. So, if you have applied a black and white effect to a clip and shrunk its scale down to 50 percent, but then replaced it with a new clip, the new clip will be in color and at 100 percent scale, just like an ordinary new clip.

A trick to work around this is to highlight the old clip you're about to replace (before you do any replacing!) and hit *Command + C* to copy the clip. Then replace your clip however you choose. Finally, select your new clip in the project and press *Command + Option + V* to perform a Paste Effects command. This will take the properties of the old clip and apply them to the new one!

A clever use for replacing clips to fix accidental audio- or video-only edits

You may have been working on your project for a very long time and come across a clip where you have accidentally placed only the video or the audio into the timeline. This may have occurred if at some point you mistakenly selected **Video Only** or **Audio Only** from the drop-down menu next to the edit buttons in the toolbar. Here's an easy way to fix that using the **Replace** command. Make sure that **All** is selected in the edit button drop-down menu, as shown in the following screenshot:

Select the clip in the timeline where you have only the audio or video. Hit *Shift + F* to reveal the clip in the Event Browser. Not only did FCPX find the original clip in the browser, it also shows you the original selected range. Click-and-drag your source clip on top of the older version in the timeline. Choose **Replace**. You have just replaced the clip with itself, but now with the video and audio intact!

Possible error messages

When trying to use **Replace from Start / Replace from End**, you might get a message that reads—**There is not enough media in the source clip to fill the range in the Timeline...** This means there was not enough duration left in your new clip to fill the duration of the old clip you're replacing. For example, if you were trying to replace a 5-second clip in your timeline and you chose a selection start point very close to the end of your source clip, it can't fill the whole 5-second space. FCPX gives you the option to continue with a normal replace edit (which will change the length of your project) or to cancel and choose a new selection start.

See also

To understand the **Replace and add to Audition** command, read the *Auditioning multiple shots or takes* recipe in *Chapter 4, Enhancing Your Editing*.

Splicing clips with the Blade tool

If you've ever recorded an interview, you know that virtually no speaker is flawless. We all "um" and "er"—it's just a fact of life. In some videos, this may not be a problem as you may be aiming for a more natural flow of language, for example if someone is recounting an old story in a documentary. It's human. However, if you're making a marketing video with a speaker giving important information in a professional manner, then it's best to try to limit these speech impediments. If your interview contains lots of "ums" and "ers," using the Blade tool is often the easiest solution to get rid of them.

Getting ready

You can do this with any footage, but if you've got some talking head shots to work with, put them in your timeline now.

How to do it...

1. First off, find the speech issue you want to remove. It could be an "um," "er," or a similar sound. Put your playhead or skimmer near the section and start hitting *Command + =* to zoom in pretty close to that point. This is a good time to make sure you can see your audio waveforms in the timeline, so if you can't, click on the light switch in the bottom-right corner of your timeline and select one of the **Clip Appearance** options that lets you see your waveforms. In the following screenshot, we have zoomed in on an "um," which you can see in the waveform:

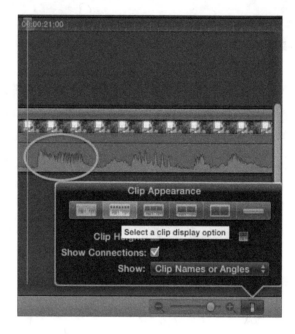

2. Choose the Blade tool from the tool palette in your tool bar or hit *B* on your keyboard. Place your cursor right on top of the clip just before the speech problem begins. Then click down with your mouse. The clip has been split into two pieces. This is commonly called a **through edit**. They play perfectly fine as long as they're touching. You'd never notice the difference.

3. Move your Blade tool cursor to just after the speech issue. Click again. Now your clip is split into three pieces, as shown in the following screenshot:

4. Press *A* to return to your Select tool.

5. Highlight the middle selection by clicking on it. Now, you have a decision to make. If you want to delete it and ripple the third section of the clip back to rest up against the first piece, just hit *Delete*.

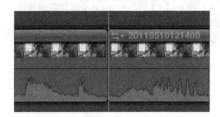

However, if you want to leave a gap, hit *Shift + Delete* to replace with a gap. You will likely have to try out both and hear which sounds better or see if leaving a gap will prevent sync issues later. The following screenshot shows a gap clip, the result of hitting *Shift + Delete*:

There's more...

Adding b-roll to bladed areas!

No matter which way you use the Blade tool, you're either going to be left with a black gap or a jump cut, where the speaker's head seems to jump bizarrely as frames have been removed from the clip. You're likely going to need to add some sort of b-roll or cutaway shot to cover this issue. Of course, you're the artist, so if that's the effect you're going for, ignore us! Otherwise, read the *Creating connected clips* recipe.

Removing a clip segment with the Range Select tool

In addition to the Blade tool, you can also use the Range Select tool. Hit *R* on your keyboard and then move your cursor to your timeline where your speech issue is. Click-and-drag across the problematic sound, much like if you were dragging across a word in a word processing program. Remember, it helps to be zoomed in and be showing your waveforms to do this accurately. Once you've highlighted the problem, choose whether to delete (the *Delete* key) or replace with a gap (*Shift + Delete*).

Blade without the Blade tool

It may sound odd at first, but you can splice a clip without activating the Blade tool! Simply move your skimmer over a clip and hit *Command + B*. It will splice the clip right where the skimmer is.

Using the Trim tool, part 1 – trimming and rippling

A rough cut should be exactly that—rough around the edges. Don't spend all your time trying to perfectly select clip ranges before you pop them into your timeline. Just get it close so that you can get a general idea of your film down in the timeline and then begin the fine-tuning process with the Trim tool.

The Trim tool is actually four tools in one—Ripple, Roll, Slip, and Slide. In the next three recipes, we'll tackle how to use each and show how they can help to perfect your rough cuts into a tightly edited final cut.

The first tool, Ripple, is used to alter the start or end point of a clip in your timeline. For example, perhaps you have an interview clip where the speaker finishes his/her sentence, but you accidentally kept the clip going too long and the speaker blinks or looks at the camera awkwardly (as so many untrained interview subjects tend to do). You need to cut out a few frames at the very end of that clip. Or perhaps you have another interview clip where you accidentally cut off the first word of a speaker's sentence (hey, it was a rough cut after all). In that case, you need to add a few frames to the beginning of that clip. The Ripple feature of the Trim tool will help us fix these sorts of scenarios with ease.

Getting ready

You can use any clips to work on this exercise, but interview clips work great, as they are one of the most common clips that will need to be rippled. In the following example, we are going to trim the end of an interview clip in which the speaker smacks his/her gums at the end of her speech.

How to do it...

1. Click on the tool palette in the toolbar and select the **Trim** tool, or hit *T* on the keyboard:

2. Move your cursor (now the Trim tool), to the end of a clip in your timeline that you want to shorten. Take note of the appearance of your cursor—this is the shape of the Trim tool when you are rippling an out point. Also take note of the waveform in the timeline where we can visibly see her gums smack. Lastly, observe the timecode where the playhead currently rests:

3. Click-and-drag your cursor to the left. The clip will seem to get a bit shorter and the following clip will be pulled along for the ride. You'll get live feedback of what you're doing in three places:

   ❑ The Viewer window will display the last frame of the clip you're rippling as well as the first frame of the following clip, which remains unchanged

   ❑ A tiny tooltip box appears near your cursor displaying how many frames you are rippling

   ❑ The timecode box will show you the current timecode of the cursor's location

Keep pulling left until you have trimmed off the necessary amount of media, then let go. In our case, we rippled to the left until we removed the last few frames containing the gum smack:

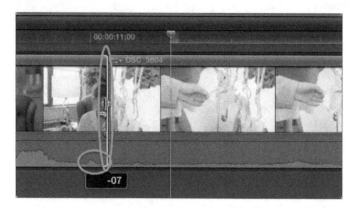

Unfortunately, there's one last issue with the sound. In the background, the camera operator bumped a table and there's a tiny audible bump heard (circled in the preceding screenshot). It's literally only in the last couple of frames of the clip, but it's still quite noticeable. Instead of clicking and dragging again (which can be difficult if only dragging a couple frames), we're going to ripple with our keyboard. Notice the fact that the last frame of the clip is highlighted with a golden bracket pointing inward toward the clip (also circled in the preceding screenshot). Because it is highlighted, FCPX knows what we want to ripple.

4. Press the comma key to ripple back one frame at a time. In our example, we pressed it five times. Those five frames were shaved off from the clip and all media following it in the project was rippled back accordingly.

5. Press *Shift + /*. This **Play Around** keyboard shortcut automatically plays the few-second area around where your playhead or skimmer is resting, allowing you to quickly judge if you have made a good edit. In our case, rippling five frames back was too much and cut off the speaker's last word!

6. Press the period key to ripple forward one frame. We rippled the out point forward by two frames, giving us back the last part of the speaker's sentence. Notice the new timecode as well. All in all, we rippled back 10 frames—seven frames by clicking and dragging, and an additional Three by using the comma key. Obviously, every scenario is different, so you will have to figure out what works best in your case!

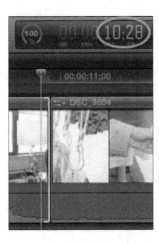

How it works...

To summarize, rippling affects the duration of one clip by adding or removing frames from one edge of that clip. In turn, your whole project will be made longer or shorter accordingly.

The previous example only talks about trimming an out point, but in points can be rippled in the exact same manner! Simply click-and-drag back and forth on a clip's in point to add or remove frames from the beginning of a clip! Thanks to the Magnetic Timeline, nothing gets overwritten, although in some cases you may cause two media clips to overlap, so be careful!

There's more...

Media limits (what are those red lines?)

Occasionally when rippling a clip longer (that is extending a clip's length), the golden brackets on the edge of clips will turn red, and you will seem to have hit a dead end. Why can't you ripple a clip further? You have hit the **media limit**. Simply put, you've reached the very end of the clip and there is no more available media to add!

More ways to ripple!

You can ripple by clicking and dragging without actually turning on the Trim tool! Thanks to the way the Magnetic Timeline works, if you simply move your regular Select tool to the edge of a clip and drag it towards the left or right, it will trim the clip and ripple sequence!

As we learned in the exercise, if you simply click and highlight a clip's in or out point, you can ripple frame-by-frame with the comma and period keys. You can also ripple by very specific amounts of actually typing numbers on your keyboard! For example, if you highlight a clip's in point by clicking on it with the Trim tool, and then type -12 and hit *Return*, the clip will start 12 frames earlier and the rest of the project will ripple back to accommodate the addition! If you type +12 and hit *Return* on the start of a clip, it will move the in point forward by 12 frames and shorten that clip accordingly.

If you find rippling by clicking and dragging difficult to do accurately, but find comma and period keys too slow, hold down the *Shift* key while pressing comma or period. This will ripple 10 frames at a time instead of one!

Trim a clip shorter, but don't ripple the whole timeline

Perhaps you want to trim a clip shorter, but you do not want to have the whole timeline ripple as well, because you want to make sure your timing doesn't get messed up. Turn on the Position tool with the *P* key and then try trimming a clip shorter. Instead of rippling the whole timeline back with the trimmed clip, it will leave behind a gap clip, keeping the original timing of your project.

Highlight an in or out point without clicking on it

You can ripple entirely without touching your mouse or trackpad! Working in your timeline, you can tap the up or down arrows to move back or forward to different edit points. Once you land on an edit point you know you want to ripple, hit *[* (left bracket) if you want to ripple the out point of the outgoing clip or *]* (right bracket) if you want to ripple the in point of the incoming clip!

See also

Read the next two recipes to make sure you have a full understanding of the capabilities of the Trim tool!

Using the Trim tool, part 2 – rolling

As we have learned in the previous recipe, using the Trim tool to ripple results in changing the length of one clip in your project as well as a change in the length of your overall project. The **Roll** tool affects two clips' timing at once—it allows you to pick a new edit point between two clips, shortening one clip while lengthening the other equally, resulting in a zero sum; your project's length remains unchanged! The Roll tool is often used in match-on-action scenarios where you have two cameras recording the same moment in time. While editing these two angles together, you might have perfectly aligned the action by trimming the two clips appropriately, but the exact moment where your clips shift from one angle to another may not be ideal.

In this exercise, we are using two clips shot by two cameras at the same time during a dance at a wedding. The two shots have already been edited into the sequence and timed so that the action matches when the timeline switches from one clip to the other. Consider this a very simple multicam edit (although the more sophisticated, proper way to do it is covered in the *Multicam, part 1 – getting your media synced and prepped* recipe in *Chapter 4, Enhancing Your Editing*. The action of the two shots match properly, but we wish the incoming angle started at a different point in time, as the dancers' faces are covered by their arms.

 Don't be confused by the filmstrip view of a clip in the timeline. The first/last images seen on a clip's filmstrip in the timeline don't accurately represent the actual first/last frames of that flip. Always trust your viewer to make sure you're looking at the first/last frame of an image!

The following is a shot of the edit point between two clips as it appears in the timeline:

And the following are the actual current frames around the edit point. Notice that the thumbnails we saw in the timeline do not accurately reflect the actual start and end frames of clips:

How to do it...

1. Click on the tool palette in the toolbar and select the **Trim** tool, or hit *T* on the keyboard:

2. Place your Trim tool right on the edit point between two clips. Take note of the cursor's appearance. This is the Roll tool. It looks similar to the Ripple tool but is subtly different. We want to move the moment when the shots change a little bit forward in time, after their arms have gotten out of the way of their own faces!

3. Click-and-drag the edit point a few frames to the right. As you drag, you will see real-time feedback in your Viewer that displays the new last frame of the outgoing clip and the new first frame of the incoming clip. If dragging toward the right, our first clip will get longer while the second clip will get equally shorter, as shown in the following screenshot:

4. Let go of the mouse when you're happy with the new timing of your edit:

How it works...

To summarize, rolling an edit point affects the duration of two clips—it changes the outgoing clip's out point and the incoming clip's in point. Depending on whether you click-and-drag towards the left or right, one gets shorter while the other gets longer, which has the added benefit of making sure your project doesn't change duration!

There's more...

Rolling and Multicam edits

As hinted in the previous exercise, one of the most common uses for the Roll tool is in true multicam scenarios. Once you've got all your clips lined and synced up and you've done a rough multicam edit, you can use the Roll tool to change the timing of your edits when your project switches from one angle to another. Read the *Multicam, part 1 – getting your media synced and prepped* recipe in *Chapter 4, Enhancing Your Editing* to get started with multicam.

Getting your timed project back in beat

There are other uses for the Roll tool and reasons to change the timing of an edit point that don't have to do with match-on-action or multicam. Perhaps you've edited a music or promo video that is cut in beat to music. Most of your edit points are supposed to fall right on a bass note or percussion beat. However, upon watching what you thought was your final cut, you realize one cut was poorly edited and fell after a beat in music. You don't want to simply trim the clip, because that will ripple your whole project and potentially move everything out of sync with the music. The Roll tool saves the day here. Simply roll your edit point until the edit point is lined up with the beat in the music! A whole recipe is devoted to this, so make sure to read the *Editing in beat to the music* recipe in *Chapter 4, Enhancing Your Editing*.

Using your keyboard to roll

Just like we learned with the Ripple tool, we can roll with our keyboard. All you have to do first is make sure your Trim tool is active and select the edit point we want to roll by clicking on it. Alternatively, you can use your up or down arrows on your keyboard to move your playhead to a particular edit point and hit the \ key. This will highlight the edit point in the same manner as clicking on it. Lastly, use your comma and period keys to roll the edit point backward or forward. Alternatively, after you have highlighted an edit point, you can type a value such as +14 and return to roll the edit point forward by 14 frames.

See also

Make sure you read the previous and next recipe to make sure you have a full understanding of the capabilities of the Trim tool!

Using the Trim tool, part 3 – slipping and sliding

Finally, we have come to the end of the road for the Trim tool. Sadly, it has nothing to do with the fun backyard game. And, realistically speaking, these tools likely won't be commonly used in your repertoire of editing weapons. But, they both have a time and a place. Much like rolling, both slipping and sliding allow you to fix the timing of clips without affecting the timing of your overall project.

The Slip tool allows you to easily use a different portion of your clip than you originally selected. Let's take an easy example. You had a clip that was exactly 10 seconds in length, but only edited the portion 02:00 to 04:00 into your project. Later, you decide you wished you had actually used a different 2-second range of the clip, perhaps 05:00 to 07:00. Slipping lets you do this easily without disrupting the rest of your project.

The Slide tool is the least used, but has its moments. It allows you to re-time when a clip starts in your timeline, shifting it earlier or later, but proportionately adjusting the two clips on either side of it so as not to disrupt the overall timing of the project.

Getting ready

Ideally, you want to have three clips to work with in this exercise. To make sure that you can practice these tools properly, make sure all three clips have media handles, that is, make sure you didn't just place the entire clip into the sequence, but rather you selected a smaller range within the clips and edited them into the timeline.

In the following exercise, we have used three clips of a playful dog with some appropriate background music:

How to do it...

1. The first two steps are optional, but will help us paint a picture of how the slipping process works. Before we turn on the Trim tool, make sure your Select tool is active by pressing *A* on the keyboard. Right-click on the clip you want to slip (that is the one in which you wish to select a different range). Select **Open in Timeline**, as shown in the following screenshot:

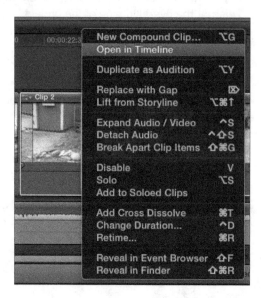

2. **Open in Timeline** takes the clip and puts it into its own timeline view so you can look at it without the distraction of what's around it and, more importantly, see your clip's handles. Hit *Shift + Z* to zoom to fit, which perfectly sizes the clip to the width of your timeline window. The shaded portion of the clip are your handles, that is, the unused portion of your clip. In this example, we wish we had used an earlier portion of the clip, starting with a good full shot of the dog staring at the camera (circled in the following screenshot). When you are ready to return to your main timeline, click on the **Go back in timeline history** button (circled in the following screenshot):

3. Click on the tool palette in the toolbar and select the **Trim** tool, or hit *T* on the keyboard:

4. Move your cursor right over the top of the clip, really anywhere except the edges of the clip. Observe the new look of the cursor. This is the icon for the Slip tool, as shown in the following screenshot:

5. Click-and-drag to the right. As you do, you will get live feedback in the Viewer, showing you the current in and out frames of the video. The further you drag to the right, the earlier in time you are moving in terms of the clip's content. It might seem counterintuitive at first, but the visual filmstrip feedback in the timeline should make it clear.

6. Let go of the mouse when you're happy with the newly chosen content. Your project is of the same length as before, but you have a new range of your clip in the project, as shown in the following screenshot:

We're happy with our clip's content but not the timing. Looking at the following screenshot, we see by our song's waveform that the song kicks into high gear a few seconds before our second clip begins. It'd be nice if the clip starts right when the song takes off. That's where sliding comes into play!

7. Once again, make sure your cursor is over the second clip. Now, press and hold the *Option* key. The cursor changes subtly into the Slide tool as follows:

8. Now click-and-drag to the left. As you do, you will see that the second clip's duration and content do not change, but its position is moved earlier in time. To accommodate this, the first clip is trimmed from the end and the third clip is extended from the beginning. The sum total length of the three clips is unchanged. Let go of the mouse when you have lined up the beginning of the second clip with the jazzy moment in the song. The following is what the timeline looks like before the drag:

The following screenshot is the result you will get after the drag:

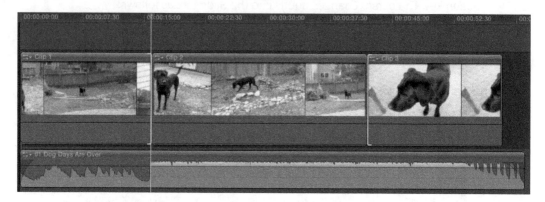

Slipping and sliding with the keyboard

Just like with rippling and rolling, we can slip and slide with the keyboard. To slip with the keyboard, simply click on the main body of the clip in the timeline with the Trim tool enabled and then use your comma and period keys, just as we did with ripple and roll. You will see two golden brackets pointing inward toward the clip to let you know your FCPX is ready to slip it. You can also use your number keys to select a specific number of frames to slip as well. To slide with the keyboard, option-click on the clip and again, use the comma and period keys. You will see two golden brackets surrounding the clip again, but this time, the first one points toward the first clip while the second points toward the third. Again, you can also use the number keys to slide if you wish.

Media limits

Don't forget about the red brackets when slipping and sliding. If you see the golden brackets turning red, it means you've run out of media on one of your clips and cannot slip or slide any further!

Read the previous two recipes to make sure you have a full understanding of the capabilities of the Trim tool!

Creating and working with gap clips

In another major change to the nonlinear editing process, Apple has reconceived the way empty spaces in the timeline work. When a clip is deleted or moved from the timeline in FCP7 and other major editing suites, you are left with literally an empty space. There is just nothing there. In FCPX, you are left with a **gap clip**. It acts just like any other piece of media in your timeline, but it is a clip of pure transparent space.

Getting ready

To practice making gap clips, just have a simple timeline with five clips inside, as shown in the following screenshot:

How to do it...

1. Click on your first clip to select it. Press *Shift + Delete*. The clip is removed from the timeline, but instead of rippling the rest of the sequence back (the normal behavior of the Magnetic Timeline), the clip is simply replaced by a gap clip:

2. Right-click on your second clip. Choose **Lift from Primary Storyline** from the pop-up menu. The clip is pulled out of the primary storyline and turned into a connected clip. What is it connected to? A gap clip that took its place! Your new lifted clip can now easily be dragged earlier or later in your timeline.

3. Turn on the Position tool by pressing *P*. Click-and-drag the third clip to the end of the timeline. When you let go, notice that the timeline did not ripple like it normally does when the Magnetic Timeline is active. Instead, the clip was moved to the end of the project and at its original location is a gap clip. Press *A* to reactivate your Select tool.

4. Place your playhead between the fourth and fifth clips in your primary storyline. Select **Edit | Insert Generator | Gap**. A three-second gap clip is inserted between the two clips and the rest of the timeline is rippled accordingly, as shown in the following screenshot:

5. Place your cursor (which should be the normal Select tool) on the right edge of the newly created gap clip. Click-and-drag left and right. The clip expands and contracts just like a regular clip, and the rest of the timeline ripples accordingly.

4

Enhancing Your Editing

In this chapter, we will cover the following:

- ▶ Making a three-point edit
- ▶ Creating additional storylines
- ▶ Trimming audio and video separately with a split edit (also known as making a J or L cut)
- ▶ Grouping clips together as a compound clip
- ▶ Adding markers and to do items
- ▶ Auditioning multiple shots or takes
- ▶ Editing in beat to the music
- ▶ Using the precision editor
- ▶ Using multicam, part 1 - getting your media synced and prepped
- ▶ Using multicam, part 2 - making the live cut
- ▶ Using multicam, part 3 - fine-tuning your multicam edit

Introduction

You've got a good handle on the basics of editing now: find a clip, select a range, add to timeline, and repeat. Now it's time to learn about some of the more advanced tools that make Final Cut Pro X unique compared to the competition. By the end of this chapter, you'll understand when and how to create secondary storylines, some of the uses of compound clips, the accuracy of the Precision Editor, and how to master the almighty multicam editing process.

Making a three-point edit

Covering interview subjects with b-roll is one of the most elementary aspects of editing video. It's simply a fact that staring at a talking head nonstop for an entire documentary is about 400 percent more likely to make your audience fall asleep! If you've read the *Creating connected clips* recipe in the previous chapter already, you know how we can easily select a piece of b-roll to accomplish this task. But if we really want to be precise with our timing, we will employ an extra technique called a **three-point edit**. Perhaps an interview subject says one particular sentence about their topic of expertise during a longer spiel, and we want to cover exactly that one sentence, beginning to end, with b-roll. The three-point edit makes this easy.

Getting ready

Our simple timeline consists of one talking head clip.

How to do it...

1. Listen to your talking head interview shot and find a sentence where the speaker verbally illustrates an idea that you may have a perfect piece of b-roll to accompany the description. In our example, our speaker is talking about the importance of playing with energetic dogs outdoors.

2. Select your Range tool by clicking on the Tool Palette in the toolbar, as shown in the following screenshot, or by simply hitting *R* on your keyboard:

3. Click on your speaker clip right where the sentence begins and drag across until the speaker finishes the sentence.

   Let's look at a couple of hints to make this easier. Remember to zoom in (by pressing *Command + =*) or out (by pressing *Command + -*) of your timeline to get to a point where it's easy to select that one sentence with the Range tool. If you're too far zoomed out, you can't accurately get your Range tool at the exact start of the sentence or let go on the exact end. And if you've zoomed in too far, it can be cumbersome to drag across the sentence, if the space it occupies is wider than your screen!

   Also, this would be a good time to turn on your waveform view if you haven't done so already. Click on the light switch in the lower-right corner of your timeline and select one of the Clip Appearance icons that displays your waveforms. This will make it easier to see when the speaker starts and stops talking.

4. In your Event Browser, find the piece of b-roll you want to cover the selected range. Select a start point by skimming to the moment in time you want the b-roll to start and hitting *I*. The end point will be automatically set for the end of the clip:

5. Hit *Q* to connect the clip. The clip is connected and only covers the exact range you had selected in the timeline:

How it works...

If you've highlighted a range in your timeline and then go up and select a range for your b-roll in your Event Browser, FCPX ignores the out point of the browser clip. If your selected range in the timeline was 10 seconds (as ours was approximately), FCPX simply uses 10 seconds from your event clip starting from your selection start (also known as the start point) and stops when it reaches your selection end (the end point).

There's more...

You can insert and overwrite with three-point edits too

The three-point edits are most commonly used in conjunction with the connect clip function, but can be used with the other edit functions as well, such as insert and overwrite. Simply select a range in your timeline again, select a start point on a clip in your browser, and perform the edit of your choice. No matter how long of a clip range you selected in your browser, FCPX contains it to the selection range in the timeline.

Errors you may encounter

When attempting a three-point edit you may get the message **There is not enough media in the source clip to fill the range in the Timeline**. It's pretty self-explanatory—perhaps you selected a five-second range in your timeline to cover but tried to connect a clip with only three seconds of media, therefore the clip can't fill the range. You are given the option to cancel and select a new, longer range or new clip, or you can proceed and accept the fact that your b-roll won't cover the entire originally selected range.

Backtiming a three-point edit

You can work in reverse with three-point edits. Perhaps you have selected a range in your timeline you want to cover and you've found the perfect clip in your Event Browser to cover it, but you want that b-roll clip to end on a specific moment in time or action. Repeat all the steps above with two minor changes—in step 4, select an end point at a point when you want to ensure your b-roll clip ends. In step 5 hit *Shift + Q* instead of just *Q*. This creates what is known as a **backtimed three-point edit**. FCPX places the end point you selected in the browser, lines it up with the end of the range you selected in the timeline, and works backwards to fill the range.

Creating additional storylines

When working in FCPX, that big black bar going across the middle of your timeline is called the **primary storyline**. Its name describes its function perfectly—it's where your primary story should be told. If you're making a documentary, talking heads and essential imagery should be placed here. However, secondary elements (b-roll, cutaways, picture-in-pictures, music, and so on), are usually going to be placed as connected clips above or below the primary story. If you haven't done so already, this would be a good time to read the *Creating connected clips* recipe in *Chapter 3, Basic Editing Mechanics*.

Connected clips are great to use and unbound by the rules of the Magnetic Timeline. But sometimes the very properties that make a connected clip what it is, can cause frustrations, especially if you do some heavy trimming. Binding connected clips into a new storyline can help mitigate these problems.

Getting ready

In the following example, we are going to work with a simple project with some voiceover narration files that are connected to the clips in the primary storyline. Using the following screenshot, you can construct a similar situation with your own media.

In this scenario, we're going to see how rippling in the Magnetic Timeline can cause connected clips to accidentally overlap and how creating new storylines can help resolve this problem.

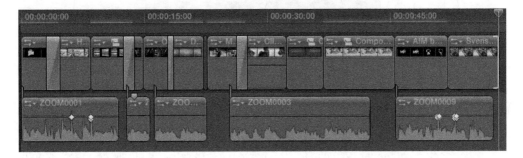

How to do it...

1. Click on the right edge of any clip preceding a clip with a connected narration file and drag to the left, rippling the clip (and timeline) shorter. If you ripple back far enough, you may encounter a situation where two of your narration files overlap with one another. In the following screenshot, rippling too far to the left leads to an overlap:

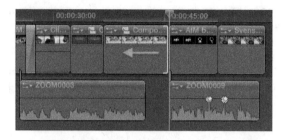

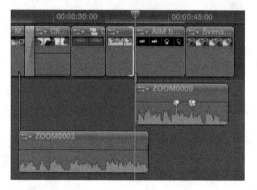

2. Hit *Command + Z* to undo.

3. Highlight all of the narration files. Right-click on any of the narration files and choose **Create Storyline** (by pressing *Command + G*). A little black bubble appears around all of the voiceovers. Also notice that there is no longer a connection point from every connected **voiceover (VO)** clip to a clip above it, but rather a single connection point attached to the clip above the first VO file:

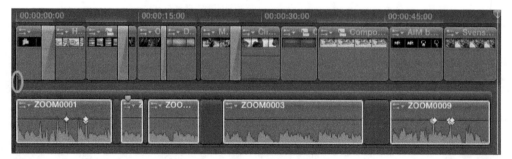

4. Go back to the same clip you tried to ripple before and try again. As you ripple, notice that the timing of the VO files has become locked in the new storyline you have created and they will not overlap with each other!

How it works...

Putting clips into a new storyline places them in a little bubble that acts like one clip (as illustrated by the single connection point). The timing will stay locked for all clips inside a storyline. Of course, you can easily re-arrange clips within a secondary storyline, thanks to the fact that they take on the properties of the Magnetic Timeline—yet another benefit!

There's more...

Transitions and extra storylines

You could easily discover this by happenstance, but there's an important concept to understand about transitions and connected clips. In order to place a transition between two connected clips, those two clips must be within a secondary storyline. What's nice is that FCPX saves you the step of having to highlight the clips and create that storyline. If your two connected clips are touching and you simply drag-and-drop a transition between them, FCPX will automatically create a secondary storyline bubble around them and place in the transition.

Inserting a gap clip at the beginning

Even if you've followed all the steps in the previous section, you can still run into goofy scenarios that can throw you and your timing off. As we saw, the secondary storyline is attached to the first clip in the timeline, but what if we wanted to move the first clip? All the VO files would move with it! If you want to prevent this, the best thing would be to insert a gap clip at the very beginning of your project by moving your playhead to the front of your timeline and hitting *Option + W*. Trim it so it's only approximately a second long, then simply drag your connected storyline earlier until the connection point is connected to the gap clip.

Adding more clips to a secondary storyline

Once you start making additional storylines, they're not closed off from adding more clips! You can simply click-and-drag more clips inside of them and watch as the storyline will expand to accommodate it. If you are a fan of using your editing keyboard shortcuts for inserting (*W*) and appending (*E*), you can tell FCPX to insert and append inside a secondary storyline by highlighting the entire thing. Simply click on the black banner across the top of the storyline and you'll see a golden box surround it. Now, when you insert/append a clip from your Event Browser, FCPX will do so in the selected (rather than primary) storyline.

See also

If you don't understand how the Magnetic Timeline works yet, read the *Working with (and without) the Magnetic Timeline* recipe in the *Chapter 3, Basic Editing Mechanics*. Also, if trimming is a new concept, go back and take a look at the *Using the trim tool, part 1: Trimming and rippling* recipe in the same chapter. Finally, secondary storylines can sometimes be confused with compound clips. Both can group your clips together, but in very different ways. To understand the differences between the two, read the *Grouping clips together as a compound clip* recipe.

Trimming audio and video separately with a split edit (also known as making a J or L cut)

You've seen and heard it a million times in movies and television shows before, but if done just right, you've never noticed it. It's the invisible form of editing known as a **split edit**. Often used during transitions from one scene to another or during conversation scenes, you will hear the next scene arrive before you see it. The audio of the second scene arrives a couple of seconds before we see the first shot of the scene. This type of split edit is nicknamed a **J cut** and it is named so for the shape of clips it creates in the timeline (you'll see it in a bit). The flipped version of a split edit is the **L cut**, in which you see the video cuts before the audio.

Getting ready

In this exercise, we've plopped two clips into our timeline that both have handles at the edit point. We'll need these handles in order to alter our clips' video or audio edit points. The first clip is a speaker talking about deer wildlife while the second shot is some nature footage of deer. We want to hear and see the speaker for a bit, but eventually cut to a shot of the deer and still hear the speaker finish her thought.

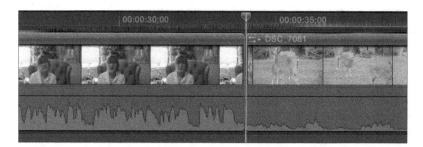

How to do it...

1. Double-click on the audio waveforms below the thumbnails for each of the two clips. A gap should appear between the video thumbnails and the waveforms. If you don't see your audio waveforms in the first place, make sure you're working in a timeline view that shows them by clicking on the light switch in the bottom right corner.

   When the video and audio has been expanded, we can now independently trim or roll each of them.

2. Turn on your Trim tool by selecting it in the Tool Palette or hitting *T* on your keyboard.

3. Place your cursor right over the edit point between the two video clips (don't hover over the edit point between the audio). Click-and-drag to the left. You will see that only the video edit point is rolling back while the audio edit point remains in place. Let go after rolling back a couple of seconds. In our example, when we play the clip back, we will see that the edit cuts to the shot of the deer while the speaker is finishing up her sentence. When she is done speaking, the audio of the second clip kicks in and the clip continues playing as normal. This is an L cut (look at the shape of the first clip in the following screenshot). If you had rolled the edit point later, it would create a J cut:

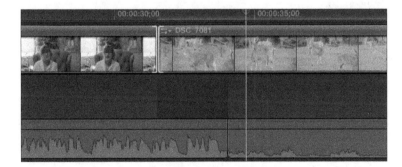

4. Play around with your footage a little bit to get a feel for the best timing of your edit. When you are done, double-click on the waveforms again to collapse the video and audio back together.

There's more...

Changing the audio edit instead of video

If you'd rather change the timing of your audio edits instead of video edits, you can; it just takes an extra step. You have to trim each audio clip once instead of just rolling the edit point like we did the video edit. In step 3, rather than place your cursor over the exact edit point between the video clips, place your cursor over the start point of the incoming audio waveform and click-and-drag to the right. The audio is trimmed back and there is now a gap in your audio. Place your cursor over the out point of the outgoing clip and click-and-drag to the right again till it clicks into place with the other clip. This is an alternate way to produce an L cut.

See also

If you haven't wrapped your brain around trimming, rippling, and rolling yet, go back and read the *Using the trim tool, part 1: trimming and rippling* and *Using the trim tool, part 2: rolling* recipes in *Chapter 3, Basic Editing Mechanics*.

Grouping clips together as a compound clip

Timelines can get messy! Once you start adding b-roll and titles and generators, or create a video with eight clips (or more!) on screen at once, your timeline can end up looking like a pile of loosely organized Lego blocks. At their most basic level, making compound clips can help tidy up a complex timeline. But the deeper you dig, the more and more functionality we can derive from them. For FCP7 users (as well as users of other pro editors), compound clips are the next generation version of nested sequences, but have much more potential as we'll learn down the line.

Getting ready

We have a timeline shown in the following screenshot, where four clips have been stacked on top of one another, and resized and moved to fit in four corners of the screen. Following these four clips is another individual clip:

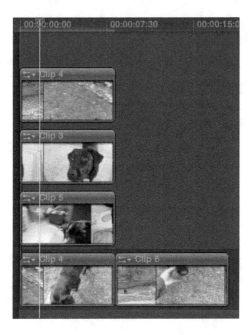

Let's see how we can we create a transition, so that our four-screen video wall fades into the following full-screen clip:

How to do it...

1. Highlight the four stacked clips. Right-click on them and choose **New Compound Clip...** (*Option + G*). The four clips suddenly seemed to merge into one, simply labeled **Compound Clip** in the timeline:

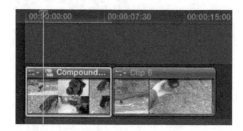

2. Play the clip. It plays identically to the way it did before. Nothing has changed in the output of our video.

3. Double-click on the new item labeled **Compound Clip**. We are brought into a little micro-universe of the clip that displays what the compound clip is made up of—our original four clips!

4. Click the Timeline History Back button (or hit *Command + [*) to return to your main timeline:

5. Click on the Transitions Browser button in the toolbar. Select the transition of your choice and drag it between the newly created compound clip and the clip following it. FCPX lets you know that **There is not enough extra media beyond clip edges to create the transition**. You might've had enough media originally on your clips that are inside the compound clip, but now that the transition is being applied to the entire compound clip itself (which is now one entire object), there isn't enough handle space to create the transition without shortening the clip a little. Click on **OK**.

How it works...

Creating compound clips takes all the selected clips and puts them inside a little pocket universe. The pocket universe is easily accessible by simply double-clicking on it, showing you that what you've created is a timeline within a timeline. Once inside, you can modify the contents of the compound clip as needed and exit to your original timeline by clicking on the Timeline History Back button.

There's more...

Transforming and applying effects to compound clips

Now that you've made a compound clip, remember that it acts just like any ordinary clip does. For example, you can take any effect from the **Effects Browser** and add it to the compound clip. If it were a Black and White effect, everything inside that compound clip would appear black and white. Or, if you highlighted a compound clip and shrunk it down to 50 percent scale with the Transform tool, everything would appear to be scaled down. Don't get confused, though—if you double-click on the compound clip after applying such an effect or transform, you won't see the change(s) once you're inside the pocket universe of the clip. It has only applied your effect or transform to the external shell of the compound clip, not each individual piece inside.

See also

There are a ton of potential uses for compound clips. This is only the tip of the iceberg! Read the *Moving clips in sync using compound clips* recipe in *Chapter 8, Get Your Movie to Move* and the *Creating and reusing a show intro* recipe in *Chapter 7, Titles, Transitions, and Generators* for a couple of excellent and advanced uses.

Adding markers and to do items

When working on a long, involved project, you're bound to come across points in your timeline where you utter "Ack! I have to fix that, but I don't have time right now!" Or perhaps you're tag-teaming a project with another editor and want an easy manner to leave notes behind for your editing buddy. **Markers** and **To Do Items** are the way to go.

How to do it...

1. Place your playhead anywhere along a clip. Hit *M* once. Take note of the blue marker icon that has appeared on the clip. This is a standard marker, simply a visual cue for a particular moment in time. If all you need to do is leave a visual icon for yourself, you're done. But we can do more!

2. Move your playhead to another point in time (on the same or a different clip). Press *M* twice. The first press adds the marker and the second press brings up the marker dialog box. Now you can type in a title for your marker. We'll type in `Trim in point to here`. Click on the box that says **Make To Do Item**. The box disappears and your marker has turned red. This is to let you know you have modified your second marker and turned it into a to-do item:

3. Click on the Timeline Index button in the lower-left corner of the screen. The index pops up from the left of the screen. Click on the **Tags** button. This shows us a list of all tagged items in our timeline, including keywords, markers, and to do items. To narrow down further, click on the marker icon at the bottom of the list. Now only your markers are displayed. Click on the marker you placed in step 1 and your playhead will jump right to it:

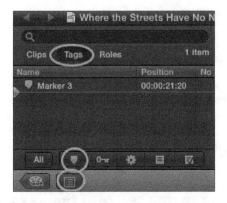

4. Now click on the fourth icon, which looks like a list icon. This shows you all your to do items. Click on the to do item and again, the playhead will jump straight to it:

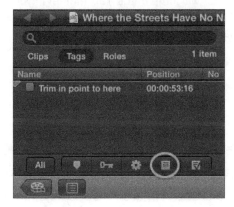

5. Click on the red box next to the to-do item. The item vanishes! Click on the fifth icon in the bottom row, which shows you completed to do items. Your marker is there, now turned green, showing that the item has been completed:

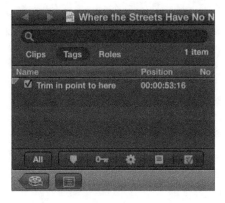

There's more...

Placing markers on connected clips

Placing markers on clips in your primary storyline is a piece of cake—just press *M*. However, if you're trying to place a marker on a connected clip, you might have a harder time because even with your playhead over a connected clip, FCPX still places the marker on the primary storyline clip. The only catch before trying to place the marker is to click on the connected clip to highlight it. Once highlighted, FCPX will know you're trying to place the marker on that clip when you hit *M*.

Jumping from marker to marker with the keyboard

If you like to move around you timeline using your keyboard as much as possible, you'll be happy to know there's a keyboard shortcut to bounce from marker to marker. If you press *Ctrl + '*, your playhead/skimmer will jump to the next marker in your timeline, regardless of whether it is a standard marker, to do item, or completed to do item. Pressing *Ctrl + ;* will take you to the previous marker in the timeline.

See also

Read the *Editing in beat to the music* recipe in this chapter to learn how to use markers to allow you to create an energetic video that cuts in rhythm to a song of your choice.

Auditioning multiple shots or takes

Decisions, decisions. The hardest part of editing isn't always the editing process—it's deciding which shots to use. What is the most dramatic shot to introduce the bride in a wedding montage? Which piece of wild animal b-roll should you use while listening to a speaker describe the African savannah? Which take is best in the scene you're editing together for a short film?

FCPX introduces a new feature called **Audition** which lets editors easily place multiple clips into one spot in a timeline and easily swap each one in and out to help decide which is the best to use.

Getting ready

In the following exercise we have a simple wedding montage set to music, but can't decide on the best shot to show the bride getting into her dress:

How to do it...

1. In your Event Browser, find another clip that you think you might want to use in place of the clip in question in your timeline.

2. Mark a selection range. Do not worry about how long the clip is (it can be shorter or longer than the original).

3. Click-and-drag the clip right on top of the existing clip. A pop-up window appears. Select **Add to Audition**:

4. Repeat steps 1 and 2 with another clip. In fact, repeat as many times as you like.

5. After you have added as many clips to the **Audition** process as you like, look closely at the original clip in the timeline. Notice a tiny spotlight icon in the upper-left corner of the clip. Click on it and the Audition window pops up:

6. In the new window, you should see your current clip and be able to skim through it with your cursor. Press your right arrow key and notice as the first clip you added to the **Audition** process appears and instantly replaces the original clip. Hit the right arrow key again and see it happen again with the next clip you added to the **Audition**. Notice as you swap the clips in and out, the clip length changes and the timeline ripples accordingly.

7. Even if you haven't decided on the best shot yet, click on **Done**.

8. Right click on the Auditioned clip and select **Audition | Preview**. Your playhead instantly jumps back in time to a couple seconds before the start of your auditioned clip, plays through it, and then loops. This helps give you a good idea of how this particular clip works in your project. After it plays through once or twice, hit the left and right arrow keys, and, without stopping, your project will switch to your other auditioned angles, allowing you to see how each and every one works in your project. When you've decided on the best shot, click on **Done**.

There's more...

Auditioning with connected clips

You aren't limited to your primary storyline when auditioning clips. The process works just as easily with connected clips. Perhaps you're trying to pick the perfect piece of b-roll to cover a speaker. You can follow the identical workflow above to accomplish the task.

Duplicating auditioned clips to test different effects

In the **Audition** window, you may have noticed a button labeled **Duplicate**. Why would you want to duplicate a clip within an **Audition**? To test out the exact same clip, but with different effects!

The easiest way to start this project is to click on any clip in your timeline and choose **Duplicate as Audition** (*Option + Y*) from the pop-up window. An **audition clip** is created which you can access by clicking on the spotlight icon on the clip. Click on the **Duplicate** button again to add a third version. Now that you've got three identical clips, try adding an effect of your choice to the first clip, switch to the next clip, and add a different effect. Repeat the process for the third. Pick which effect looks best and click on **Done**!

See also

If you know right away that you simply want to replace a clip in your timeline and you know what clip you want to use, Auditioning is not the right tool. Read the *Replacing a clip* recipe in the previous chapter.

Editing in beat to the music

Your client just asked you to make a snazzy promo piece that really grooves with its soundtrack. A common way to make this happen is to edit your video in pace or beat with your music. Creating that link between your sound and image really helps separate a video from the rest of the crop. This method can be used to create some pretty stellar photo slideshows to boot.

Getting ready

Find a piece of music in your iTunes library that really has a great beat to it. We'd love to make our own recommendations, but beauty is in the eye... er, ear of the beholder here, so find one that suits you!

There are a couple of different ways to approach this topic, but we're going to go about it by starting with an empty timeline. It is not required to do so, but it's the simplest way to demo the task.

How to do it...

1. Edit your music track into your timeline with the append function (by pressing *E* on your keyboard). Make sure you can easily see the tune's waveforms. If not, change your clip appearance by clicking on the light switch in the bottom right corner of your timeline.

2. Click on the song track to highlight it. This is important to ensure your markers are added to the song clip, rather than any other clips that might be present.

3. Skim to the beginning of the tune or to a place in the song where you want to start marking the beats (perhaps before the refrain):

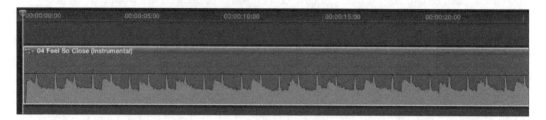

4. Hit the Space bar to begin playback. As you listen to your song, listen specifically for the beats. As you do so, keep your finger hovering over the *M* key, which is the keyboard shortcut to add a marker.

5. Each time there is a beat in your song or a point where you want to make a cut, hit *M* to add a marker. As you do, a blue marker is added to that point in time. When you are done, hit the Space bar to pause again:

6. Turn on your Range tool by pressing *R* on your keyboard.

7. Move your cursor to the very first marker in your timeline. There should be a reasonable amount of space between markers on your screen. If not, zoom into your timeline by pressing *Command + =*.

8. Click-and-drag right on the body of the clip from the position of the first marker to the position of the second marker. We have now highlighted that range between beats:

9. Up in your Event Browser, find a clip you want to place in the range we have selected. Mark a start point by skimming to the point in the clip you want to start at and hit *I*:

10. Hit *Q* on your keyboard. The clip should connect to the song clip and be timed perfectly to end at the second marker:

11. Repeat steps 9 and 10, selecting the next range in your timeline between markers two and three, then selecting a new clip in your Event Browser and connecting it to the music clip:

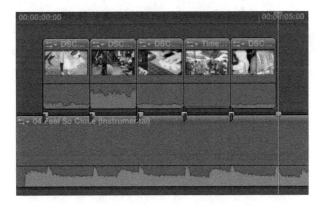

There's more...

Using the Roll tool to fix timing issues

Placing markers in beat to the music is only as accurate as you are. The markers are placed manually by you as you try and hit *M* in time with the beats. Some of us are better at this than others. If you've laid down a ton of clips over your markered music and you find that some of the edits don't seem to fall right on a beat, you can use the Roll tool to course-correct.

The best workflow is to first zoom in on the area pretty tightly in your timeline. Turn on your Trim tool (with the *T* key). If the edit falls after the beat (meaning you hit *M* too slowly the first time around), roll back the edit point to the left until it lines up. If the edit falls before the beat, roll to the right. You might need to listen to that area of your timeline to check your edit, so don't forget one of the most overlooked keyboard shortcuts in FCPX, Play Around Edit (*Shift + /*).

Adjusting marker timing

Markers can be easily nudged to left or right one frame at a time. Simply click on a marker to highlight it (it becomes slightly larger in your timeline). Then press *Ctrl + ,* or *Ctrl + .* to nudge the marker to left or right one frame. A different workflow than the one in the previous exercise (rolling to fix timing after you've edited clips in) is to nudge any misplaced markers into the right place before you begin dropping clips between markers.

Backtiming a clip into your timeline

Step 9 in the previous section mentions marking a start point for your clip with the keyboard shortcut *I*. However, if you prefer, you can make a backtimed edit, which will line up the selected end point of the range in the timeline with an end point you pick on your clip in the Event Browser and works backwards when placing the clip between the two markers. Do this when you want to care more about the ending image of your shot rather than the start. To backtime a clip, follow step 9, but mark an end point with *O* instead of a start point with *I*. When you are ready to add the clip between two markers, press *Shift + Q* instead of simply *Q*. This will create a backtimed edit.

This exercise makes use of markers, three-point edits, and the Roll tool, so if any of these concepts are new to you, read the *Adding markers and to do items* recipe and *Making a three-point edit* recipe from this chapter, and *Using the trim tool, part 2: rolling* from the previous chapter.

Using the Precision Editor

The Ripple tool lets you easily trim clips shorter as needed, but also extend them when needed. The tricky part is often not knowing how much you are able to extend a clip because you don't know how much additional handle space you have. In fact, you usually won't know until you hit a brick wall by seeing a red bracket appear, indicating you have run out of media.

The **Precision Editor** is a tool allowing you to see all available media of two clips on either side of an edit point and easily trim both and roll the edit point in one, easy-to-use interface. It is commonly used when trying to perfect timing of match-on-action shots or conversation scenes.

In the following example, we have two shots from a father/daughter dance at a wedding. Two cameras were used to record the moment. However, when creating our rough cut, we were a little too rough and accidentally created an overlap of action when we laid down the two clips to our timeline. The father of the bride twirls her in the first shot, the video cuts to the second camera, and we see the same twirl again. While we could fiddle with the Ripple tool to fix this situation, let's try another approach.

How to do it...

1. Double-click on the edit point between the two clips. The clips suddenly spread apart and overlap one another, separated by a gray bar. In addition to seeing the two edited clips, we also get to see their handles, as illustrated by the shaded portion of the clips. This is the Precision Editor view in the following screenshot:

2. You must pay close attention to the location of your cursor when playing clips in the Precision Editor view as its location will determine what you see in the Viewer.

    Hover over the gray bar in the middle and hit the Space bar. The clips play as you had originally edited them. Hover over the top clip and hit the Space bar. The clip plays, including the original unused handle of the clip beyond the original end point. Position your cursor over the shaded area of the second, lower clip and hit the spacebar. The clip plays starting with the original unused handle media before the original start point.

3. It would be nice if our new edit cut right in the middle of the twirl for some added visual flourish.

4. Hover over the first clip again and move your skimmer to a point in the middle of the action (obviously, the footage you're working with is different than the images in this recipe):

5. Click once with your mouse or trackpad. The end point of the clip is suddenly trimmed to that exact frame. We've perfected where we want the first clip to end, but have yet to fix the beginning of the second clip:

6. Move your cursor over the second clip. You could repeat the process in steps 4 and 5, but there's one other way to go about it. Instead of skimming to the matching frame and clicking, simply click and hold down on the clip and drag to the left and right. As you do this, you will alter the start point of the clip. You will see visual feedback in the Viewer, which will allow you to find the perfect frame that aligns the action with the first shot:

7. Let go when you have found the frame with the matching action.
8. Click on the button labeled **Close Precision Editor** in the lower right corner.

There's more...

The tool for type A editors

The Precision Editor is by no means a required tool to learn to improve your editing technique or perfect your timing of a scene. Using the regular Trim tool allows you to have all the same capabilities as the Precision Editor; you simply get the added benefit of seeing the additional media handles available around an edit point.

Rolling in the Precision Editor

Not only can you trim two clips easily in the Precision Editor; you can also roll the edit point where they meet! After you've synced up the action of two clips, hover over the gray knob in the middle of the Precision Editor window. Click-and-drag it to the left and right to roll the edit point:

Multicam part 1 – getting your media synced and prepped

Editing multi-camera shoots is rarely a pleasant experience. Interfaces for most editing software are cumbersome and far from straightforward to set up. Plus there's that whole syncing thing you have to deal with before you can even start editing! If you were lucky enough to work in a professional production environment where all the cameras had timecode synchronized, then you're multicamming life is easier. But for the rest of us, we need extra tools to help us out.

FCPX re-built how multicam projects are created, put together, and edited, and all for the better. In many cases now, editors no longer have to worry about marking exact sync points to line up clips. FCPX (using what we swear must be magic) analyzes the audio waveforms of each clip and syncs them automatically! And trust us when we say it works very well, even if one or more of your sources has pretty terrible audio. We tried!

Getting ready

There's a lot of prep work for you to get to this point and it has nothing to do with FCPX. You need at least two video clips that were shot with two unique cameras at the same time and place. In the example used in the next three recipes, we created a fake news broadcast with three camera angles.

You can ignore the fact that it was shot in front of a green screen. We use these clips again in the *Going green (screen)* recipe.

How to do it...

1. Highlight all the clips you want to use in your multicam project. Right click them and select **New Multicam Clip...** . A new dialog box opens. Name your new multicam clip and do not change any custom settings for now (more on these in the following sections). Make sure **Use audio for synchronization** is checked. Click on **OK**:

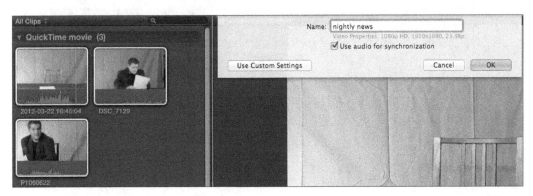

2. FCPX begins to analyze the clips, and will create a new multicam clip in your event after it has synced them up:

3. Click on the light switch in the upper-right corner of the Viewer and select **Show Angle Viewer**:

A new piece of the interface pops up in the left of the Viewer. Move your cursor over your multicam clip in the Event Browser. You should see up to four of your angles. As you skim back and forth over the clip, you should be able to see they are all in sync:

Now you have to make a critical choice. Think ahead to your finished product. When you imagine your movie cutting from angle to angle, does the audio switch with each cut as well? Or do you have one clip with the best, clearest audio that you want to use for the whole project and only cut video angles?

For example, in a two-camera, two-person interview, both subjects are likely mic'd. Therefore, you'd want to swap both video and audio angles simultaneously. However, on the flip side, perhaps you recorded a concert with multiple cameras, but only one was patched into the soundboard. Then you'd want to be able to switch video angles while using the one good audio source the whole time.

Notice the yellow box surrounding one of your angles. In the upper-right corner is an icon with a filmstrip and audio waveform (circled in the previous screenshot). This indicates that when you click from angle to angle, it will switch BOTH the audio and video angles.

Look toward the upper left region of your Angle Viewer. You see three icons, one for video and audio, one that is solely an audio waveform, and one that is solely a filmstrip (again, circled above). These buttons let you select what element(s) you want to switch when cutting angles.

In our example, the angle that is currently selected in the previous screenshot had the best audio and we want to use that camera's audio for the whole sequence. So we are going to click on the filmstrip icon in the upper left to tell FCPX to only switch video angles moving forward. Now when we click on any other angle, we see that a green, audio-only bounding box surrounds the original clip we had highlighted, and a blue, video-only box surrounds the new angle we clicked. As we click around, the audio angle will stay set on the original angle we selected and we can easily switch the video angles.

Keep in mind, we aren't doing any editing yet, just setting the stage for when we are ready to do the live edit.

There's more...

Other methods to sync besides audio

Our example was very easy to set up because we were able to use the audio to sync all of our angles. But that won't always be the case. Perhaps you had no audio on an angle or the sound was just so different between angles that FCPX couldn't properly sync them automatically. Luckily, you have other options.

Back in the **Make Muticam Clip...** window (see in step 1), you can click on **Use Custom Settings** and select other options under **Angle Synchronization**. You can tell FCPX to sync using **Timecode** (rare unless you were in a very professional shoot), **Content Created** (risky unless your time and date settings in your cameras were perfect), **Start of First Clip** (unlikely that you hit Record on the cameras at exactly the same moment), and finally **First Marker on the Angle**. This last option is usually safest. Before you make your multicam clip, simply place one marker on each clip at a **sync point**—an identical point in time on each clip.

This is usually easiest using an audio cue such as a clapper/slate's loud clack noise, but any obvious noise will do. If you also keep **Use audio for synchronization** checked, you get a two-for-one deal—FCPX will try to align by the markers you placed, but even if they weren't perfectly timed, FCPX will still try and look at the audio near those markers to perfectly align them!

Changing overlays and the number of viewable angles

You can overlay extra info on top of your angles in the Angle Viewer if you need help keeping them sorted. Simply click on the **Settings** button in the upper right of the Angle Viewer and you'll see options to display timecode, angle name/number, or clip name. You can also change settings to view two, four, nine, or 16 angles at once. Just know that the more you select, the more of a strain you put on your hard drive and processor!

See also

Keep reading the next two recipes to get the whole picture on multicam editing!

Multicam part 2 – making the live cut

The stage is set! We've synced up our media and made the important decision as to whether or not we want to cut both video and audio or only audio. Now it's time to place our multicam clip into a project and make our real-time rough cut!

Getting ready

Just make sure you've read the prior recipe to create your multicam clip.

How to do it...

1. Select your multicam clip in your Event and add it to a project of your choosing. You can insert, overwrite, connect, or append a multicam clip just like any other clip. For simplicity, we will append our multicam clip into an empty project.

2. Skim through your clip. You are only seeing one angle right now, the one you had selected most recently in the Angle Viewer. Do not be alarmed if you see black frames at the beginning or end of your clip. Because your clips may vary in length, FCPX creates black frames as needed during the syncing process.

3. Move your playhead to the beginning of the multicam clip. If you do not see the angle you want to start with, hover your cursor over the appropriate angle in the Angle Viewer. Notice the cursor changes to a blade icon. When you click on the icon, it will cut the video to that angle. You may also need to trim the front end of the clip with the Ripple tool if you see any black frames:

4. Double check that your playhead is still at the beginning of the clip. Start playback of your clip by hitting the Space bar.

5. As playback begins, keep your cursor in the vicinity of the Angle Viewer. As the clip plays, start clicking on the different angles. In your timeline, you will see FCPX automatically cut to the angle you selected. Go through your entire video and keep cutting! Don't worry if you cut a little too soon or too late on some cuts. We'll fix this in the next recipe.

6. Press the Space bar again when you are done to pause playback.

See also

Continue on to the final multicam recipe to really be able to polish off your multicam edit!

Multicam part 3 – fine-tuning your multicam edit

You've done it! You've done real-time multicam editing! But, chances are, you didn't do it right! That's not an insult, but the truth is, it's almost impossible to perfect the timing of your cuts the first time through simply by clicking on your angles in the Angle Viewer. Do you have to do the edit all over again? Absolutely not. FCPX has easy tools that let us fix the timing of our cuts and swap angles entirely.

Getting ready

Make sure you've read the last two recipes to understand how to set up a multicam clip and edit it into a project.

How to do it...

1. The most common desire when tweaking a multicam edit is to change the timing of some of your edits. You say to yourself "Oops, I wish I had cut from Angle A to Angle C a little sooner." It happens all the time! This can be accomplished very easily with the Roll tool.

    Move your Selection tool cursor on top of the edit point where you wanted to change the timing. Once you place your cursor right over the edit point, you should see the Roll tool cursor appear. Normally, you have to turn on the Trim tool to be able to use the Roll tool function, but specifically with multicam clips, FCPX makes it even easier by allowing you to skip that step!

2. Click-and-drag the edit point to the left (if you wanted to move the timing of the edit earlier). Let go. Because this is a multicam clip and everything was properly synced up, you can use the Roll tool all day long without worrying about any sync issues!

Upon further thought, we've also decided we wished we had cut to a different angle in that previous edit.

3. Right-click on an angle that you wish to swap out. Select the **Active Video Angle** option and then select from your list of angles:

The angle is immediately replaced. Also take note that the audio waveform did not change because we chose to only change the video angle. This is very important in our example as we are aiming to use one good audio source.

There's more...

Adding effects

You can absolutely add effects to multicam clips as well. After you've created your multicam edit, each piece acts like its own individual clip. Drag effects onto them as you so choose. If you like one particular effect and have tweaked it to your liking on one clip, you can copy and paste the effect with its settings onto the other clips! After adding and tweaking an effect on one clip, just highlight the clip, hit *Command + C*, select all the additional clips you want to paste the effect onto, and then select **Edit** | **Paste Effects** (or hit *Command + Option + V*).

5
Sweetening and Fixing Your Sound

In this chapter, we will cover the following:

- ▸ Reading and understanding the audio meters
- ▸ Lowering your music during speakers
- ▸ Lowering a loud, unexpected background sound with manual keyframes
- ▸ Replacing bad audio with a cleaner recording
- ▸ Sound effects, part 1 – browsing, connecting, and panning
- ▸ Sound effects, part 2 – animating with keyframes
- ▸ Sound effects, part 3 – working in a surround sound space
- ▸ Removing unwanted audio channels
- ▸ Unlinking audio from video
- ▸ Using FCPX's auto audio enhancements
- ▸ Recording a voiceover

Introduction

Ask any editor and he/she will tell you he/she would rather have to deal with editing and fixing bad video any day of the week over bad audio. Nothing can turn an audience off faster than horrible sound. If you can't understand your primary content, you might as well not have made a film to begin with! If you want to make your life easy, make sure you do everything in your ability to record good audio in the first place. While FCPX does have some tools to help us with bad audio, you'll make your life much easier if you take this into consideration while shooting.

Producing the right sound for your film is still an artistic endeavor, just like getting the right look, but there are some very important concepts you have to understand on how sound and volume are measured in a digital world. Rule number one—never trust your speakers. If you learn nothing else in this chapter, just remember that (but hopefully you'll learn lots more)!

Once you understand how to balance your audio levels, we'll move on to some more fun and fancy audio work including how to autofix some bad audio scenarios, record voiceovers, and work with surround sound!

Reading and understanding the audio meters

Before you can really start tackling and improving your audio, you simply have to understand how it is measured in the first place. An editor must observe the audio meters. These meters give a proper and consistent reading of the output level of our audio, whether our speakers are muted or at full blast.

Getting ready

You can work with any project you like for this recipe, however, if any of your timelines contain clips with yellow or red color in their waveform, those would be the best to practice on, as shown in the following screenshot:

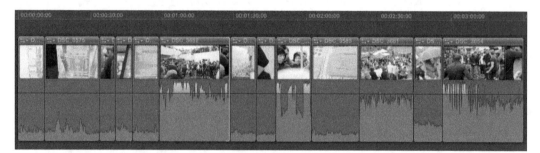

How to do it...

1. Click on the tiny audio meters icon inside the dashboard, located in the toolbar:

A larger version of the audio meters will appear to the right of your timeline. If you are working on a stereo project, you will see two bars for the left and right channels. If you are working on a surround project, you will see six bars for all the possible channels (left, right, center, left surround, right surround, and **low-frequency effects (LFE)** also known as your subwoofer).

2. Click-and-drag to the left on the dividing line between your timeline and the audio meters. They will get wider. Keep dragging until you see numbers appearing at the top of the meters. You may at first see -∞ instead of an actual number, but you can disregard this for the moment:

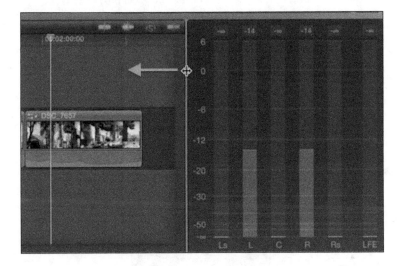

3. Play a clip in your timeline. Watch the meters bounce up and down. Audio is constantly changing in volume, so these meters will almost always be in motion. In our example, we have a surround sound project but we only see two levels in motion (left and right channels), because our source clips were only recorded in stereo. This won't have a negative impact on our output.

As audio is constantly fluctuating and different clips will have different levels, there's no magic cure-all to adjust all your clips perfectly. But the most important rules are as follows:

❑ You never want your audio to peak over 0 **decibels (dB)**. If it does, your audio will possibly clip or distort. You can easily see any clips that are peaking by looking for red spikes in the waveforms inside your timeline.

❑ Your primary audio (perhaps your interview clips in a documentary or your music bed in a music video) should average around -12 dB and ideally not peak much over -6 dB. If it does, the peaks will turn yellow, indicating you're still safe, but getting close to distorting your audio. Secondary audio (often music beds for your video are a little trickier to gauge, but if you don't want it to overwhelm your primary audio, you probably want it peaking in the area of -18 db. But again, this requires a little more trial and error to find a level that doesn't wash out any speakers, but still allows the listener to hear the music.

❑ Audio is additive, meaning if you have two audio clips playing simultaneously, they will peak at a higher level than either clip by itself.

So, if we find a clip is too loud or quiet, what do we do?

4. Find a clip that has audio levels that seem to frequently peak into the red (positive dB) territory. Click-and-drag downward on the black-level line that appears directly on the body of a clip, as shown in the following screenshot:

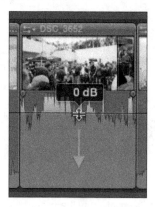

The waveforms will shrink in size. Keep dragging until the red (and most of the yellow) color disappears. Play back the clip and ensure that the clip peaks well below 0 dB, as shown in the following screenshot:

5. Find a second loud clip, and simply click on it to highlight it. Then press *Command + -*. This will lower the level of the clip by 1 dB at a time. Keep doing so until any red and yellow peaks in the waveform disappear.

6. Lastly, find a third clip, one where the waveforms are very low. Click on it and then open your Inspector window (*Command + 4*). Click on the **Audio** tab, and click-and-drag the **Volume** slider to the right to raise the volume of this clip. You can also right-click on the dB number and type in a value of how many decibels you want to raise the volume by. These methods of changing volume are identical to using the black-level line on clips in the timeline.

There's more...

Raising a clip's volume by more than 12 dB

Note that you can only raise a clip's volume by 12 dB using the steps listed previously. There is an audio effect in the **Effects Browser** called **Gain** that you can apply to raise the volume further if necessary. However, note that if you need to raise a clip's volume by more than 12 dB, then it was recorded too low in the first place and the more you raise it, the more it will amplify background noise!

Changing the volume of multiple clips at once

You can save a lot of time if you need to change multiple clips' volumes simultaneously. Simply highlight all the clips you want to adjust the volume of. Then use the *Command + =* or *Command + -* shortcut and all highlighted clips will adjust up or down by 1 dB at a time.

Lowering your music during speakers

If you're piecing together a documentary or any video with a mix of talking heads and images, adding a soundtrack is very common. However, you'll often find that simply throwing a song into the project will overwhelm your speakers. You might think, "Ok, let me just lower the volume of my music track." You would be correct, however, this can lead to the music being too quiet when there isn't anyone talking (that is, you're showing some other visual image between interview clips). FCPX makes it easy to select a range within a clip and adjust its volume by automatically adding keyframes. This process is sometimes referred to as **ducking your audio**.

Getting ready

In the timeline shown in the following screenshot, we have an interview clip at an appropriate level, but we've also added a music track. The music track is at an appropriate level when played over b-roll or other silent images, but unfortunately overwhelms our speaker.

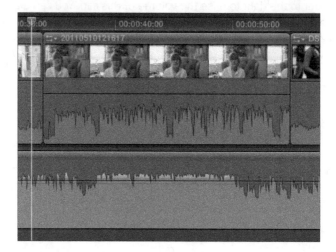

How to do it...

1. Turn on your Range Selection tool by pressing *R*.

2. Move your cursor right on top of the music clip approximately one second before the interview clips starts.

3. Click-and-drag to the right until you have highlighted the full portion of the music clip underneath the speaker as well as about a second beyond the end of the speaker clip, as shown in the following screenshot:

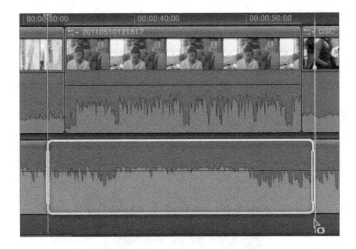

4. Move your cursor over the black volume-control line and drag down. As you do, FCPX automatically places four audio keyframes onto your clip. The first two create a dip in the volume from the original level down to the level where you have dragged the volume-control line. The next two bring the volume back to its original volume as follows:

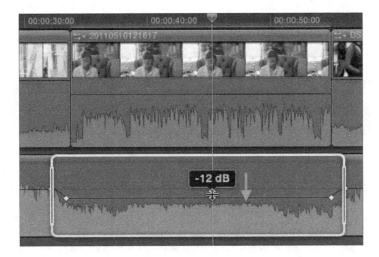

5. Play back your clip and see if you are happy with the results. Can you hear your speaker more clearly? If not, drag the volume control lower.

Adjusting the length of the dips

If you feel as though the automatic dips created by the Range Selection tool were too fast, you can adjust the timing of them easily right in the timeline. For example, perhaps you wished the music dip leading into the interview clip dipped a bit slower. First, make sure you switch back to your Select tool (press A). Move your cursor on top of the first keyframe that was created by the Range Selection tool. Right-click on the keyframe itself and drag it to the left. This will pull the first keyframe earlier in time, therefore creating a lengthier and longer dip.

Read the next recipe to learn how to add keyframes manually to adjust the volume of a clip any way you want!

Lowering a loud, unexpected background sound with manual keyframes

Keyframes are an essential tool to all aspects of video editing. Occasionally, we want to make adjustments not just to an entire clip, but within a clip. A **keyframe** is a kind of marker placed at a precise moment in time that locks in a value for a parameter. When a second keyframe is placed later on the same clip and a parameter value is changed, FCPX knows to animate the difference between the two.

The previous recipe, *Lowering your music during speakers*, was actually a special function of FCPX that automatically created four keyframes for us. But, sometimes you need to do a little bit of work yourself to achieve the right sound.

In audio editing, we often encounter scenarios where the clip's audio may be perfect with the tiny, but obnoxious exception of a loud, quick sound in the background; or perhaps when a speaker let out a large laugh that was much louder than the rest of his/her interview. We can use a few keyframes to adjust the volume of a small (or large) area of a clip.

Getting ready

In our example shown in the following screenshot, we have a clip where a background speaker let out a large "Oh!" during an interview that sent that one small portion of the clip into peaking territory. We want to lower this "Oh!" without lowering the volume of the entire clip. Take note of the timeline ruler that shows how long of a space we are looking at (about 2 seconds):

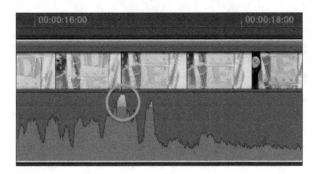

How to do it...

1. Zoom in significantly on your timeline with *Command + =*. Press it many times until you are zoomed into what is called the sample level of the audio. Audio is made up of samples, which are similar to the idea of frames in video, except that audio is made up of thousands of these samples each second—commonly 44,100, which is often displayed as 44.1 kHz.

    After zooming in, it looks like our audio waveform of the "Oh!" has changed to multiple peaks. In reality, we're so far zoomed in that we are seeing the vibration of the human voice! Our whole screen is now only three frames wide, or one-eighth of a second.

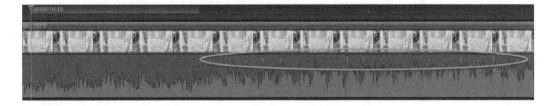

2. Put your cursor over the volume-control line before the beginning of the loud peak. Hold down the *Option* key and click. A keyframe, represented by a diamond shape, will appear on the volume-control line. Place a second keyframe right around the middle of the peaking audio and a third one right after it ends, as shown in the following screenshot:

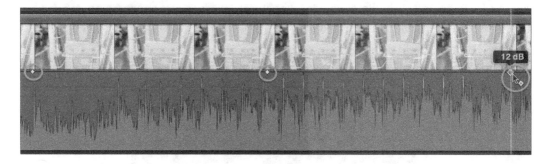

3. Move your cursor back to the middle keyframe. Click-and-drag downward. Watch as the audio waveform warps and shrinks. In our example, we're lowering the volume from 12 dB to -2 dB in order to bring the peak to an acceptable, balanced level as follows:

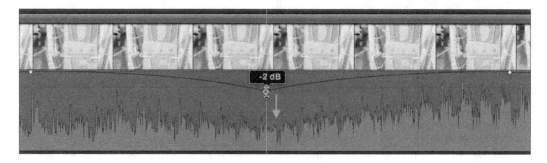

4. Use the Play Around shortcut (*Shift + /*) to play that part of the timeline back. Adjust the keyframes as necessary by dragging upward or downward to alter the volume, or left and right to adjust timing.

How it works...

The first question you might ask is, "Why didn't we use the Range Selection tool like we did in the last recipe?" The only limitation with the Range Selection tool is that it can only select a range using whole frames on a video clip. The fix we wanted to make required a much higher level of precision than that. Keyframes can be dropped anywhere along an audio clip's waveform, which, as mentioned previously, is made up of thousands of samples per second!

Replacing bad audio with a cleaner recording

As more and more videographers today are experimenting with the quickly advancing world of DSLR video, they quickly learn one rule—the recorded audio on DSLRs sucks! A true professional would almost never use their camera's built-in microphone, but most DSLRs have especially bad audio. While some DSLRs have microphone inputs, they still don't often have the best recording capabilities or feature sets, so many professionals use external audio recorders for their audio needs.

There are many out there, but a couple I highly recommend looking into are the Zoom H1 and H4n models (`http://www.zoom.co.jp/?lang=en`). They both record pristine audio quality in the WAV and MP3 formats to SD cards that can be imported instantly into FCPX. The H4n model also allows you to plug in XLR microphones directly into it.

So, once you've imported your video with bad audio and your separate high-quality audio file, what do you do? You used to have to spend a ridiculous amount of time lining the two clips on top of one another and perfecting the sync manually. FCPX introduced the ability to synchronize a video and audio clip by matching waveforms. Look at it as the little sibling process of full on multicam editing.

Getting ready

All you need to make this work is two clips—a video clip and an audio recording that were recorded at the same time. The video clip's audio doesn't have to be bad, but it helps us illustrate the point!

How to do it...

1. In your Event Browser, find and highlight both your video clip with the poor audio and the audio file with the good audio (click on one, hold down the *Command* key and click the other).

2. Right-click on either clip and choose **Synchronize Clips** (*Command + Option + G*). A new clip is created in your event called **synchronized clip** plus the name of the video clip used in the sync process. If you don't see it appear within a few moments, make sure you're looking at your whole event and not just a keyword collection or some other subset of your media.

3. Select your newly created clip and rename it if you want.

4. Open the Inspector window by pressing the **I** icon to the far right of the toolbar (or press *Command + 4*). Click on the **Audio** tab at the top, as shown in the following screenshot:

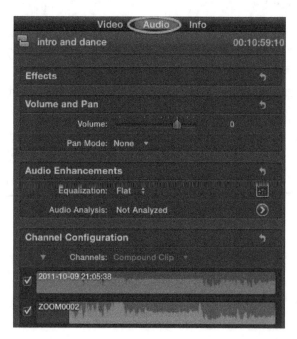

5. Look at the box named **Channel Configuration**. You will see two boxes for your audio labeled with their respective clips' names. Uncheck the box next to the clip with the bad audio. The video clip's audio has been turned off, but the newly synced clean audio is still active and attached to the clip, as shown in the following screenshot:

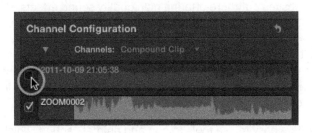

6. Add the clip however you deem fit to your project.

How it works...

When you synchronize clips, FCPX analyzes the waveforms in a shockingly short amount of time and then glues the two clips together into one clip. All you have left to do is to select which audio you want to use!

There's more...

Silent start to your clip

If after completing the recipe you have a silent start to your newly synchronized clip, there is a simple explanation—you didn't hit the Record button on your audio recorder until after you hit Record on your camera. You may need to trim off part of the beginning of your clip if this happens.

See also

As mentioned earlier in this recipe, synchronizing clips is a simplified version of how multicam editing works in FCPX. To learn more about full-fledged multicam editing, read the *Multicam, part 1 – getting your media synced and prepped* recipe in *Chapter 4, Enhancing Your Editing*.

Sound effects, part 1 – browsing, connecting and panning

There are loads of websites out there offering high-quality sound effects. However, few are free and the few that are rarely offer high-quality material. Luckily, Final Cut Pro X comes with more than 1,300 royalty-free, high-quality sounds effects for you to use. And while there are some cheesy ones (that is, 35 variations of "Cartoon Accent"), there are plenty of genuinely useful ones such as crowd noises, Foley effects, transportation sounds, and more. You'd be amazed how much a crowd sound in the background of a public scene or insect noises in an outdoor night time scene can add atmosphere and realism to your video.

Additionally, FCPX offers easy to use tools to pan and animate sound, which we will explore in the next few recipes. **Panning a sound** refers to shifting a sound from its original channel(s) to another. For example, perhaps we have a scene in a movie where a person walks off the left of the screen after an argument with a friend and slams a door. We would want to take a slamming-door sound effect and make sure that it only comes out of the left channel. In that case, we would need to pan the sound effect to the left. We'll cover animating a sound in the next recipe.

Getting ready

FCPX's free sound effects library is an optional download after you've installed the program. If you've recently downloaded FCPX, make sure you run your Mac's Software Update application to get the sound effects download package.

In our following example, we are going to find a gunshot sound effect to add to a clip from a shooting range and make sure the sound only comes out of one of our speakers.

How to do it...

1. Click on the **Music and Sound** browser in the toolbar as follows:

2. Click on the disclosure triangle next to Final Cut Pro sound effects, then click on the folder labeled **Weapons**. A list of various weapon-related sound effects appears, as shown in the following screenshot:

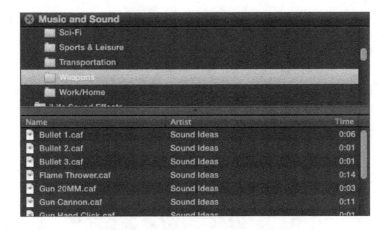

3. Double-click on **Bullet 2.caf** to preview the effect. Notice in your audio meters that the sound effect uses both the left and right channels. This is a stereo sound effect, as shown in the following screenshot:

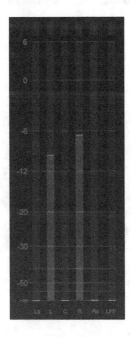

4. Click-and-drag the sound effect to the left and drop it underneath a clip in your timeline in order to connect it to that clip as follows:

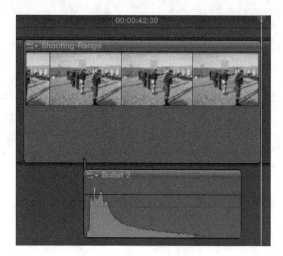

5. Make sure the clip is highlighted and open the Inspector (*Command + 4*). Notice near the top of the window the section labeled **Pan Mode: None**.

6. Click on the drop-down indicator next to the word **None** and select **Stereo Left/Right**. A new slider labeled **Pan Amount** appears underneath.

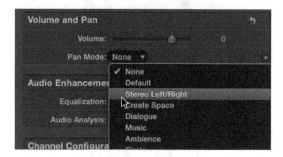

7. Drag the new **Pan Amount** slider all the way to the left (a value of **-100.0**) and play your sound effect in the timeline again.

This time, it only plays out of the left speaker as follows:

8. Drag the **Pan Amount** slider all the way to the right and play the sound once more. Now it only comes out of the right speaker.

There's more...

Downloading sound effects

FCPX has a ton of sound effects, but it won't have everything you need. Just about any sound effect you can find on the Internet will work in FCPX including files in the WAV, MP3, AAC, AIFF, CAF, and BWF formats. Once you've acquired your file, simply bring it into FCPX by clicking on **File | Import Files** as you would with any ordinary piece of media. Of course, don't forget to make sure you are allowed to use the effect freely. Always ensure you have rights to use any content that wasn't directly created by yourself!

See also

Read the next recipe to learn how to make our bullet sound effect travel from one speaker to another!

Sound effects, part 2 – animating with keyframes

Now that we've learned how to add sound effects to our projects and pan them to different speakers, let's take a look at how we can animate our audio with keyframes. The term animating sound might seem a bit odd at first, but it actually fits perfectly. Animation involves movement and we are going to make our sound effect move from one channel to another.

Getting ready

It's a good idea to have completed the prior recipe before jumping onto this one. For our next examples, we're going to pick up from right where we left off in the last recipe. To make sure you're caught up, double-check that the sound effect is highlighted in the timeline, the Inspector window is open, and the **Pan Mode** option has been set to **Stereo Left/Right**.

How to do it...

1. Zoom in on your timeline (*Command + =*) until the sound effect takes up most of the width of your screen. This will allow us to be very accurate with placing our keyframes.

2. Place your playhead right at the beginning of the sound. Use the waveforms to determine when the sound starts, not necessarily the left edge of the clip. Notice in the following screenshot how the sound effect doesn't start right at the clip's beginning:

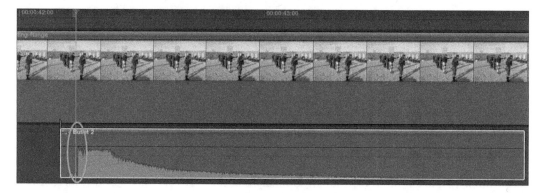

3. In the Inspector window, drag the **Pan Amount** slider all the way to the left (**-100.0**).

4. Move your cursor to the right of the slider and click on what looks like a diamond shape with a plus sign inside of it. It should turn orange with an x shape inside (clicking again would remove the keyframe).

   Clicking on this button adds a keyframe at the exact frame our playhead is currently sitting at. By adding a keyframe, we're saying "Hey, FCPX, make sure the pan amount is -100 at this exact moment in time." By adding the keyframe, we're also giving FCPX a heads up that we are about to change this parameter's value later in the clip.

5. Back in the timeline, drag your playhead later in the sound effect, close to its end. Again, use the waveform to make this decision, not the right edge of the clip.

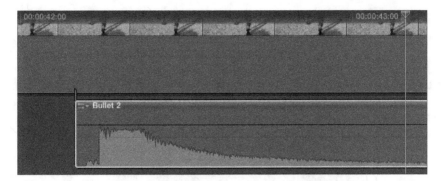

6. In Inspector, click-and-drag the **Pan Amount** slider all the way to the right. Take note that as soon as you do, FCPX automatically inserts a second keyframe at this point in the clip. You can confirm this by checking the keyframe icon next to the slider, which turns orange, as shown in the following screenshot:

7. Play back your sound effect and hear it pan from the left channel to the right one.

How it works...

Once you get the hang of keyframing, the sky is the limit with how you can make your sound and video move. To boil it down, keyframing essentially includes the following five steps:

1. Move your playhead to a point in time of a clip where you want a parameter to start changing.

2. Set the parameter you want to animate (that is **Pan Amount**).

3. Add a keyframe.

4. Move to a second point in time.

5. Change the parameter value (FCPX automatically sets the second keyframe).

You may repeat steps 4 and 5 as many times as you want along a clip.

There's more...

Deleting the audio keyframes on a clip

Keyframing is a tough art to master. It takes quite a bit of practice, trial and error before getting it perfect. If you had trouble placing keyframes on your sound effect and want to remove them all to start over, it's very easy to do. In the clip's **Audio** Inspector tab, simply click on the curved reset arrow to the far right of the category label—**Volume and Pan**. This removes all keyframes you've added in that category. Other keyframes you may have added to the clip other than ones involving volume and pan will remain.

See also

Make sure to read the *Making your image move by keyframing in the Viewer* recipe in *Chapter 8, Get your Movie to Move* to have a better understanding of how keyframes work in FCPX and how to animate video properties.

Sound effects, part 3 – working in a surround sound space

Although possible in FCP7, creating surround sound elements was complicated and limited, and users were often forced to take their projects into Soundtrack Pro for more robust options. Although Soundtrack Pro has fallen off of Apple's product map, the developers did integrate some of Soundtrack Pro's features right into FCPX, including the (mostly) easy-to-use Surround Designer.

Getting ready

Unsurprisingly, to properly complete and appreciate this recipe, you must have a surround sound setup at your home or workplace. It may be an easier setup than you think. If you already have a home stereo receiver, you can probably plug your Mac right into one of the HDMI inputs—all you need is a Mac with an HDMI port or a Mini DisplayPort to HDMI adapter, which can be purchased at most Apple stores or on their online store site (`http://store.apple.com/us`). Note that some older Macs don't support sound through the Mini DisplayPort, but if you've got a Mac that old and you're a video editor, you should consider upgrading! All Thunderbolt-enabled Macs support surround sound through the port as well.

Additionally, to work in a surround sound space, make sure that when you create a new project, you select the default audio settings in the **New Project** dialog box, as that creates a surround sound project file by default.

How to do it...

1. Insert any sound effect into your timeline. We are going to use a fresh, unedited version of the Bullet 2.caf effect from the previous two recipes with no keyframes.

2. Click and highlight the sound effect, and open the **Audio** Inspector tab.

3. Next to **Pan Mode**, select **Create Space**, as shown in the following screenshot:

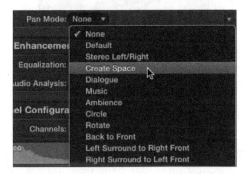

4. A parameter called **Surround Panner** appears underneath **Pan Mode**. If you do not see the **Surround Panner** interface appear, click on the disclosure triangle to the left of **Surround Panner**. The full interface appears as follows:

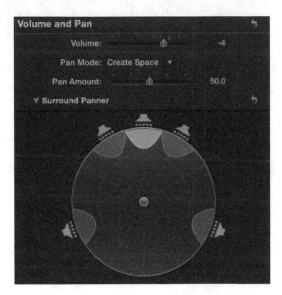

We see five arcs of various colors positioned around the inside of the circle at the location of five speaker icons. The blue arcs represent the left and left surround channels of sound, the red arcs represent the right and right surround channels, and the green arc represents the center channel.

5. Play your sound effect and observe your audio meters as you do so. Notice that as we have created a surround space for the effect, the sound effect plays out of all five channels as follows:

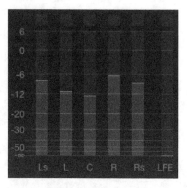

6. Back in **Surround Panner**, take note of the puck in the middle of the circle. Drag it straight down to the bottom of the circle. Notice that the left, right, and center channel arcs are all shrunk away to nothingness and the left surround and right surround arcs have grown a bit, as shown in the following screenshot:

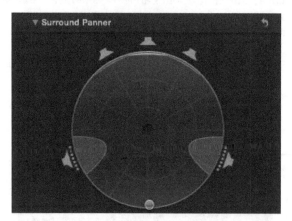

7. Play your sound effect again. Your audio meters should only show activity in the **Ls** and **Rs** channels. You should only hear the sound effect behind you in the left surround and right surround speakers. Note that you will only hear an appreciable difference if you are working in a true surround sound environment. Otherwise, you will have to rely solely on your audio meters.

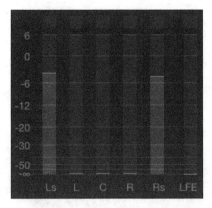

8. Now drag the puck to the right channel (the speaker icon that looks like it's at 1 o'clock), as shown in the following screenshot:

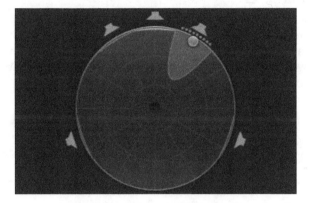

Play your sound effect again. The audio meters should show that it is only coming out of the **R** channel and you should only hear the sound in that one speaker:

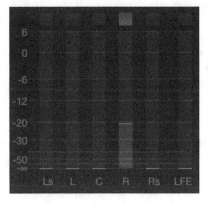

There's more...

Keyframing and animating sound in Surround Panner

If you had a keen eye (and read the last couple of recipes), you may have noticed a keyframe icon in Surround Panner. Following the steps outlined in the *Sound effects, part 2 – animating with keyframes* recipe, you can totally make your sound effects move around the room as they play in any way you want!

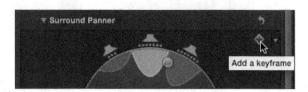

Turning off a channel

If you've moved your puck to a specific location in the Surround Panner and for whatever reason, your sound effect is still playing out of a particular speaker that you do not want it to, you can turn off a channel on a particular sound effect. Simply click on the speaker icon of the channel you wish to disable on the sound effect. The following screenshot shows the left channel deactivated on a sound effect. The blue arc still appears, but no sound will come from the left speaker with this particular sound effect.

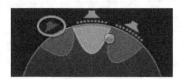

The other pan modes

This exercise reviewed the most manual way to move your sound effects around the room. And, as mentioned a couple of paragraphs before, you can animate your sound with keyframes any way you like. To make things ever easier, FCPX built in a few commonly used surround sound animations to make the keyframing process a bit easier. In the **Audio** Inspector tab, under **Pan Mode**, you will see a bunch of options including **Circle**, **Back to Front**, **Left Surround to Right Front**, and more. Selecting one of these will pop up the **Pan Amount** slider that easily lets you pan and keyframe your audio from one specific location to another without having to drag the puck around manually in the Surround Panner.

For example, if you have selected **Left Surround to Right Front**, you can drag the **Pan Amount** slider to the left side, forcing the sound effect into the left surround speaker. Then, add a keyframe, move your playhead to a later point in time in your sound effect, and drag the slider all the way to the right, making the sound effect travel to the right front speaker. FCPX will animate the process so that it sounds like the effect is moving from one corner of the room to another!

See also

Make sure you read all three recipes on sound effects to get a full understanding of how to use them to their full potential. For more on keyframing with image elements, read the the *Making your image move by keyframing in the Viewer* recipe in *Chapter 8, Get your Movie to Move*.

Removing unwanted audio channels

When going out and shooting in the field, it's good to have multiple recordings of your sound to use as a backup in case something goes wrong. One of the most common scenarios in a real-world shoot is to have a boom mic plugged into your camera to record high-quality audio while also recording with the on-board microphone as a backup.

When importing into FCPX, all audio channels will be brought in by default. This can lead to messy sounding audio as on-board microphones sometimes offer clear sounding audio, but often pick up far more background noise than higher-quality mics.

How to do it...

1. Find and highlight a clip with audio channels that you wish to remove. You can turn off channels on a clip straight from the event it is contained in.
2. Open the **Audio** Inspector tab.
3. Scroll down to the bottom of the Inspector window and take a look at **Channel Configuration**. In the following screenshot, there are two stereo files attached to this video clip:

Look closely at the audio waveform at the bottom. It is slightly flatter than the top one, which has more obvious peaks and valleys. Chances are that the top waveform is the high-quality boom mic and the bottom is the on-board microphone.

4. To be sure, place your cursor over the more defined waveform and hit the Space bar to play just that channel of sound. It will likely sound pretty clear.
5. Place your cursor over the flatter waveform and hit the Space bar to play. The audio is probably decidedly murkier.

6. Click on the checkbox next to the murkier waveform to deactivate it, as shown in the following screenshot:

Unlinking audio from video

In FCPX, when you edit a video clip in a project, the clip's video and audio appear as one unit in your timeline. This can be a bit disconcerting at first for long-time digital video editors, who are used to seeing video and audio as separate entities in the track-based timeline used in FCP7. Video and audio are not tied together permanently, however, and can be separated and manipulated individually in the timeline.

Getting ready

In a documentary project, you may have a talking head clip where you decide you only want to use the spoken words, rather than see the speaker's face, and then use that spoken portion as voiceover for some b-roll. Instead of removing the clip, go back to your Event Browser, find the clip again, and re-edit the audio portion into your timeline. It's much faster to unlink the audio in the timeline and drag it wherever you want.

How to do it...

1. Right-click on the clip in your timeline that you want to detach the audio from and select **Detach Audio** (or press *Command* + *Shift* + *S*). The audio gets separated from the video. There are no visible waveforms now in the blue box representing the video, and a green audio-only clip is appearing below it, as shown in the following screenshot:

2. Drag the audio clip wherever you like. It now operates totally independently from the original video clip.

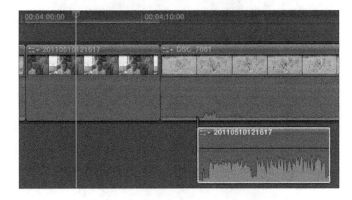

3. Click and delete the original video clip if you need to.

There's more...

Relinking after detaching

As stated in this recipe, once detached, the audio and video clips truly act as independent pieces. There is no true way to relink them if needed. However, a workaround can be found by using compound clips. Highlight both the video and audio pieces at the same time, right-click on one of them, and choose **New Compound Clip...** The clips will get visibly compressed down into a compound clip that makes it look and act like a solid clip again.

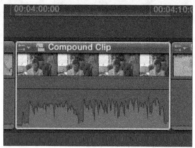

See also

If you know in advance that you want to edit only a clip's video or audio in a timeline, there's an easier way! Read the *Appending, inserting, and overwriting clips to a storyline* recipe in Chapter 3, *Basic Editing Mechanics*.

If you want to know more about compound clips, read the *Grouping clips together as a compound clip* recipe in Chapter 4, *Enhancing Your Editing*.

Using FCPX's auto audio enhancements

It is said that there are two certainties in life—death and taxes. Except if you're a video editor, then there are three—death, taxes, and bad audio. We have all encountered or will encounter bad audio and nothing can be more frustrating to try and fix. FCPX gives us a few automatic quick fix options to try and clean up a few common bad-audio scenarios, such as balancing clips with both loud and quiet moments, removing background noise, and removing hums.

Getting ready

Obviously, this exercise is a bit challenging if you only have a clean audio to work with at the moment.

How to do it...

1. Highlight a clip in your event with any of the following audio issues—the audio is unbalanced within the clip (that is, very loud and very quiet parts), the audio has background noise, or the audio has a hum caused by an electrical signal at 50 or 60 Hz (common if there was a power cable overlaying an XLR cable when the video was shot).

2. Open the **Audio** Inspector tab. (*Command + 4* and click on **Audio** at the top). Notice the box labeled **Audio Enhancements**, and, within it, the attribute called **Audio Analysis**. Depending on whether or not you have told FCPX to analyze for audio problems upon import, this will either read as **Not Analyzed**, **No Problems Detected**, **Potential Problems Detected**, **Problems Detected**, or **Problems Resolved**:

3. Click on the arrow inside the circle to the right of the **Audio Analysis** reading (circled above). This will bring you to the **Audio Enhancements** window, as shown in the following screenshot:

If it hadn't done so already, FCPX will automatically analyze the clip for potential problems in the area of loudness, background noise, and hums. It will then display the results with either a green check mark, yellow warning symbol, or red warning symbol. In our example, FCPX detected some background noise that needs to be removed.

4. To activate any of the fixes, simply click on the black box next to the label name to turn it blue. Play back your clip to see if it sounds any better. The following is a brief explanation of all three fixes:

   ❑ **Loudness**: The **Amount** slider will increase the volume of a clip while the **Uniformity** slider is used to try to balance the clip, that is, to flatten the audio a bit if there are large peaks and valleys in the waveform.

   ❑ **Background Noise Removal**: This one is pretty straightforward. If activated, FCPX tries to remove what it perceives as background/white noise. Be careful with this one. It can make human voices sometimes sound like they're talking underwater. Try and drag the slider to the left to decrease the intensity of the removal if this happens. It can take a bit of work to find the sweet spot.

❑ **Hum Removal**: This one is also very straightforward. You'll know if you have a hum in your video! If you hear one, it was likely caused by an electrical signal from a power cable. Luckily, these usually operate at very specific frequencies, so FCPX can nullify them pretty easily once this is turned on.

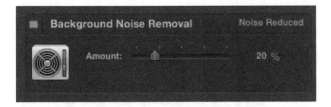

How it works...

When you turn on any of the audio enhancements, FCPX will actually borrow some of the power that belongs to another pro software suite—Logic Pro, and some features that used to belong to Soundtrack Pro. FCPX actually integrates many of Logic's advanced audio tools and filters into the application, even if you don't own Logic.

There's more...

Audio effects from Logic

For those of you who are audio buffs and know Apple's Logic Pro, you'll be happy to know that many of Logic's advanced filters are available in FCPX. Click on the **Effects Browser** and scroll down to take a peek at all the categories of audio effects pulled from Logic. Read *Chapter 6, Practical Magic Also Known As Useful Effects* for information on how to work with audio filters.

Don't expect miracles

Any auto enhancements, like the ones found in the Audio Enhancements pane, are not magical panaceas to your audio woes. They're simply a computer's attempt to find a best solution to a problem. But in an artistic field such as video editing, you have to be the judge of what sounds good and what doesn't. Often, FCPX overcompensates with its auto fixes and you're given something worse than what you started with. Don't forget the most important keyboard shortcut of all time—*Command + Z* (Undo)!

Recording a voiceover

If you have a face for radio, here's your chance to shine! We've all wanted to record a voiceover for a movie trailer and sound like some of those baritone narrators we hear during previews at the movie theater. Or, more realistically, you're making some informational video and need to get your point across with a mix of picture and sound. FCPX lets you record live into your timeline using either your Mac's built-in mics or any professional ones you've got plugged in.

How to do it...

1. Select **Window | Record Audio**. The **Record Audio** window pops up, as shown in the following screenshot:

2. Select which event you want your voiceover(s) to be recorded to under **Destination**.

3. Select **Input Device**. For the Mac's built-in microphone, select **Built-In Microphone**. For any attached microphone, select it from the drop-down menu.

4. Start talking while watching the audio meters to get a sense of whether or not you need to adjust the **Gain** slider. If the peaks of your voice are falling too low, increase the gain (that is, drag the slider to the right). If your voiceover is going to be your primary audio in your project, you want your voice to peak around -6 dB.

5. Do not turn monitoring on unless you are wearing headphones, otherwise you are likely to experience a piercing feedback noise. In fact, you almost always want to be wearing headphones when recording voiceovers regardless. We are about to record a voiceover live while watching and listening to our movie and we don't want the microphone to pick up the sound of the video as it plays!

6. Place your playhead where you want to begin with recording your voiceover.

7. In the **Record Audio** window, press the red record button next to **Ready to record**.

8. Your video will start playing and you should start talking! Record your voiceover as long as necessary and press the red record button again when you are done. A green audio clip appears under your timeline. An audio clip has also been created in the event you chose in step 2.

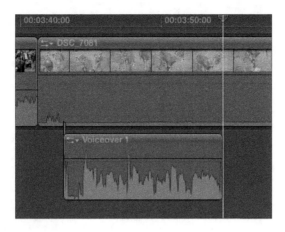

There's more...

Auditioning voiceovers

You'll often have to make multiple attempts before you get your voiceover right. If you want to try out multiple takes, follow all the steps, repeating steps 6 through 8. Each time you record a voiceover, it will plop the new version underneath the previous take.

This next step sounds wacky, but trust us! When you are done with your takes, delete all but one of them from the timeline. Then, go back to the event where they are contained and find the list of voiceovers. Highlight the ones you deleted and drag them on top of the remaining voiceover clips in the timeline. Select **Add to Audition** in the window that pops up. Voila! You can now easily use the audition process to pick your best take!

Good voiceover microphones

The built-in microphones on most Macs are surprisingly good, but far from perfect. While very clear sounding, they have a habit of picking up every little sound in a room rather than just your voice. What you need is likely some form of cardioid microphone, and luckily there are companies that make some very good USB powered ones without breaking the bank. One company to take a look at is Blue Microphones (`www.bluemic.com`). They make a few sub-$100 portable USB mics that are great for recording voiceovers and podcasts in a home studio.

See also

If you haven't learned how the audition process works, go back and read the *Auditioning multiple shots or takes* recipe in *Chapter 4, Enhancing Your Editing*.

6

Practical Magic a.k.a Useful Effects

In this chapter, we will cover:

- ► Adding an effect and changing its parameters
- ► Animating parameters of an effect over time with keyframes
- ► Adding a watermark or logo to your video
- ► Downloading and installing more effects
- ► Blurring out a face or logo
- ► Disguising someone's voice using an audio effect
- ► Copying and pasting effects onto multiple clips
- ► Going green (screen), part 1 - the basics
- ► Going green (screen), part 2 - improving your key
- ► Going green (screen), addendum - using the mask effect to cut out unwanted parts of an image

Introduction

Effect is a rather vague word. At its most basic definition, an **effect** is a change that is a result or consequence of an action or other cause. We are merely changing our video (or audio) in some way or another. It might be a special effect used to transport our viewers to another time and place. It might be disguising a person's face or voice. It might be simply making your video black and white instead of color. Sometimes it can be used to improve your clip and sometimes used to purposely distort it.

FCPX has more than 100 built-in effects, and, as we'll show in one of the recipes in this chapter, you can download many, many more on the Internet (some are free, but of course, others may require payment).

Adding an effect and changing its parameters

We'll start with the basics of adding an effect and seeing what parameters there are to change. We've got some footage of monuments around Washington D.C.'s National Mall and we want it to have the campy look of an old educational film from the 1950s. Obviously, this can be accomplished by any clips you may have.

Getting ready

You can work with any clips at all in a project of your choice for this recipe.

How to do it...

1. Highlight a clip in your timeline that you want to give the old film look. Make sure your playhead is parked somewhere over the clip:

2. Open your **Effects Browser** by clicking on its icon in the toolbar or by hitting *Command + 5*:

3. Click on the category named **Basics** and find the effect **Black & White**.

4. Skim your cursor over the effect box and you will see a preview of the effect on the clip without even adding it yet! Hit the Space bar to get a real-time preview of the effect on the clip:

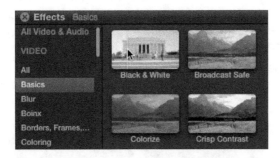

5. Double–click on the **Black & White** effect to actually apply the effect to the clip. Alternatively, drag-and-drop the **Black & White** effect on top of the clip(s).

6. Skim through the clip in the timeline and see it is now black and white. The thumbnail in the timeline doesn't update, but you will see the result in the Viewer:

7. Now our clip is black and white, but that's not enough to make it look old so we need to add another filter to get that old film look.

8. Back in your **Events** Browser, click on the category **Stylize** and skim over the effect **Aged Film**:

9. Double-click on the **Aged Film** effect to add it to the clip. Playback the clip and see we now have an old-looking black and white clip. However, the intensity of the old film look is a bit too high, so let's soften it up a bit.

10. Open the Inspector (*Command + 4*) and click on the **Video** tab if it isn't already selected. We see both effects listed as well as any parameters we can tweak on each effect:

11. Drag the **Amount** slider on the **Aged Film** filter down to about **70**. The effect has been slightly muted. You may also try changing the **Style** from **iMovie Grain** to **Realistic Grain** and see which results you like better.

There's more...

Other ways to apply effects to multiple clips at once

We applied an effect to one clip. This would be very time consuming to do it to 50 clips. There are a few tricks to apply effects to many clips at once, each with pros and cons.

One way is to highlight all the clips in the timeline you want to apply an effect to, find the effect, and double-click on it. This will apply the effect to all highlighted clips. This is often the fastest way, but can be a pain if you decide you need to tweak one parameter of an effect because then you'd have to go in and tweak it on every single clip one at a time.

An alternative is to highlight all the clips you want to add an effect to and create a compound clip (by pressing *Option + G*). As a compound clip acts like one solid clip, you can apply an effect to just the compound clip and the effect will be applied to all clips inside. You can read more about compound clips in the *Grouping clips together as a compound clip* recipe found in *Chapter 4, Enhancing Your Editing*.

You can also copy and paste effects, but that is covered in greater detail in an upcoming *Copying and pasting effects* recipe.

Changing the effect order for different results

You may have noticed that when we added the **Aged Film** effect to the clip that it was no longer truly black and white, despite having added the **Black & White** effect beforehand. This is because FCPX applies effects in a certain order. First we applied the **Black & White** effect, and then we applied the **Aged Film** effect afterwards, so that the **Aged Film** effect (which contained a slight color tint) was applied to the **Black & White** effect. You can reverse this by clicking and dragging on the lower effect's name and drag it up above the upper effect. This will reorder the effects so that **Aged Film** is applied first and then we apply the **Black & White** effect to it:

Here's what the shot looks like with the effect order reversed. Which one looks better? That's for you to decide.

Animating parameters of an effect over time with keyframes

Effects are incredibly easy to apply and manipulate in FCPX, but at first, they're quite static. You throw on an effect and boom! It's there, as is, for the entire clip. But what if you wanted to have an effect to fade in? Or to change intensity throughout the clip? Welcome to the world of **keyframes**.

The keyframing process works like this: you tell FCPX what you want a certain parameter's value to be at one point in time on a clip, then change that value at a different point in time and FCPX animates (or **interpolates**, if you want to use fancy wording) the difference.

Getting ready

Add a **Black & White** effect to any clip. Ideally, make the clip about six seconds long. Here's what we want to happen. We want this clip to start off in color and then, about two seconds in, we want the clip to fade to black and white within the next two seconds.

How to do it...

1. Place your cursor about one-third of the way (approximately two seconds) through the clip and click. This should both highlight the clip and place the playhead at that point in time.

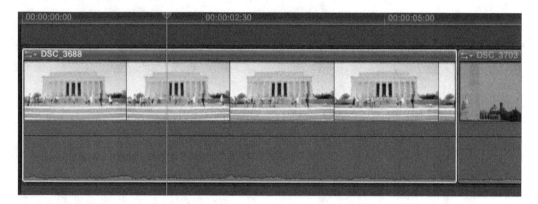

2. Open your Inspector window (by hitting *Command + 4*) and ensure that the **Video** tab is visible.

3. Change the **Amount** slider for the **Black & White** effect to **0**.

4. Move your cursor to the right of the **Amount** parameter until it is hovering over a gray diamond shape. This is the **Add/Remove a keyframe** button:

5. Click on it! The keyframe icon should turn orange indicating you have successfully placed a keyframe at that point in time for that parameter (clicking on it again would remove the keyframe). We have now told FCPX that at this exact moment in time, we want the amount of black and whiteness of the image to be zero percent (basically, we want the clip to look normal).

6. Hit *Ctrl + P*. This is the Move Playhead Position command. It lets you specify a timecode you want to jump to in your timeline or a specific amount of time you want to move ahead or back. Type *+2.* (press the + sign, number two, and period) and hit *Return*. Alternatively, you can also type *200* (press the number two, and the number zero twice) and hit *Return*.

   Either way, your playhead will jump ahead exactly two seconds in time (if you only type *+2* without the period, it will only move you ahead two frames!). Make sure the clip remains selected. If you accidentally deselect it, click on it again:

7. Back in the Inspector, drag the **Amount** slider in the **Black & White** effect to **100**. As soon as you do, you should see the keyframe icon light up again. FCPX automatically inserted the second keyframe at this point in time. Because you had already placed a keyframe for that parameter earlier in the clip, FCPX correctly guessed you wanted to place another one here and now. Don't press the keyframe button or you will remove the new keyframe!

Play back the clip with / (forward slash) and see the clip fade to black and white.

How it works...

To review, we added an effect to a clip and told FCPX what we wanted the clip to look like at one point in time (zero percent black and white at about two seconds) by changing the parameter and adding a keyframe. Then we went ahead to four seconds into the clip and dragged the parameter slider again to 100 percent. FCPX added the second keyframe automatically and animated the difference.

There's more...

Adding as many keyframes as you want

This was a very simple approach to keyframing. We only put in two keyframes, but you can put in as many keyframes as you wish on a clip. There's no limit! After adding two keyframes, just keep moving around in time and changing a parameter again and again to keep adding new keyframes and adding to the animation.

See also

To learn about keyframing the size, shape, position, and other physical properties of your clip, read the *Making your image move by keyframing in the viewer* recipe.

Adding a watermark or logo to your video

Often in the promo video world, a client will ask to have their logo embedded in their video through the duration of the video. This is a relatively easy task, you may think, until they e-mail a JPEG image of their logo. When you plop it into your timeline, you are presented with this annoying white background that is very distracting. Even if you make the image semi-transparent, you still get this ugly rectangular halo around the logo. With this help of the **Luma Keyer** effect, we can easily get rid of this solid color background.

Getting ready

Simply import any JPEG image/logo into FCPX.

How to do it...

1. Connect your logo to the first clip in the timeline where you want the watermark to appear. This is often right at the beginning of the video, but not always. Don't worry about the clip's length just yet.

   Here's what the clips look like in our timeline:

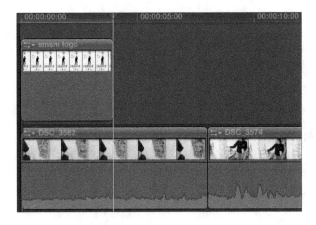

And here's what the result looks like in our Viewer:

As we can see, the image currently is overlayed on top of the video, taking up most of the frame. Don't worry about the size just yet either.

2. Open up the **Effects Browser** by clicking on the icon in the toolbar:

3. Click on the category labelled **Keying**:

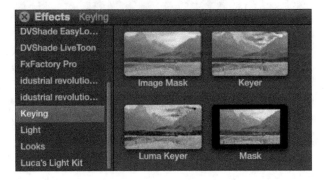

4. Drag the effect called **Luma Keyer** onto your logo clip:

At first, it seems to have the opposite effect of what we want—the white background is still visible, and the actual logo shape has gone transparent!

5. Make sure the clip is highlighted and open the Inspector. Here we can see all the properties than can be adjusted for the **Luma Keyer** effect:

6. Click on the box next to **Invert**. From here, your results will vary widely from logo to logo. In many cases, this will take care of 90 percent of the problem!

7. You may have to tweak some of the other parameters if your logo appears semi-transparent (and you don't want it to). There are numerous parameters within the effect and a couple ways to try to approach fixing your image, but one of the easiest steps is to first try dragging the handles on the **Luma** gradient box back and forth a bit to find the sweet spot. Keyframing and applying effects often requires a little trial and error:

8. When you are happy with your image, you can use the Transform tool to shrink the logo down and move it into a corner of your video frame:

How it works...

The purpose of the **Luma Keyer** effect is to make a matte that is based on the luminance, or lightness in an image. It is used to remove the black (or white if you used the **Invert** option, as we did) areas of an image and control how transparent the in between (gray) areas of luminance should be.

There's more...

The advantage of using PSDs, GIFs, and PNGs

You may have already experienced the benefit some other image formats have, such as PSDs, GIFs, and PNGs—when you drop these kind of images into a project, there's (usually) no solid color background! This is because these image formats support a transparency (also known as **alpha**) channel that knows if there was originally a background element or not. JPEGs, although a very common file format, do not support this, thus the white background you often see with them.

See also

If you don't know how to use the Transform tool as mentioned in step 8, read the recipe, *Using the Transform tool* in *Chapter 8, Get Your Movie to Move*.

Downloading and installing more effects

FCPX comes with tons of video and audio effects, virtually every one of them made using Motion. That's one of the coolest features of the relationship between FCPX and Motion—Motion users can create their own effects, transitions, and generators, and then easily share them with other FCPX users, even if those other users don't have Motion on their machines!

Getting ready

All you need is an Internet connection, as we're going to download video effects we'll be using in the next few recipes. Also, make sure FCPX is shut down while installing effects. It technically doesn't have to be, however, sometimes you won't see newly downloaded effects until FCPX restarts, so we might as well close up shop for a few minutes now!

How to do it...

1. Open your web browser and visit www.rippletraining.com/using-the-rt-face-obscure-effect-in-final-cut-pro-x.html. Ripple Training is a fantastic resource for video editing tutorials, tips, and tricks. Once in a while they post free downloads for FCPX as well.

2. Click on the link near the top of the page to download the **RT Face Obscure Effect** (we'll use this in the next recipe to blur someone's face out easily). The effect should download quickly.

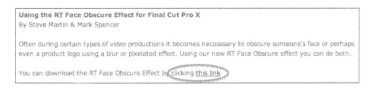

3. When it's done, find the file (likely in your **Downloads** folder) and double-click on it.

4. This effect is easy to install because it came downloaded as an installer package. Follow the instructions to install:

    Not all effects are that easy to install, however. Some don't come with built-in installers and we have to manually put it in just the right place for FCPX to find it.

5. Back in your web browser, visit http://alex4d.wordpress.com/2012/03/06/mask-plus-fcpx-effects/. Here is a link to an effect that allows editors to create an eight point mask, another effect we will be using later in this chapter.

6. Scroll down the page until you find the download link and download the effect.

As well as two ways of changing the overall shape and position of the mask, there is also the option for applying an additional mask which can be based on the luminance or transparency of another clip. The additional mask can add to, subtract from or intersect with the main mask.

So that the effect's result can be used as an input to other effects, you can choose to show the computed alpha as a luminance map (as well as see the additional mask).

Installation

Download this disk image:

7. In your **Downloads** folder, open the **DMG, Alex4D_Mask+_1.0.dmg**, and then open the folder **Alex4D Mask+ 8**.

8. Examine the contents of the folder. Inside are a few items, but the most important one is the one ending in the extension `.moef`. That tells us that this is an effect (as opposed to a title, transition, or generator). Click on the back button to return to the previous folder.

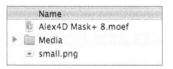

9. Open an additional **Finder** window by pressing *Command + N*, navigate to your user's home folder, then open the **Movies** folder. Inside, there should already be a folder called **Motion Templates**. If there is not, create one. (If you can't find your home folder, simply click on the **Go** menu in the menu bar of the **Finder** window and select **Home**.)

10. Open that folder and look for a folder called **Effects**. Again, if it does not exist, create it.

11. Drag the entire **Alex4D Mask+ 8** folder into the **Effects** folder. Do NOT just drag the contents of the folder, but the entire folder itself:

12. Relaunch FCPX.

13. Open the **Effects Browser** if it is not already open. Click on **Custom**. You will see both of the downloaded effects:

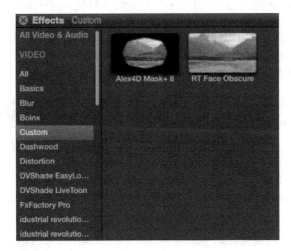

How it works...

First off, note that downloaded Motion projects come in the form of a whole folder, not just a project file. This is important as the whole folder must be moved into a very specific location in order for it to show up in FCPX's browsers, as we saw in this recipe. All downloaded or created Motion project folders must go into the **Motion Templates** folder in a user's **Movies** folder. In addition, they must then be added to the appropriate subfolders such as **Effects**, **Generators**, **Titles**, or **Transitions**.

There's more...

The best sites to visit for effects, animated titles, and more

There are an enormous number of websites and resources on the web for finding plugins and add-ons for FCPX. Of course, some are free and some are not. www.motionvfx.com has dozens of downloadable packs of themed Motion projects that include animated text, titles, and transitions. The website www.fcp.co is a great resource for FCPX news, but also contains a useful message board where other Motion users post often free Motion projects they've put together. The site www.noiseindustries.com makes a great piece of software called **FXFactory**, which, simply put, is much like an app store for FCPX plugins. Also be sure to check out www.rippletraining.com, www.fcpeffects.com, and www.crumblepop.com.

Did I just download a generator, title, effect, or transition?

If you downloaded a Motion project and are unsure of which folder it belongs to within the **Motion Templates** folder, you can cheat by looking inside the project folder and checking the file extension of the actual Motion project file. The .motn file extension is for generators, .motr is for transitions, .moti is for titles, and .moef is for effects.

Blurring out a face or logo

If you're shooting a documentary, reality TV show, news package, or countless other similar run-and-gun, man-on-the-street style shoots, you're often going to play it safe and blur out certain elements on screen. Does an interview subject not wish to be recognized? Is someone wearing an offensive shirt? Maybe someone flashed an inappropriate body part! Who knows.

While FCPX can create localized blurs without any installed extras through a rather cumbersome process, we're going to use the downloaded effect **RT Face Obscure**, downloaded in the last recipe to make this process much, much easier.

Getting ready

It's recommended you read the previous recipe before jumping into this one, but at the very least visit www.rippletraining.com/using-the-rt-face-obscure-effect-in-final-cut-pro-x.html and download the **RT Face Obscure** effect and install it.

How to do it...

1. Find a clip in any timeline that contains a portion of the frame you wish to blur out. Set your playhead at the first frame of the clip.

2. In your **Effects Browser**, click on the **Custom** category, and then drag the **RT Face Obscure** effect onto the clip. Immediately, a blurred circle appears in the center of the frame:

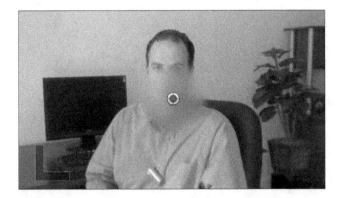

3. As the element you want to blur is likely not centered, click-and-drag the puck in the center of the screen the move the blur over the object/face you want to blur:

4. Open the Inspector (by pressing *Command + 4*). Observe the parameters that can be changed for this effect. **Mask Position** was the parameter you altered by dragging the puck in step 3. But now you can modify the shape and size of the blur as well:

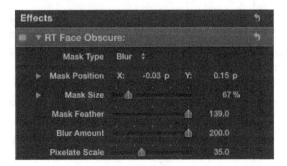

5. Click on the disclosure triangle next to **Mask Size**. Here are independent controls for the X- and Y- axes. Increasing the X axis, for example, will make your mask stretch wider. This might be useful if you're trying to block out lines of text:

6. Click on the word **Blur** next to **Mask Type**. Select **Pixelate**. You've now created a pixelated effect sometimes seen on Cops and other reality programs. You can also control the size of the pixels with the **Pixelate Scale** slider:

Animating blurs with keyframes

Consider yourself lucky if the subject/object that you're trying to blur doesn't move much within the frame. However, in many run-and-gun shoots, this is rarely the case. Luckily, the parameters within the **RT Face Obscure** effect can be keyframed, which means they can be altered throughout the duration of a clip.

Keyframing an effect is explored in the *Animating parameters of an effect over time with keyframes* recipe, but the short version is this:

Follow steps from 1 to 3. In the Inspector, hover your cursor over the right of the **Mask Position** parameter. Click on the add keyframe icon to add a keyframe. Move your playhead forward in time a bit (perhaps a few frames or seconds) until your subject has moved out from behind the blur. Drag the puck in the Viewer to move the blur on top of the subject again. A new keyframe will be automatically added. Keep repeating this process each time the subject moves significantly.

Disguising a voice

We just easily made someone's face unrecognizable, but sometimes that's not enough to ensure a person's anonymity. We have to take it up one more notch by not only hiding someone's face, but by altering their voice as well. FCPX has a number of voice-altering audio effects to accomplish this.

How to do it...

1. Highlight the clip with the speaker whose voice you want to alter.

2. Open the **Effects Browser** and scroll down into the **Audio Effects** categories and select the **Voice** category.

3. Find the effect called **Disguised**. Hover your cursor over the left edge of the effect and hit the Space bar. You will hear an instant preview of the effect. It makes our speaker sound a bit like a cross between a Dalek from Doctor Who and Darth Vader, but let's see if we can improve it.

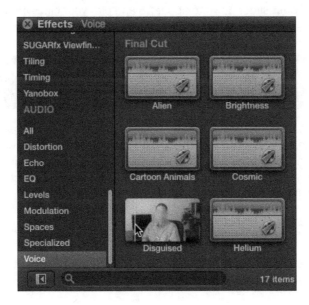

4. Double-click on the effect to add it to the clip.

5. Open the Inspector and click on the **Audio** tab:

6. If your speaker is female, click on the **Disguised Male Voice** preset and choose from one of the two female options.

7. Drag the **Amount** slider down to about **25** and play your clip with the / (forward slash) key. Now your speaker sounds a little less creepy, but the voice is still disguised.

Copying and pasting effects onto multiple clips

In the last two recipes, we have successfully disguised the person's face and voice, making them unrecognizable. In addition, we tweaked the parameters of both effects that we used (**RT Face Obscure** and **Disguised**). What if we have a dozen more clips later in our timeline of the same interview subject? Reapplying and remanipulating both effects would be a major hassle. It's a good thing we can copy and paste effects!

Getting ready

Although it's not necessary to have completed the previous two recipes, it may help as we will continue to use the same example.

How to do it...

1. Highlight the clip with the effects you want to apply to other clips.

2. Hit *Command + C* to copy the clip.

3. Find the next clip in your timeline where you want to apply the effects and click on it to highlight just that clip.

4. Look for other clips you want to add to the selection and press *Command* + click on them. Highlight as many clips as you need to.

5. Choose **Edit** | **Paste Effects** (*Command + Option + V*). All the highlighted clips will have the effects applied with the changed settings you made as well.

How it works...

When you choose the command **Paste Effects**, it will paste all changes to a clip. This means almost any parameter you modified in the **Video** or **Audio** tabs in Inspector on a clip (with the one exception of **Channel Configuration**) will be transferred to the clip you pasted the effects to. This is usually what you want, but not always, so you may have to go and do some cleanup work to remove any effects changes you didn't want on certain clips.

There's more...

Other time-saving uses

As mentioned above, copying and pasting effects actually does more than just effects. For example, perhaps you color-corrected an image perfectly and you want to apply the same color corrections to other clips. One way to accomplish (among many others) would be to copy the corrected clip and paste the effects onto other clips.

Going green (screen) part 1 – the basics

Perhaps you need to transport your subjects to another planet in your indie sci-fi flick or maybe you're just trying to create a virtual set for your high-end video podcast. Either way, you're going to have to get comfy with the **Keyer**. The **Keyer** effect has been vastly improved in FCPX and can get rid of most well-lit green screens with a click or two.

Getting ready

For this to work, you need to have some solid color background that can be keyed out, or made transparent. It doesn't have to be green, but that's the easiest to work with as that is the color FCPX tries to key out by default without changing any complex parameters.

In our example we have some poorly lit green screen, but it will show just how good FCPX is at removing the background, even in less than ideal circumstances such as this one.

How to do it...

1. Add your green-screened video clip into a timeline.

2. Go into the **Generators** browser and find a generator you like from the **Textures** or **Backgrounds** categories. We chose the **Underwater** generator from the **Backgrounds** category. This is going to replace our green screen in a few steps.

3. Connect the generator underneath the beginning of your green screen clip by clicking and dragging the generator icon from the browser into the timeline and not letting go until the generator is under the main clip.

4. Drag the right edge of the generator to the right to match the length of your clip:

5. Open your **Effects Browser** and browse to the category **Keying**.

6. Drag the **Keyer** effect on top of your clip with the green screen background.

Instantly, you should see most of your green screen disappear. In our example, it did a very good job, however, due to the overexposed portion of our green screen near the lower left corner, we can still see the news anchor over the **Underwater** background. Also, it actually keyed out a bit of our table surface.

We'll fix these things in the next recipe.

How it works...

When you add the **Keyer** effect, FCPX is set to identify and remove a certain range of green pixels from the image, making that part of the image transparent. As we then applied a generator underneath that clip, we were able to see the underwater animation once the effect was applied.

See also

Read the next recipe to learn how to fix the problems we were left with from the auto-keying process.

Going green (screen) part 2 – improving your key

FCPX's **Keyer** effect did an excellent job of getting rid of most of the green background. However, because our green screen was not very well lit, the final result was not good enough. But these were just the automatic settings. Now we'll see how we can manually tweak the parameters of the **Keyer** effect to get a much more accurate color sample and make sure our green background is totally invisible.

Getting ready

We pick up right where we left off in the previous recipe, so it's a good idea to complete it if you haven't done so already.

How to do it...

1. Make sure your clip with the green screen is highlighted and open the Inspector (by pressing *Command + 4*) and click on the **Video** tab. You will see all the parameters for the **Keyer** effect:

2. Drag the **Strength** slider to **0**. The background doesn't return entirely, but there is no automatic color sampling going on which will allow us to manually tell FCPX what colors to look for:

3. Click on the **Sample Color** button next to **Refine Key** in the Inspector. Your cursor will change into a crosshair:

4. Move your cursor back into the Viewer and drag a selection rectangle over a portion of your background. You will instantly see the results. However, they're still not likely to be perfect:

5. Click on **Sample Color** again and repeat the process of taking a second sample on another portion of your background that has not yet become full transparent. Repeat this a few times if you need to.

We still have an issue where the **Keyer** has keyed out too much—the very bottom-left corner of the image on the brown surface, which we did not want it to.

6. Drag the **Fill Holes** slider to the left—slowly. As you do, the **Keyer** will do exactly that—find keyed out holes in your image and slowly fill them in. But be observant because if you drag the slider too far to the right, you may once again reintroduce part of your green background back into the image.

7. Next to the **View** parameter, you see three small boxes with a face inside. Click on the center one, called **Matte**. This view gives you a grayscale representation of your image where white is opaque, black is totally transparent, and gray is somewhere in between. Use this as an easy way to see if you've keyed out what you want and if you need to do any further refinements.

There's more...

Picking color samples throughout a clip

In steps 3, 4, and 5, we took multiple color samples from a frame of our clip to make sure we keyed out the entire background properly. You are not limited to taking a color sample from one frame, however. You may move your playhead to other frames later or earlier in the clip and take additional samples if you need to. This should only be necessary if the lighting against your backdrop changed significantly, such as if your subjects moved and cast an accidental shadow on the background.

Fine-tune flowing hair with an edge matte

When you think you're done and you look at your image in the **Matte** view (described in step 7), you may find that the softer edges of your subject need more work, most commonly around a frizzy, flowy hairline. Hair is always a tricky part of perfecting a key. Edge mattes can be improved with the Edges parameter control.

Click on the **Edges** button in the **Refine Keyer** parameter. In the Viewer, click-and-drag your cursor from the inside of your subject (starting near the hairline) to the outside:

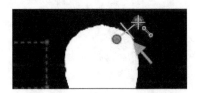

The line that intersects the line connecting the two dots (seen in the previous screenshot) can then be dragged in order to refine the edge.

Getting your image to blend in with the surroundings

Another difficult aspect of keying has always been making your subject look as though they're actually in the background environment. Mediocre green-screening is always easy to spot from a million miles away. It can be a challenge, but the **Keyer** effect does provide a few extra parameters that can help the edges of your subject blend slightly with the background elements.

Two groups of parameters to experiment with, are the **Light Wrap** and **Matte Tools** set of sliders. Both can help blend the pixel colors on the edges of your subject with the background so that the lighting and color from the background are seemingly affecting the subject.

Going green (screen) addendum – using the mask effect to cut out unwanted parts of an image

We had a pretty easy time fixing our image in the previous two recipes. Our green screen, while poorly lit, covered the background entirely so we only had to tweak a couple of parameters to finesse the key.

However, you may run into a scenario where you have a green screen backdrop that isn't large enough to cover the entire background of your shot. We can mask out edges of our image to fix this. Another example is when a light, stand, or boom mic is in the shot.

Getting ready

We're going to use a different angle of the same fake news broadcast from the previous couple of recipes. Notice that on the right of the frame, we can see the background of the room.

How to do it...

1. Add the **Keyer** effect to your clip and tweak the parameters as necessary to key out the backdrop, while temporarily ignoring any obvious background element not covered by the green screen that is still in the shot.

2. Make sure your green screen clip is highlighted in the timeline. In your **Effects Browser**, in the **Keying** category, find the **Mask** effect and double-click on it to add it to your green screen clip. You should immediately see four pucks appear on screen that have seemingly cropped out part of the frame.

If you followed the *Downloading and installing more effects* recipe, you can optionally use the slightly more advanced mask you've acquired, **Mask 8 points Alex4D**.

3. Drag these four pucks around as necessary to adjust your matte.

In our example, we dragged the two left pucks back to the far corners. We took the bottom right puck and dragged it to the bottom of the screen and to the right, but just short of where the background became visible again. And with the upper-right puck, we dragged it up and near the upper right corner, making sure not to reveal the background on the right edge of the original clip. Take note that the matte effect does not have to be a rectangle with two parallel sides, but merely a quadrilateral:

There's more...

When a four point mask isn't enough

A four point mask isn't always enough points to properly cut out the shape you want. While you can make your own multi-point mask in Motion and publish it to the **Effects Browser** in FCPX, it's sometimes just easier to download an effect if someone's already thought of it! If you followed the *Downloading and installing more effects* recipe, you've now got a mask effect with more than four points!

7
Titles, Transitions, and Generators

In this chapter, we will cover the following:

- ▸ Adding transitions to clips
- ▸ Adjusting the transition's parameters in the Viewer, Inspector, and timeline
- ▸ Creating counters and countdowns
- ▸ Adding a timecode overlay
- ▸ Inserting a placeholder clip
- ▸ Creating a text style template
- ▸ Creating a credit sequence
- ▸ Creating a video-in-text effect
- ▸ Creating a custom animated title
- ▸ Creating and reusing show intro

Introduction

Not every visual element that makes up your movie is shot with a camera. Almost all produced videos have some added visual elements to them in the form of titles, transitions, and generators. Before FCPX, titling in previous versions was a real drag, with limited options and visual flair, often leading to users to head over to Motion or elsewhere to create anything animated and visually worthwhile. But with FCPX, Apple upped the game and integrated many of Motion's titling powers right into the program.

As for transitions, Apple started over, dumping almost all previous effects for a new generation of transitions. Sure; many of them are still tacky, but they look as though they were built for the 2010s, not the 1990s!

Lastly, generators are an often overlooked tool when you have the simple needs of generating a background for text, making shapes, displaying timecode, and more.

All of these tools should always be used in moderation, however. It's easy to get carried away when you see all the neat bells and whistles you can add to your movie, but you always need to take a step back and ask yourself whether you should really add them. The overuse and abuse of these tools can distract a viewer from the core content of your video. It's like the auto-tune of the video editing world!

Adding transitions to clips

Since the early days of digital video editing, editors (or people who call themselves editors) have always abused the art of transitions. When it's as easy as a click or two to make your video disappear in the shape of a star or explode into dust, many people think, "Why not?" (On a side note, George Lucas is the only artist who can get away with a wipe transition).

The world of transitions is often an area of editing where it's important to remember the adage, "less is more". But, then again, transitions do have a time and a place, and with dozens built into FCPX, you're bound to experiment.

Getting ready

We've created a timeline with four clips in the primary storyline and three connected clips above the primary storyline. While not required to have this exact setup, it will make this exercise easy to follow along with, as shown in the following screenshot:

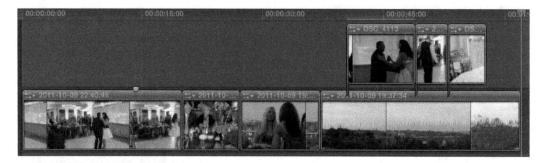

How to do it...

1. Click on either side of an edit point between the first two clips to highlight it as follows:

2. Hit *Command + T*. If you get a message that says, **There is not enough extra media beyond clip edges to create the transition...**, click on **Create Transition** (there's more info in the *There's More...* section of this recipe).

   The most basic of all transitions—the cross dissolve—is added to those clips as follows:

3. Highlight the next edit point by clicking on it. Again, it's ok that only one side of the edit point displays a bracket.

4. Open your **Transitions** browser and find the transition called **Earthquake** in the **Movements** category, as shown in the following screenshot:

5. Double-click on the **Earthquake** transition. It will be applied to the edit point. Again, if you get any message about not having enough extra media, click on **Create Transition**.

6. Back in your Event Browser, find the transition called **Bloom** in the **Lights** category.

7. Click-and-drag it to the edit point between the third and fourth clips and let go. The transition will be added, as shown in the following screenshot:

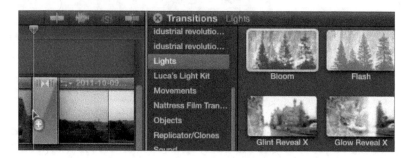

8. Highlight all the connected clips above the primary storyline and hit *Command + T*. A cross dissolve is added to all edit points on the clips. In addition, all the connected clips were placed into a secondary storyline. This is a requirement for transitions placed on connected clips—they must be in a secondary storyline. If they are not, FCPX automatically creates one. Also note that there is now only one connection point between the connected clips and the primary storyline, rather than three:

9. Click on the black banner above your newly created secondary storyline to highlight the entire storyline and not just the individual clips inside as follows:

10. Go to **Clip | Break Apart Clip Items** (*Command + Shift + G*). This command is to disassemble the secondary storyline. A pop-up box will inform you that connected clips cannot have transitions. Click on **Break Apart**. Your clips will return to their normal connected state, without transitions.

11. From your **Transitions** browser, click-and-drag the **Bloom** transition on top of the rightmost connected clip. When you let go, the transition will be applied to both edit points on the clip and the clip will be joined in a secondary storyline with the preceding clip, as shown in the following screenshot:

12. When you let go, the transition will be applied to both edit points on the clip and the clip will be joined in a secondary storyline with the preceding clip as follows:

There's more...

Transitions and media limits

What does it mean when you try and add a transition and FCPX spits back, **There is not enough extra media beyond clip edges to create the transition...**?

By nature, transitions exist by overlapping two video clips at the same time. One clip leaves the frame in some way while another comes in. In order to prevent disrupting the timing and length of your project, FCPX tries to use extra media from your two clips beyond the clips' original selected range in order to create a transition that doesn't alter the length of your project. If that extra media doesn't exist (that is, you have used the entire length of a clip in a project, not just a shorter range within), then FCPX will let you know that in order to make the transition, it must force an overlap using your existing project clips, and therefore, shorten the project.

This is fine and dandy most of the time, but if you were editing a video in beat to music, it can throw the timing off farther down the project, or if you were editing a 30-second commercial, it might become 29.5 seconds long!

Adjusting the transition's parameters in the Viewer, Inspector, and timeline

It's easy to tack on a transition, but many of them have multiple parameters that can only be tweaked in certain places such as the Inspector, on-screen controls in the Viewer, or even in the timeline itself.

Getting ready

Simply create a timeline with two clips in it that you can add a transition to.

How to do it...

1. Open your **Transitions** browser and make sure **All** is highlighted in the categories box.

2. In the search box below, type in black hole, as shown in the following screenshot:

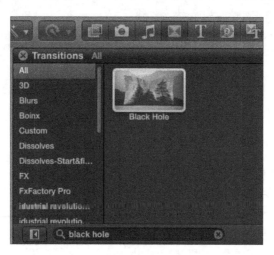

3. Drag the black hole transition between the two clips in your timeline. If you get a message that says **There is not enough extra media beyond clip edges to create the transition...**, click on **Create Transition**, as shown in the following screenshot:

There is not enough extra media beyond clip edges to create the transition.

Do you want to overlap (ripple trim) your media to create the transition?

This will decrease the total duration of your project.

Cancel   Create Transition

4. Play the area around the transition. This transition sucks in the first clip into a vortex and reveals the second clip underneath.

5. Click on the transition itself in the timeline to highlight it. A puck should appear in the middle of the black hole.

6. Click-and-drag the puck around. It will distort the center point of the black hole. Drag the puck to the bottom right. When you play back the transition, the first clip is sucked into its own bottom-right corner, rather than the center, as shown in the following screenshot:

7. Open the Inspector (*Command + 4*). Additional parameters for this transition will appear as follows:

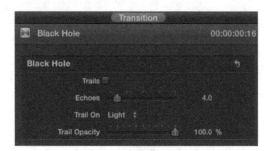

8. Select the checkbox next to **Trails** and increase the **Echoes** parameter to **15.0**. Play back the transition to see how it has changed as follows:

As we can see, sometimes certain parameters are only accessible in the Viewer, and some are only accessible via the Inspector.

Let's take a look at a transition whose parameters are decided in the timeline itself.

9. In the **Transitions** browser, search for **Clone**.

10. Drag the clone spin transition right on top of the black hole transition to replace it, and then play back the transition. It's interesting, but seemingly repetitive with the images from the same two clips being shown over and over on the video wall.

11. Click and highlight the transition in the timeline if it has not already been done. Numbered golden medallions will appear over the surrounding clips. These medallions control the images seen in the transition, as shown in the following screenshot:

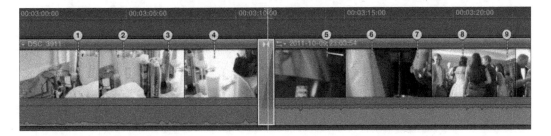

12. Click-and-drag around on the medallions and place them on other clips in your timeline.

    Hint: you may need to zoom out of your timeline a bit with *Command + -* (the minus sign) in order to see more of your clips that you can drag the medallions to.

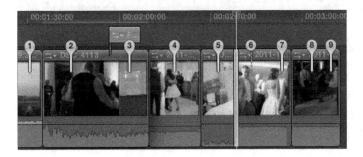

13. Play through your transition again to see a whole new and more varied video wall, as shown in the following screenshot:

There's more...

Changing the duration of a transition

If you find a transition's animation moving too fast to appreciate it, you can adjust its length. Simply click on the transition itself and hit *Command + D*. Your dashboard lights up in the central toolbar. Type a number like 200 or 2. (the number 2 and a period) to change the length of the transition to two seconds. If it does not let you, it means you do not have enough media handle space to create the overlap!

See also

If you don't understand the message—**There is not enough extra media beyond clip edges to create the transition...** when trying to apply a transition, read the last recipe—*Adding transitions to clips*.

Creating counters and countdowns

Whether you're calculating the GDP of a foreign country or simply trying to count down from 10 to 1, the ability to create animating counters is a handy tool, even if it's not a tool you're going to use every day.

How to do it...

1. Open your **Generators** browser.

2. Click on the **Elements** category, as shown in the following screenshot:

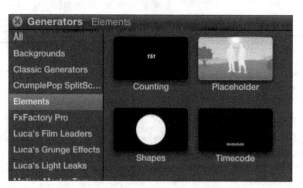

3. Highlight the **Counting** generator and hit *E* to append it to your storyline. In reality, you can place this clip where you like—hit *Q* if you want to connect it to a particular clip or *W* if you want to insert it between two clips. Just beware of your playhead's position!

   Take note that the default length of the **Counting** generator is 10 seconds long. This will be important in a moment.

4. Skim through the generator. By default, the **Counting** generator counts up from **1.0** to **300.0**.

5. Highlight the generator in your timeline and open your Inspector if it isn't already visible (*Command + 4*).

   We see a large number of parameters that can be manipulated. Let's say we want to first make a countdown from 5 to 1.

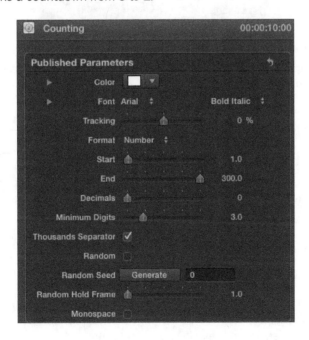

6. Click on the parameter value **1.0** next to the **Start** slider. Type in 5 and hit *Return*.

7. Click on the parameter value **300.0** next to the **End** slider. Type in 1 and hit *Return*.

8. Drag the **Minimum Digits** slider to **1.0**, as shown in the following screenshot:

9. Play back your video and watch how the counter counts down from **5.0** to **1.0**. However, the **Counting** generator is 10 seconds long, so each number appears for two seconds. Rather than try and trim the clip ourselves to be exactly five seconds long, we'll use the Duration command to set a length for the generator.

10. Double-check that the generator is highlighted in the timeline. Hit *Command + D*. Your dashboard will light up in bright blue.

11. Type in 500 or 5. (the number 5 and a period). These are two different ways to indicate FCPX that you want to change the duration to 5 seconds. Hit *Return*. Your generator will shrink to exactly **5:00** seconds in length, as shown in the following screenshot:

12. Play your clip again. You will now have a perfect 5-second countdown with each number lasting 1 second.

There's more...

Modifying the text

You're not limited to using white font in the center of the screen. Notice that in the Inspector, you can change the font and font color. You can also reposition the counter anywhere you want on the screen by using the Transform tool.

Currency, percentages, binary and more – the Format parameter is key!

We just did an extremely simple countdown with whole numbers, but the **Counting** parameter is capable of much more. The most important parameter to know about in the Counter's Inspector is the **Format** parameter. You can change the **Number** setting to **Currency**, **Percent**, **Spell Out**, and more, as shown in the following screenshot:

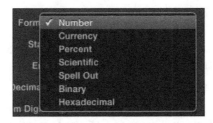

See also

If you want to move your counter off center, you can do so easily with the Transform tool. If you haven't learned how to use this tool yet, read the recipe, *Using the Transform tool* recipe in *Chapter 8, Get Your Movie to Move*.

Adding a timecode overlay

Timecode has been around for decades and is a tool that easily allows an editor to identify each and every frame within a clip. Timecode essentially gives every frame a name. They're often overlayed in rushes and rough cuts so a director or producer can say, "Hey, can you change the transition at 00:34:52:17?" rather than "Hey, can you change the transition that's about a half an hour in, between the shot of the monkey shooting lasers out of his ears and the shot of the couch falling from the sky and landing on the sad clown?"

FCPX can easily apply a timecode reader to appear over your video so that it can be viewed right in FCPX's Viewer (if your director/producer is right there with you) or in any exported version of the video.

Getting ready

You can add timecode at almost any point in the editing process. Usually, however, it's easiest to do it towards the end, right before you are either going to export a version of your video or show it to someone right there in FCPX. In our upcoming example, we have a simple finished project that we're going to add timecode to.

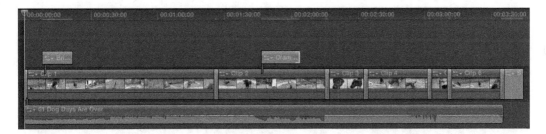

How to do it...

1. Set your playhead at the very start of your timeline. You can do this by pressing the Home key or *fn* + left arrow.

2. Open your **Generators** browser.

3. In the **Elements** category, find the **Timecode** generator and highlight it. Press *Q* to connect it. The generator will be added as a connected clip at the very beginning of your project, but will only be 10-seconds long.

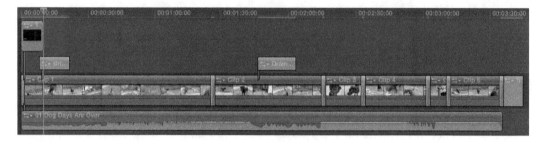

4. Click on the out point of the generator clip.

5. Press the End key or *fn* + right arrow to move your playhead to the end of the timeline (you could also just move your playhead to the end of the timeline by directly clicking on it).

6. Press *Shift* + *X* to perform an Extend Edit command. Because we highlighted the generator clip's out point, it will extend the generator to the location of our playhead (or skimmer, if it's showing).

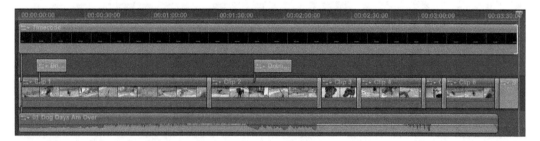

Our timecode now displays across the entire project.

7. Highlight the **Timecode** generator in the timeline and open the Inspector (*Command + 4*). A number of parameters will appear as follows:

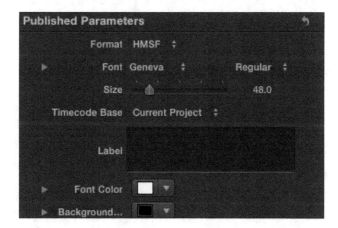

8. Tweak the parameters to your liking. You can adjust the basic font properties, add a custom label to the timecode, and change the format of the timecode to display only a frame count as follows:

There's more...

Moving the location of the timecode

Although it doesn't show up as one of the **Timecode** generator's parameters, you can easily move the location of the timecode display, you just need to think outside of the box—or tab, in this case. Instead of looking in the **Generator** tab in the Inspector, click over to the **Video** tab and adjust the clip's Position parameters under the **Transform** category. Of course, you could also simply click on the **Transform Tool** button under the Viewer and pick up and drag around the timecode clip in the Viewer itself!

Inserting a placeholder clip

The editing process doesn't always begin after all shooting on a project has wrapped up. Sometimes editors are given footage to start editing far before a shoot has wrapped. When editing together a music video, a scene from a movie, or a promotional video, you may have 80 percent of what you need, but are still waiting on a few last-minute pickup shots or reshoots.

With the **Placeholder** generator, you can drop in temporary clips and make it display some basic elements of what the shot will look like and replace them later when needed. This is especially helpful when you are editing a timed piece that must be of a specific length and you want to get the timing down accurately and quickly, even before you have all your material.

How to do it...

1. Place you playhead between any two clips in a timeline of your choosing.

2. Open your **Generators** browser and find the **Placeholder** generator in the **Elements** category, as shown in the following screenshot:

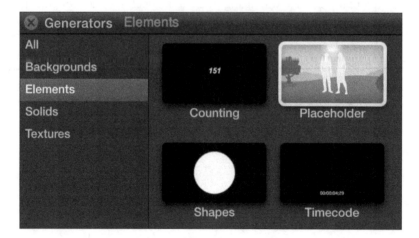

3. Double-click on the **Placeholder** generator to insert it at the playhead's location. You will see a simple illustration of a man and woman standing in a field. Chances are, this is not the exact image you're going for! Also, the new clip is 10 seconds long and may not be of the desired length:

4. Click and highlight the generator in the timeline. If you know exactly how long this clip needs to be, press *Command + D*, type in the length of the clip, and hit *Return*. For example, if you knew the shot needed to be exactly 5 seconds and 17 frames long, you would highlight the clip, press *Command + D*, and then type 517 and hit *Return*:

5. Open the Inspector (*Command + 4*). A number of parameters are revealed, as shown in the following screenshot:

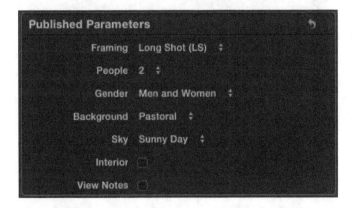

6. Click to the right of the **Framing** parameter name to change **Long Shot (LS)** to **Medium Shot (MS)**. Change **People** from **2** to **3**, **Gender** from **Men and Women** to **Women**, **Background** from **Pastoral** to **Distant City**, and **Sky** from **Sunny Day** to **Clear Night**.

7. Select the checkbox next to **View Notes**. In the Viewer, you can now double-click and type any notes or description of the shot to come!

Whether its hours, days, or weeks later, eventually you'll get the shot that's supposed to fit in this space. Once you do, it's time to replace the placeholder clip.

8. Select a selection start of your new clip in the Event Browser.

9. Drag the clip from the Event Browser and drop it on top of your **Placeholder** generator, as follows:

10. In the pop-up box, choose **Replace from Start**, as shown in the following screenshot:

The clip will replace the placeholder without disrupting the timing of your project:

See also

If you're unsure of how the other Replace options work, read the *Replacing a clip* recipe in *Chapter 3, Basic Editing Mechanics*.

Creating a text style template

Modifying text parameters in the Inspector is a relatively painless process, but it can be quite time-consuming if you modify 10 different stylistic parameters and then realize you need to create the same style over and over again for multiple title clips later in your project.

While you can duplicate title clips for reuse in a project and modify the duplicates, this can get a bit tedious. It's much more efficient to make one title clip look the way you want and then save those settings as a preset.

How to do it...

1. Add a Basic Title clip to your timeline. You can connect it to another clip or just place it in your primary storyline.

2. In the Basic Title's Inspector window, under the **Text** tab, type in `Presets Save Time`, one word on each line. Adjust the font and size so that it takes up most of the screen (we chose Snell Roundhand and a font size of 224). Adjust the tracking to around 50 percent. These parameters are known as your **basic attributes**.

The white text is a bit hard to read on brighter images. Let's fix that.

3. Scroll down further on the **Text** tab and click on the boxes next to **Outline** and **Drop Shadow** to turn them on. **Face** should already be on (otherwise, you wouldn't see your text!). This group is known as the **style attributes**:

4. Hover your cursor over **Outline** and click on the word, **Show**. Change the **Color** parameter to black and set the **Width** parameter to **3.0**, as shown in the following screenshot:

5. Hover your cursor over **Drop Shadow** and click on the word, **Show**. Set **Distance** to about 12 and set the **Blur** value to about 3.

The text is far more legible now:

6. Back at the top of the **Text** tab, click on the box that reads **Normal** in the style you've just created.

7. Select **Save All Basic+Style Attributes**, as shown in the following screenshot:

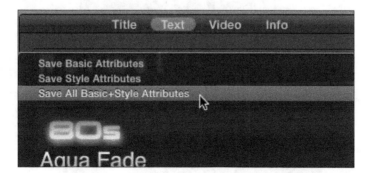

8. Name the preset with whatever you like and click on **Save**, as shown in the following screenshot:

9. Add a new Basic Title clip to another location in your timeline.

10. Modify the text to say whatever you like, but don't bother changing any of the basic or style attributes.

11. Highlight the text and at the top of the **Text** tab in the Inspector, click on **Normal**, scroll down to your newly named preset, and click on it. The clip will change all parameters to match that preset automatically:

There's more...

Deleting a preset

Adding a custom preset is a piece of cake, but deleting one is not. You cannot delete a preset directly from FCPX. You must find the tiny preset file FCPX created somewhere deep on your computer! The file's path is `Users/username/Library/Application Support/Motion/Library/Text Styles`. There you will find the actual files of your custom presets and you can delete them accordingly!

If you're using Lion or Mountain Lion, your user's `Library` folder is hidden. The easiest way to get there is in finder; click on **Go** in the menu bar and hold down the *Option* key. The `Library` folder will magically appear in the menu!

Saving just a basic or style preset

In our exercise, we chose to save both the basic and style attributes, but remember that the menu lets you save one or the other, depending on your needs!

Creating a credit sequence

This one needs little introduction—we've all needed/wanted to create a cinematic style credits sequence before and FCPX makes it easy to do.

How to do it...

1. Open your **Titles** browser and click on the **Credits** category, as shown in the following screenshot:

2. Click on the **Scrolling** title and hit *E* to append it to the end of your storyline. The title clip is displayed as a purple box, as shown in the following screenshot:

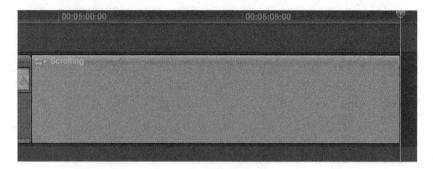

3. Skim through the title. There is some placeholder text, which we've got to change:

4. Highlight the title in your timeline and open your Inspector if it isn't already visible (*Command + 4*). We see some, but not all, of the parameters that we can tweak for the title. Some options are under the **Title** tab while others are under the **Text** tab.

5. Under the **Title** tab, set the **Font** and **Color** parameters to whatever style you deem fit for your film. In this example, we'll choose **Times New Roman** and keep the color of the font white, as shown in the following screenshot:

6. Click on the **Text** tab in the Inspector. A new slew of parameters appears, as follows:

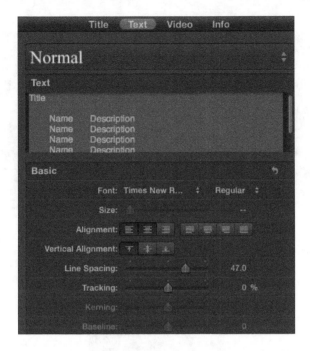

7. In the **Text** box, replace the **Name** and **Description** placeholders with your actual credits. You should instantly see the changes in the Viewer. Highlight and delete any unneeded lines of text.

 You can double-click and edit text directly in the Viewer, but it is often easier to do so in the Inspector.

The following screenshot shows the updated **Text** box:

8. Play back your credits. They roll a bit too fast for our liking so we would like to slow them down.

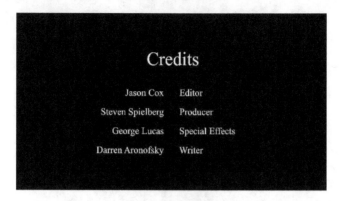

9. Move your cursor to the right edge of the title clip in the timeline until you see the trim icon:

10. Click-and-drag to the right. As you do so, a pop-up window will show how many seconds and frames you are adding to your title. The longer the scrolling title, the slower the text will move. Add about 5 seconds:

11. Watch your clip once more and see how the speed of the scroll has decreased.

Adding extra lines to the credits

The default **Scrolling** title only gives you a few lines for credits. If you're editing a large-scale production, however, you will likely need many more lines for **Name** and **Description**. The only tricky part here is the fact that, in cinematic credit style, the **Name** parameter is right justified and the **Description** parameter is left justified, even though they're on the same line.

To add another credit line, move your cursor to the end of your **Text** box in the Inspector and hit *Return* to create a new line of text. Immediately hit the *Tab* key. This will justify the cursor for the **Name** field. Type in the name you want, then hit *Tab* again. This then justifies the line for the **Description** field. Type in the description you want:

It might not look properly justified in the Inspector, but check your Viewer to confirm that the alignment is indeed correct. To summarize adding another line, hit *Return*, hit *Tab*, type name, hit *Tab*, type description, repeat.

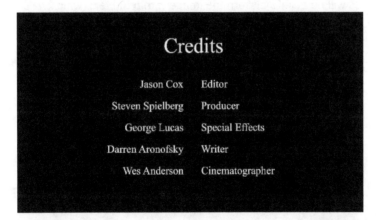

Creating a video-in-text effect

Sometimes placing text on top of an image can get a little too straightforward and boring. However, using colors for fonts is not the only way to go! Using blend modes in FCPX, we can make FCPX carve out an image based upon the title clip stacked along with the clip.

How to do it...

1. Move your playhead to the beginning of the clip where you want to create your video-in-text effect and connect a title effect of your choice to the clip with the shortcut *Q*. We've inserted **Basic Title**.

2. Trim the length of the title clip to match your clip length, as follows:

3. Customize the title to look exactly the way you want using the Inspector window.

    You will likely want to make your text rather bold and/or large to make sure your audience will be able to discern the image within the text (which we'll do in a couple of steps). Don't worry about the color of the font. We will choose the Impact font at a font size of 426:

4. Make sure the title clip is still highlighted and open the Inspector (*Command + 4*).

5. In the **Video** tab, scroll down to the bottom and find the box labeled **Compositing**.

6. Change **Blend Mode** from **Normal** to **Stencil Alpha**, as shown in the following screenshot:

Your image will disappear except for the parts that were obscured by the text. Replace the colored font now.

How it works...

There are more than 20 blend modes in FCPX. Each one is a different algorithm used to analyze the pixels of a selected clip as well as the one(s) underneath it to create a new visual outcome. In the case of **Stencil Alpha**, all the white pixels from the text kept the image underneath opaque, while all transparent pixels (which appear black) from the title clip made the rest of the clip invisible. Thus the image was stamped out by the white pixels.

There's more...

Experimenting with blend modes

With more than 20 blend modes, not only would it be difficult to try and define each one here, but it's nearly impossible as each has such a radically different result depending on the clips you use. Most of them (the ones that don't mention Alpha or Luma, which are usually better suited for effects like the one we just did with text) are intended to mix two full-screen images with one another. Try stacking clips and experimenting with the different blend modes to see the different results you can attain. Just remember you usually apply the blend mode to the uppermost clip!

Creating a custom animated title

FCPX has dozens of built-in animated titles that are flashy and easy to use, but fairly rigid in their customization options. A few you can barely manipulate at all with the exception of the content of the text. Although intimidating at first, the **Custom** title option lets you build your own text animation from scratch using more than a dozen possible parameters.

How to do it...

1. Open up your **Titles** browser and click on the **Build In/Out** category. Find the **Custom** title and add it to your storyline wherever you like.

    Skimming through the title clip at first doesn't seem all that interesting—it's simply the placeholder text, Title and is totally static.

2. Make sure the title clip is highlighted and open your Inspector (*Command + 4*). Ignore the **Title** tab for the moment and click on the **Text** tab.

3. Change the placeholder text to say what you like. Also, change any of the basic and style attributes while you're at it (**Font**, **Size**, **Drop Shadow**, and so on). We wrote a title card for a promo video using the Menlo font with size of 130 and adjusted the tracking up a bit. We also threw on a subtle glow and drop shadow for good measure (although it's hard to see on a black screen).

4. Click back on the **Title** tab, and you will see a long list of parameters, as shown in the following screenshot:

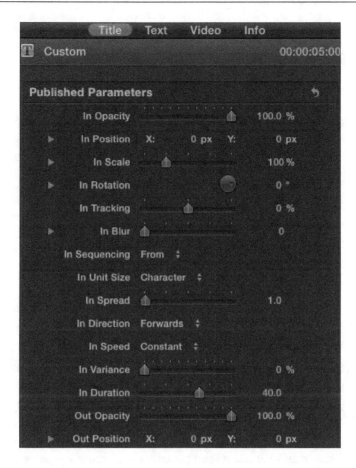

There seems to be 26 parameters listed here, but there're only 13 in reality. The first half (all starting with the word **In**) are animation parameters affecting how your text will animate in on screen while the second half (all starting with **Out**) are parameters that will affect how your text animates out.

5. Drag the **In Opacity** slider to **0.0%** and skim through your clip. Your text now fades in.

   In this step, we told FCPX to make sure the opacity was **0.0%** at the start of the clip and then FCPX animated the text to **100%** opacity.

   Let's try another example.

6. Change the **In Scale** parameter to **0%** and **In Rotation** to **180**, and play your title back. Your text should animate in three ways now—it should fade in, grow in size from infinitesimally small to the font size you set, and rotate from upside down to right-side up, as follows:

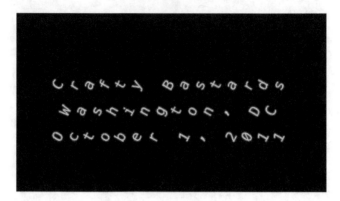

If you find that the animation is happening too quickly, there are a couple of parameters to help with that.

7. Click on the **In Unit Size** parameter and set it to **Word**. Instead of your text fading in character by character, it will fade in word by word. You could also select **Line** to fade in line by line. This may be preferable with a longer title.

8. Drag the **In Duration** slider to **60**. This number determines how many frames the **In animation** parameter lasts for. The longer the animation, the slower it goes.

9. Drag the **In Spread** slider to **4.0**. Instead of each word fading in one at a time (as we have set in step 7), it will spread the animation across the value of **In Spread**. In our case, at any given moment, four words are fading in. This results in a slightly smoother animation:

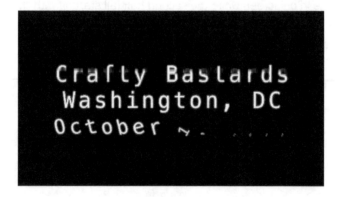

10. Play around with the other parameters and don't forget to set all the **Out** animations if you choose to do so.

Creating and reusing show intro

If you're producing a regular series of videos for the Web or even for broadcast, chances are, you have a show intro that will stay relatively consistent each and every episode. A 30-second show intro may include a ton of clips, titles, generators, and transitions, and obviously no one wants to have to recreate that for each and every project.

Through a sneaky use of compound clips, we can create a reusable show intro that can be dropped into any number of projects and tweaked from episode to episode as well.

Getting ready

This task requires a bit of forethought. Ideally, you want to have all the elements of what will go into your show's intro together in one event. Don't worry about titles, transitions, or generators yet, just get the raw video and audio material collected into an event. It's ok if there's excess material in the event.

If you haven't read the *Grouping clips together as a compound clip* recipe in *Chapter 4, Enhancing Your Editing* yet, now would be a good time to do so!

How to do it...

1. Highlight all the clips in your event that you want to use in your show intro. This can be video, audio, or still images.

2. Right-click on one of the highlighted clips and choose **New Compound Clip...**, as shown in the following screenshot:

3. In the pop-up window, type in a name for your new compound clip and click on **OK**, as shown in the following screenshot:

The newly generated compound clip appears in your event. Note the unique icon that marks it as a compound clip, as follows:

4. Double-click on the compound clip. The clip will be loaded into its own timeline. All the clips we added to the compound clip will be lined up in the timeline, as shown in the following screenshot:

 This is *not* a project. We have not created a new project in the Project Library. We can confirm this by looking at the path listed above the timeline. In our example, it shows that we are viewing the **Bridie Show Intro** compound clip contained within the **Play with Bridie** event.

5. Now comes the creative part. Build your show intro! This might take you 60 seconds to do or 60 minutes, but take your puzzle pieces in the timeline in front of you and work with, it as you would with a normal project. Add titles! Add generators! Add transitions! Add effects! The following screenshot shows what our timeline looks like when we wrap up:

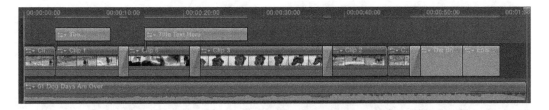

We rearranged our clips, we added some titles and transitions, and although you can see them in the timeline, we tacked on some effects to our clips as well. Our last title clip says Episode 1: Bridie Out Back. This is obviously a textbox that will change from episode to episode. We'll see how to do this in just a couple of steps.

6. Click on the **Project Library** button in the lower-left corner of the interface or hit *Command + 0*:

7. Find a project you want to add this show intro to. We've opened up our **TBS – Episode 2** project we have created for The Bridie Show.

8. Back up in the Event Browser, highlight the compound clip you've created and edit it into your timeline (likely right at the beginning, if this is a show intro). The show intro now appears in your timeline, as follows:

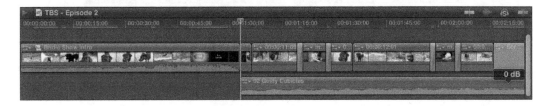

There's only one problem left. Our show intro contains the placeholder text, Episode 1. But this is Episode 2!

9. Double-click on the compound clip in the project to load it into the timeline. Do *not* double-click on the one in the original event or you will modify the original! You can safely confirm which version of the compound clip is loaded up by again looking at the path given just above the timeline. The following screenshot shows that this is the **Bridie Show Intro** compound clip inside the project, **TBS – Episode 2**:

10. Make any modifications to title clips that you want in order to differentiate or customize them for this episode. We have simply changed the ending title card to Episode 2: Bridie at the Vet, as follows:

11. Once you've made any necessary changes, click on the **Go back in Timeline History** button to return to your main timeline and continue editing your show, as shown in the following screenshot:

Adding more clips to a compound clip after you've created it

When putting your show intro together, you may decide you want to add some extra clips or music to it after you've already created the compound clip. Luckily, you don't have to recreate the clip! Assuming the compound clip is loaded up into the timeline, simply drag any additional media from an event and it will immediately become part of the compound clip.

If you're having a tough time with how compound clips work, go back and read the *Grouping clips together as a compound clip* recipe in *Chapter 4, Enhancing Your Editing*.

8

Get Your Movie to Move

In this chapter, we will cover the following:

- ▸ Making freeze frames and speed changes
- ▸ Creating speed ramps
- ▸ Showing an instant replay
- ▸ Using the Transform tool
- ▸ Cropping or trimming a clip
- ▸ Panning and zooming over a photo or clip with the Ken Burns effect
- ▸ Creating a video wall
- ▸ Making your image move by keyframing in the Viewer
- ▸ Moving clips in sync with compound clips
- ▸ Changing keyframe timing in the timeline
- ▸ Customizing motion paths with Bezier handles and modifying interpolation

Introduction

Welcome to the most important chapter in this book! In the next batch of recipes, you will get to essentially mess with the space-time continuum of Final Cut Pro X. We will start off with the "time" component by learning how to play around with the speed of clips. We will go beyond simply speeding up or slowing down whole clips and will freeze them, replay them, and ramp them as well!

After that we will move on to the "space" portion where we will alter the position, size, and rotation of clips, as well as learn how to animate these changes with keyframes!

Hop in your DeLorean, buckle up, and prepare to hit 88 mph (if you didn't understand that, please do yourself a favor and go rent Back to the Future).

Making freeze frames and speed changes

Life moves at one speed—1x (although, I'm sure we all feel differently sometimes, for example when writing a book), but unlike real life, movies can be a lot cooler when they move slower or faster than real time. Final Cut Pro X makes it easy to slow down or speed up clips to fit your needs within a project down to the frame.

Getting ready

Any clips at all can be used to illustrate speed changes. We're going to experiment on three clips in this exercise.

How to do it...

1. Click on any clip in your timeline. Our first shot is a pan of a produce aisle in a grocery store. The shot is nice and smooth, but the pan is a bit fast, so we need to slow it down to appreciate the imagery.

2. Click on the **Retime** button in the toolbar and choose **Slow** | **50%**, as shown in the following screenshot:

In the timeline, the clip appears longer, but the Retime Editor that appears over the clip tells us that the clip is merely playing at **50%** speed. We are not seeing any new frames of video that we did not see before:

Now it's playing a little too slow, though. To speed it up just a little, we need to take a close look at the Retime Editor.

3. Find the two tiny vertical lines at the right-hand edge of the Retime Editor. Click and hold on them, dragging slowly to the left. You will see the clip grow thinner (and therefore slightly faster as indicated by the increasing speed percentage), as follows:

4. Click on another clip in your timeline to highlight it, and hit *Command + R*. This is another way to bring up the Retime Editor. In our clip, we have a crowd shot, which we want to speed up a lot to create a sort of time-lapse look:

5. Click on the triangle next to the **100%** label and choose **Fast | 20x**, as shown in the following screenshot:

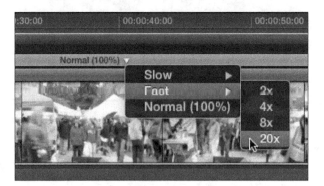

The clip shrinks tremendously, now appearing with the speed of **2000%** above it. You may need to zoom in on your timeline in order to properly see the label:

6. Highlight yet another clip, find a frame that would make for a good moment to freeze on, and drag your playhead to that spot. We've got a clip of a break dancer at the peak of a handstand, as follows:

7. Click on the **Retime** pop-up menu button and choose **Hold** (*Shift + H*), as shown in the following screenshot:

8. The clip has been broken down into three speed segments—the first part plays at normal speed until it reaches the frame we had parked our playhead on; the second segment shows the label, **Hold (0%)** for two seconds; and the third one plays the rest of the clip at normal speed again, as follows:

Maybe we only want the freeze frame to last about one second.

9. Find the two tiny vertical lines at the right-hand edge of the second segment (the frozen segment), as follows:

Click and hold on those vertical lines, dragging slowly to the left to shorten the hold frame, as shown in the following screenshot:

10. Click on **X** on each Retime Editor window to close them or highlight all the clips where the Retime Editor is viewable and hit *Command + R*.

How it works...

FCPX has three different ways in which it will play back a clip that has a speed change applied to it—**Normal**, **Frame Blending**, and **Optical Flow**. When a clip has been highlighted and a speed change has been applied, you can select which quality level is to be used by navigating to the **Video Quality** option under the **Retime** button, as shown in the following screenshot:

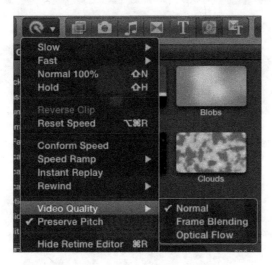

Let's say a clip is slowed down to 50 percent of its original speed. In **Normal**, every frame is played for the length of two frames, creating rather stuttered playback. In **Frame Blending**, FCPX applies a quick and dirty algorithm which blends two frames together, sometimes creating an undesirable ghosting effect. Finally, you can apply the **Optical Flow** algorithm. This is the granddaddy of all FCPX algorithms, and when selected, automatically becomes a background process that can take a while to finish. FCPX analyzes every frame of the clip for motion and creates a much smoother slow-motion playback than **Frame Blending**, by creating whole new frames based upon its analysis. Of course, depending on the quality of video, results will vary. Video with a lot of high-speed motion or poor stabilization will often result in a video with a jelly-like quality!

There's more...

Changing the speed while using the Range Selection tool

It's easy to change the speed of a small portion of a clip. Perhaps you have a gymnast running across a mat and you want to slow down just the middle section of the video when he/she does a large flip into the air.

First, simply select your Range Selection tool (with the *R* key), and highlight a range of a clip in your timeline, as follows:

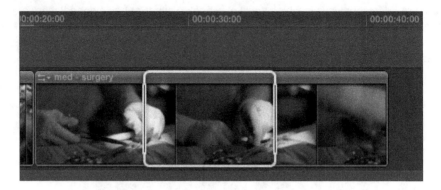

Then select the speed level of your choice from the **Retime** pop-up menu in the toolbar, as follows:

Rendering a sped-up video

You'll often find that if you speed up your video by very large amounts (for instance, 20x), then the video will likely play back pretty jittery at first. You will also likely see an orange render bar appear over the clip, indicating that FCPX needs to render it in order to play back the clip smoothly. You can wait for the background rendering to kick in or you can force it to render the clip by highlighting it and choosing **Modify | Render Selection** (*Command + R*).

Play a clip backwards

To make a clip play backwards simply highlight it, and choose **Reverse Clip** from the **Retime** pop-up menu. A **-100%** speed appears above the clip. You can manually tweak the speed by dragging the retime handles on the right-hand edge:

Creating speed ramps

For a little extra time-warping flair, we can slow clips down as they play along, making them go slower and sloowwer.... and slooooowweeer........... Or inversely, we can make them start at a snail's pace and keep getting faster and faster and faster until they're up and running at normal speed even faster than real time.

How to do it...

1. Highlight a clip in your timeline.

2. Click on the **Retime** button to bring up the pop-up menu and select **Speed Ramp | from 0%**, as shown in the following screenshot:

Your clip will stretch out in length and be split into four segments, each with a different speed percentage getting closer to 100%, as follows:

3. Play back the clip with the / key. Watch as the clip starts in slow motion and gets close to regular speed by the end.

   The one thing that might feel a bit odd is that the clip doesn't ever reach 100% speed at the end. Let's fix that.

4. In the fourth segment, click on the two vertical lines at the right-hand edge of the segment and drag left until the speed reads 100%:

Now the clip ramps up and finishes off at **100%** speed (real time).

We now know we can adjust the speed of any one of the four segments. However, we never picked the frames/points in time when one segment ends and another begins. Adjusting a segment's speed does not change the frame the segment ends on. For example, if the clip is 100 frames long, each segment is showing 25 frames of the original video, no matter what speed each segment is set to. This may not be an issue most of the time, but if you want a particular speed segment to start/end at a particular moment, we can alter the frame that a segment starts on.

5. Click on the disclosure triangle next to the second speed segment label and select **Change End Source Frame**, as shown in the following screenshot:

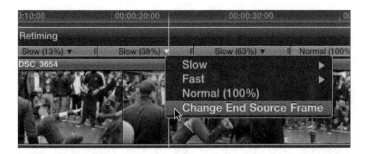

An icon that looks like a cell of film appears between the second and third segments, as follows:

6. Click-and-drag the icon towards left and right. Notice how the segments' speeds (shown by the percentages) do not change but the duration of the second and third segments do. If we drag the icon towards right, we are picking a later frame in the clip to end the second speed segment on. The third segment shortens and the clip as a whole ripples the timeline accordingly, as follows:

Think of it as rolling the edit point between the speed segments.

See also

If the idea of "rolling the edit point between the speed segments" was confusing, head back and read the *Using the Trim tool, part 2 – rolling* recipe in *Chapter 3, Basic Editing Mechanics*.

Showing an instant replay

Sometimes a clip is just so good that you simply need to watch it twice. Of course, you're unlikely to use this in a film production, but for sports or related videos, the instant replay technique is one of the most commonly used. FCPX's speed change tools give us a couple of options for applying this type of effect.

Getting ready

You can use any clip to perform this exercise. In our case, we've got a clip of a breakdancer bouncing in a circle on the ground using only one hand, as shown in the following screenshot:

How to do it...

1. Highlight a clip you want to turn into an instant replay.

2. Choose **Instant Replay** from the **Retime** pop-up menu (or go to **Modify | Retime | Instant Replay**), as follows:

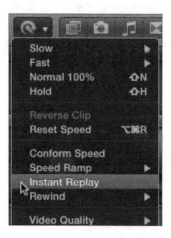

Your clip will now appear twice as long, with two identical sections at **100%** speed. Visually, it looks as if we have duplicated the clip right after itself, as follows:

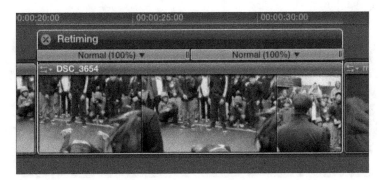

3. Click-and-drag the retiming handle (marked by the two vertical lines on the right-hand edge of the Retime Editor) of the second speed segment and drag left to speed up the replay, as shown in the following screenshot:

4. Make sure the clip is still highlighted and select **Reset Speed** from the **Retime** pop-up menu or hit *Command + Option + R*. The clip should return to its original **100%** speed state, as shown in the following screenshot:

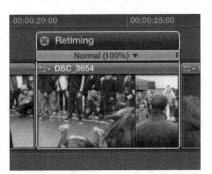

5. This time, choose **Rewind | 4x** from the **Retime** pop-up menu. Now the clip plays normally all the way through, rewinds at **400%** speed, and then plays through once more, as follows:

6. Click-and-drag the retiming handle of the third speed segment and drag it rightwards to slow down the replay, as shown in the following screenshot:

There's more...

Adding the Instant Replay title clip for added effect

For a little extra visual flair, FCPX offers a specific title clip that pairs nicely with an instant replay. Open up your **Titles** browser, click on the **Elements** category, and look for a title clip called (unsurprisingly) **Instant Replay**. Connect it above your instant replay clip in the timeline!

Only want to rewind/replay part of the clip?

It only makes sense that you may not want to create a replay of an entire clip. This is very easy to accomplish using the Blade tool. Simply activate the tool by hitting *B* on your keyboard. Next, move your cursor to the frame within the clip in your timeline right before the portion of the clip begins that you want to replay. Click to split the clip in two (playback will not be affected). Finally, apply either the **Instant Replay** or **Rewind** change to that second clip!

Using the Transform tool

If you were to ask us, we might call this the most important recipe in this book. Once you have a foundational understanding of how to use the Transform tool to modify a clip's "physical" properties, it unlocks a tremendous amount of creative potential in FCPX. The Transform tool lets editors resize, reposition, and rotate a piece of media. This can be accomplished visually in the Viewer or with numeric values in the Inspector.

Getting ready

You can practice on any clip in your timeline for this exercise.

FCPX can measure and display the parameters, which we will change in this exercise in two ways—percentages and pixels. We're going to do the next few exercises by pixel value. To make your settings match ours, go to **Final Cut Pro | Preferences**, click on the **Editing** tab, and make sure **Inspector Units** is set to **Pixels**, as shown in the following screenshot:

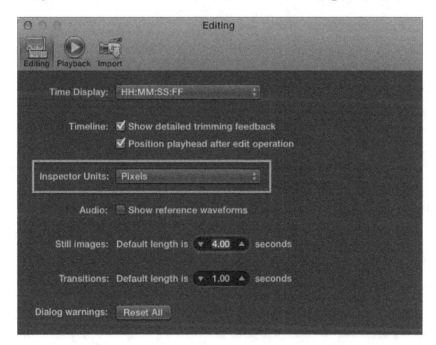

How to do it...

1. Highlight a clip in your timeline and double-check to make sure your playhead is somewhere over the clip. Your playhead *must* be over the clip in order to see which changes we are about to make to our clip in real time.

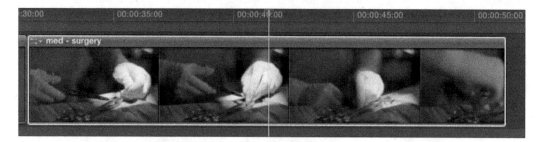

2. Click on the **Transform tool** button in the lower-left corner of your Viewer, as shown in the following screenshot:

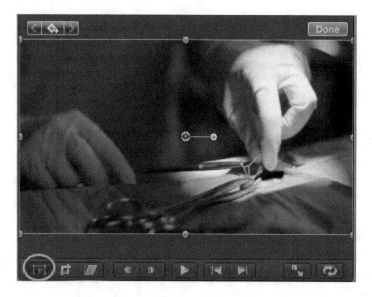

Some on-screen controls appear on your clip. The blue handles around the edges allow you to resize a clip. The blue circle extending from the central circle allows you to rotate a clip. Lastly, you can click-and-drag directly on the body of the clip itself to reposition the clip.

3. Click and hold on the blue resize handle in the bottom-left corner. Drag inward towards the center of the clip. The clip will begin to shrink in size. Let go when you've reduced the clip to approximately 30% in size (the value will show up in the upper-left corner of the Viewer while dragging), as shown in the following screenshot:

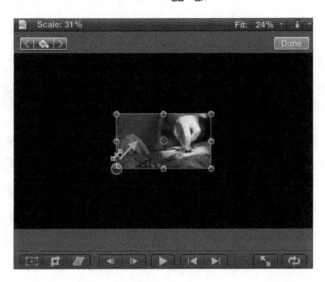

4. Click on the blue circle extending from the center, and drag up and down slowly. This allows you to rotate your clip, as follows:

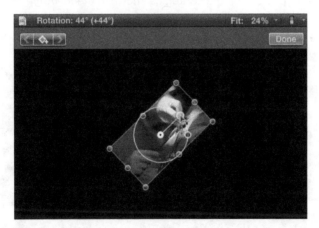

Often while rotating, you want to rotate in 90-degree increments, which can be tough to nail down precisely by dragging in the Viewer.

5. As you are dragging, hold down the *Shift* key, which will lock the rotation to 45-degree increments, making it much easier to rotate in common amounts. Drag until the image has been rotated 135 degrees (again, the value will be displayed in the upper-left corner), as shown in the following screenshot:

6. Lastly, click anywhere on the body of the clip and drag towards the upper-left corner of the frame. Your video will be repositioned. In the following screenshot, we can see that we have dragged the image to the left by 585 pixels (thus the negative number) and up by 185 pixels from the center, as shown in the following screenshot:

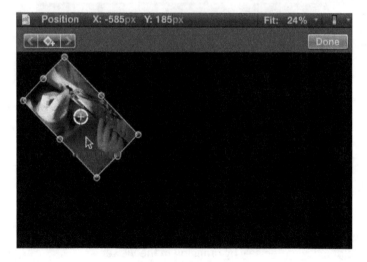

Now that we've made some changes in the Viewer, let's take a look at entering specific values in the Inspector.

7. Open your Inspector (*Command + 4*) or click on the **Inspector** button on the far right of your toolbar). Make sure the **Video** tab is highlighted at the top:

We see a long list of parameters available to us here, but we want to focus just on the **Transform** category. Notice that the **Position**, **Rotation**, and **Scale** values have all been altered from their default values (**Position** is normally (0, 0), **Rotation** is normally 0 degrees, and **Scale** is normally 100%). Your current values will likely differ a bit from the preceding screenshot.

8. Click on both the **X** and **Y** position values and type in o for both, followed by *Return*. The clip returns to the center of the frame.

9. Click on the **Rotation** percentage and type in o, followed by *Return*. The clip's rotation returns to normal.

10. Lastly, drag the **Scale** slider to **100%** or click on the **Scale** value itself and type in 100, followed by *Return*. The clip returns to its original size, filling the frame.

There's more...

What the heck is Anchor?

If you start fiddling with the **Anchor** parameter, you might be confused at first as it seems to have an effect similar to the **Position** parameter. When you adjust the **X** and **Y** values, the clip seems to be repositioned on those axes. However, take note of one important difference—when you adjust the **Anchor** parameter, the puck in the center of the clip and rotation handle extending from it move off center from the clip. This has a significant impact on both rotation and scale.The **Anchor** parameter is the center point for the **Rotation** and **Scale** parameters.

If you have a normal high-definition clip that is 1920 x 1080, put in the values **X: 960**, **Y: -540**. You will see the anchor point move to the lower-right corner of the clip. If you try and rotate or scale the clip, it will no longer rotate or scale around the center of the clip, but rather the newly positioned anchor!

The anchor point cannot be changed via onscreen controls.

Reset all Transform parameters

If you've heavily tweaked all four parameters within the Transform tool and you simply want to quickly reset them all to their default settings, simply click on the curved arrow that appears in the upper-right corner of the **Transform** panel within a clip's Inspector window, as shown in the following screenshot:

See also

To learn how to animate the Transform parameters, read the *Making your image move by keyframing in the Viewer* recipe.

Cropping or trimming a clip

Cursed boom poles! They always have a tendency to drop into the top of a shot! Or perhaps your amateur cameraman simply didn't frame an interview subject particularly well, leaving way too much headroom. The Crop tool in FCPX is split into three subtools—Trim, Crop, and Ken Burns.

Trim lets us slice off lines of our video from any of the four sides in any manner and amount we want. This can be useful when you're being creative and want to show many clips of different shapes and sizes on the screen at once. Crop lets us select a proportional section of a clip so that it still fits the full frame. We'll cover Ken Burns in the next recipe.

Getting ready

You can use any clip you like for this exercise. In our example, we'll use an interview clip that was poorly framed with too much headroom and containing a bright window in the background we want to try and crop out.

How to do it...

1. Highlight your clip and click on the **Crop** button below the Viewer. A dotted line appears around your clip with blue handles on the sides and corners. Also note the three options that appear in the upper-left corner—**Trim**, **Crop**, and **Ken Burns**. Trim is highlighted by default, as shown in the following screenshot:

2. Click-and-drag inward on the blue handles to shave, or trim off part of your video:

This would be useful if we wanted to show multiple clips on screen at once and only wanted to see certain regions of each clip.

We can also apply the Transform tool to our newly trimmed clip.

3. Click on the **Transform** tool underneath the Viewer, or press *Shift + T*.

4. Scale down the clip using the scale handles on the clip's corners. Of course, you can also reposition the clip by clicking and dragging on the body of the clip, or rotate it using the rotation handle at the center, as follows:

It's now time to reset the trim and transforms we've applied to the clip.

5. Open your Inspector (*Command + 4*) and scroll down to find the **Crop** controls. Click on the curved arrow to reset the parameters:

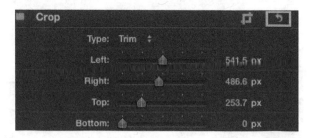

Our untrimmed clip returns, but it still has the transformed properties:

6. Scroll up to find the **Transform** controls and click on the curved reset arrow there as well, to return the clip to normal.

7. Click on the **Crop** button below the Viewer window if it isn't already active (highlighted blue).

8. At the top of the Viewer, click on **Crop**. We will now see a solid border around our clip with blue handles in each corner, as shown in the following screenshot:

9. Click-and-drag inward on any corner. Unlike the Trim effect, Crop removes part of the image proportionally so that our frame doesn't lose its original shape (16:9 in our case).

In our example, we're dragging from the upper-left corner for two reasons—to cut out as much of the blown out window as possible and also to reduce the headroom above our subject:

The only issue here is that, in our illuminated area, the subject is off center now.

10. Click on the body of the image within the illuminated portion of the clip and drag around. We can select a different (yet still proportional) area of our frame. In our case, we dragged the box slightly leftwards to recenter our subject, as follows:

11. Click on **Done**. The cropped image now fills the entire frame automatically, unlike the Trim effect, which left behind an empty space:

If steps 3 and 4 confused you because you haven't learned how to use the Transform tool yet, read the previous recipe, *Using the Transform tool*.

To learn about the Ken Burns effect, the third effect within the Crop tool, read the next recipe!

Panning and zooming over a photo or clip with the Ken Burns effect

Static photo montages aren't exactly the most dramatic, engaging way to present your images. Famous film documentarian Ken Burns popularized the technique of panning and zooming across still images in order to give a little more life and flair to his films, and thus was born the Ken Burns effect. In FCP7, this process was manual and a bit tedious (especially if you had tons of photos), involving keyframes, but now FCPX has a built-in tool to make it happen in seconds.

Getting ready

Drag any photo into your timeline. In reality, this technique can also be applied to video clips, but we'll work with a photo in this exercise as it's more commonly used on still images.

How to do it...

1. Click and highlight your image in the timeline and click on the **Crop** button under the Viewer, as follows:

2. Click on the **Ken Burns** option in the upper-left corner of the Viewer. Two boxes will appear over your image—a green box labeled **Start** and a red box labeled **End**. We are going to reposition and resize these boxes to tell FCPX which portions of the image we want framed at the beginning and end of the clip, and FCPX will animate the difference.

The default animation is just a straight zoom in on the image. In our mountain peak image (shot in the Mount Cook National Park in New Zealand), we want to start low and wide, and zoom in to the upper-right portion of the image.

3. Click on a corner of the green **Start** box to resize it. Remember, we're deciding which portion of the frame we want to be focused on when the photo actually begins.

4. Click and hold down on the body of the green **Start** box and drag it to reposition it wherever you want on the photo. We've kept our **Start** box pretty wide and moved it to the lower-left corner of the photo, as shown in the following screenshot:

Don't be confused by any black edges you may see in the frame. You won't see any black space in the final outcome, as long as you don't include any of it within the **Start** and **End** boxes. While you can include black space within a **Start** or **End** box, your end result will usually look better if you don't.

5. Click on the red **End** box to highlight it. Even if it is underneath the space taken up by the **Start** box, FCPX will highlight it regardless, as follows:

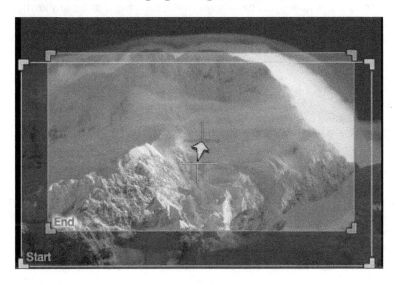

6. Resize and reposition the **End** box as necessary. In our image, we've shrunk it and moved it towards the upper-right corner, as shown in the following screenshot:

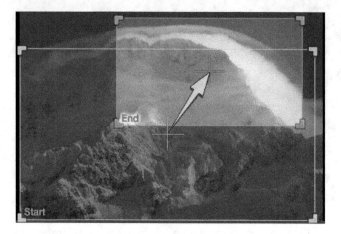

7. Click on **Done** and hit the / key to play back the clip. The photo now pans and zooms as you have defined it.

How it works...

For all intents and purposes, we just did a keyframing exercise without any keyframes. Despite the lack of keyframes, the process worked the same. We defined how we wanted our image to look at two different points in time and FCPX animated the difference. We'll work with manual keyframing later in this chapter!

There's more...

Speeding up or slowing down the Ken Burns effect

Depending on how much you have panned and zoomed, you may find the animation moving too quickly or slowly. The speed of the Ken Burns effect is a direct result to the length of the clip itself. To slow down the effect, make the clip longer. To speed it up, make it shorter. This is incredibly easy to accomplish with photos, as they can be infinitely long. Simply trim them in the timeline by clicking and dragging towards left or right on their in or out point. If you want them to have a very specific length, highlight the clip and hit *Command + D*. The dashboard in the toolbar lights up, letting you type in a very specific timecode length. If you wanted the clip to be 6 seconds long, type in 600, followed by *Return* or *6.* (6 period), followed by *Return*.

Don't zoom too much!

Don't get too carried away with the Ken Burns effect. If you choose to zoom too much into a photo, your photo can become blurry or pixelated. This is less likely to happen with a high-quality photograph, but can happen quickly if you use the effect on video. Here's a little piece of trivia. A 1920 x 1080 video is equivalent to only a 2-megapixel image! That's a lot smaller than your point-and-shoot or DSLR, which likely shoots over 10 megapixels!

Ken Burns and video

As mentioned previously, you can use the Ken Burns effect on video. There are a couple of practical applications for this. Think about a still interview shot. Perhaps you wish the cameraperson had done a very slow, subtle zoom-in on the subject as he/she spoke. You can easily accomplish this with the Ken Burns effect by making sure the **Start** box takes up the whole frame and the **End** box is just slightly smaller and tighter around the speaker. Voila! Instant fake camera zoom.

Creating a video wall

Sometimes one image on the screen just isn't enough. Whether it's for a music video, multiple angle view, or a video where you just need to cram in more visual information in a short amount of time, it's easy to stack clips in FCPX and play them all back simultaneously on the screen wherever you want, at any size. In this exercise, we'll create a video wall with four, evenly spaced clips, as follows:

Getting ready

If you haven't read the *Using the Transform tool* recipe, now would be a good time to do so. Also, this exercise assumes you are using HD video that is 1920 x 1080. If not, some of the **Position** numbers we'll be manipulating will not work exactly. Read the *There's More...* section at the end of this recipe to figure out the math and numbers you'll need if you aren't using full HD video.

How to do it...

1. Find and edit four clips into your timeline on top of one another. That means you will likely append (*E*) or insert (*W*) the first clip to the primary storyline and then connect (*Q*) the other three right on top of it. Make sure none of the clips are shorter than the duration you want your video wall to appear. For example, we want a 7-second video wall, so none of the clips we are using are less than 7 seconds in length:

   Obviously, we only see the topmost clip, as all of the clips are in the same position and at 100% scale. We'll tackle this shortly.

2. Trim the clips so that they are of the same length, as follows:

3. Highlight the topmost clip and open the Inspector (*Command + 4*). We're going to focus on the **Transform** properties, as shown in the following screenshot:

4. Change the **Scale** parameter to **50%**, and set the **Position** parameter for **X** to **-480**, and for **Y** to **270**.

 If next to the **Position** coordinates you are seeing a percentage sign (%) and not the letters **px**, then go to **Final Cut Pro | Preferences**, click on the **Editing** tab, and change **Inspector Units** to **Pixels**).

Your video is now wedged in the upper-left corner of the screen. To understand how we have arrived at these numbers, read the *How it works...* section of this recipe. Also note that we can now see the clip underneath, which is the second clip from the top in the timeline.

5. Click on the second clip from the top in the timeline, as follows:

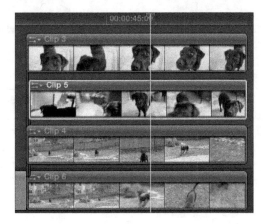

6. In the Inspector, again set **Scale** to **50%** and this time, set **Position** to (**480,270**). Now the clip will be scaled down and wedged into the upper-right corner, as follows:

7. Repeat the process for the last two clips. Both should have **Scale** set to **50%** and one in the lower-left corner should have **Position** set to (**-480,-270**) while **Position** for the one in the lower-right corner should be set to (**480,-270**).

How it works...

How did we come up with the **Position** numbers (-480,-270) to perfectly fit a clip at 50% scale in the lower-left quadrant? The clip has a resolution of 1920 x 1080. That's 1,920 pixels across and 1,080 pixels down. The original position (0,0) is dead center on the clip so it is 960 pixels inward on the x axis (half of 1920) and 540 pixels in on the y axis (half of 1080). We wanted to move our image to the left and down by half of those pixel values.

When you think of a quadrant, think of quarters. Half of 960 (one-fourth of 1920) is 480 and half of 540 (one-fourth of 1080) is 270. They are both negative values because anything moving towards left of center is negative while moving to the right is positive, and anything moving down is negative while up is positive. Basically, if you know your video's horizontal and vertical resolutions, just divide each by four and you're done!

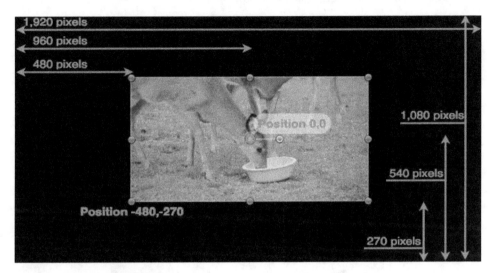

There's more...

Why 50% scale and not 25%?

Entering a value of 50% might seem odd at first. If we want an image to fit into a quadrant of the screen, one might think we'd want a scale of 25%, but 50% scale means half the original width and half the height, resulting in an image that takes up 25% of the screen!

Quadrant math for standard definition video

The math used previously was calculated for HD video. But what if you're working with **standard definition (SD)** video in an SD timeline? The formula is the same; you just need to know your frame size. If your video is 640 x 480, and you want to move the video into the upper-right quadrant, you would scale the video down to 50% (this parameter doesn't change no matter what size your video is of) and use the coordinates 160,120 (640 / 4=160 and 480 / 4=120).

Extra pizzazz

What else would make this video wall a little more interesting? Should two clips be in black and white or have some other sort of effect applied? Maybe they shouldn't appear all at once, but rather fade it one at a time. Try staggering each connected clip by 1 second and adding transitions to the beginning of each clip, as follows:

Or don't make a perfect video wall. Place the clips in all different sizes helter skelter all around your video frame:

Making your image move by keyframing in the Viewer

As mentioned before, the Transform tool unlocks a lot of creative potential in FCPX. Being able to resize and reposition clips within your frame gives you a lot of flexibility to show multiple images at once in limitless creative ways. Let's turn the volume up to 11 using keyframes!

A keyframe allows us to lock in a parameter and its value at a specific moment in time on a clip. When we add a second keyframe later in the clip with a different parameter value, FCPX animates the difference between the two keyframes!

For example, we might drop a keyframe on the **Scale** value at **100%** on the first frame of a clip. Then, on the last frame of the clip, we will set the **Scale** value to **0%**. FCPX is pretty darn smart and automatically adds the second keyframe (as we have added the previous one already). The result is our clip scales down from 100% to 0% during its lifespan.

Getting ready

If you haven't read the *Using the Transform tool* recipe, now would be a good time to do so. We're going to use what we have learned from that recipe and animate our video! We will modify a clip to start off playing normally at full size, then make it shrink down to the lower-left corner over a period of 2 seconds, then finish playing in the corner.

To get a good grasp on this exercise, place a clip of approximately 6 seconds in length into your timeline.

How to do it...

1. Click on your clip approximately one-third (about two seconds) of the way through it. This will simultaneously highlight the clip as well as place the playhead at that location, as follows:

2. Open the Inspector (*Command + 4*) and take a look at the **Transform** controls. At this moment in time, we want the image to start shrinking down in size and moving towards the lower-left corner. This involves two parameters, **Scale** and **Position**.

3. Move your cursor over the **Position** parameter and a gray diamond will appear with a plus sign. This is the **Add a keyframe** button. Click on it, and it will turn orange.

We have now placed a keyframe at this moment in time telling FCPX that we want to make sure that **Position** is **0,0**. This may seem obvious as the clip always plays at 0,0 by default, but by inserting this keyframe, we're also giving FCPX a heads up that we are going to be changing this parameter later in the clip.

4. Add a keyframe for the **Scale** parameter as well, as shown in the following screenshot:

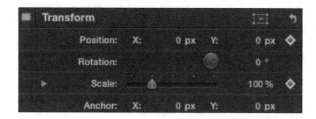

5. Click-and-drag your playhead forward in time a couple of seconds until it rests about two-thirds of the way through the clip, as follows:

6. Back in the Inspector, drag the **Scale** value to **50%** (or click on the percentage value, type in `100` and hit *Return*). Notice the keyframe icon next to the **Scale** parameter turns orange right away. FCPX is smart and knew that, as we have placed a keyframe for this parameter earlier; we must have another one here!

Lastly, we need to change the position, or center point, of this clip.

7. Click on the **Position** parameter **X** and type in `-480`. Click on the **Position** parameter **Y** and type in `-270`. (If how we have reached these numbers is confusing, read the previous recipe). Just like when we changed the **Scale** parameter, a new keyframe will immediately be added to the **Position** parameter at this moment in time, as follows:

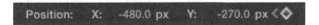

In the Viewer, we can see a red dotted line showing us the motion path we have created that takes the clip from the center of the screen to the lower-left quadrant, as follows:

8. Play back your clip and the image will play for about 2 seconds, shrink and move to the lower-left corner over a course of 2 more seconds, then finish playing.

Moving clips in sync with compound clips

Let's say you've created a video wall much like we did in the *Creating a video wall* recipe. Now, we want to add some animation to it, to give it a bit more oomph. What if you were asked to create an animation where this four-clip grid started off infinitesimally small, then grew in size (and in sync) from the left corner to eventually fill the frame? Oh, and we want to make it spin once for good measure! Your eyes might start rolling into the back of your head trying to figure out how you're going to keyframe all four clips in synchronous motion. We wouldn't blame you! But once again, we'll use the fine art of compound clips to make this task just as easy as keyframing one single clip.

Getting ready

This trick involving compound clips can be used in a variety of circumstances, but to illustrate it in this exercise, we've simply stacked four clips on top of one another and created a grid by resizing and repositioning the clips. We did this task in the *Creating a video wall* recipe, so hop back and read up if you haven't already done so.

How to do it...

1. Highlight all four clips in your timeline that comprise the video wall, right-click on them, and choose **New Compound Clip...** (or press *Option + G*), as follows:

The four clips are consolidated into one clip. Because of this, the four clips will now be extremely easy to keyframe in a synchronous motion. As we want the animation to end, looking just as it does now, we're going to do our keyframing backwards in time.

2. Position your playhead roughly at 2 seconds into your clip. Make sure the clip is still highlighted, as shown in the following screenshot:

3. Open your Inspector (*Command + 4*) and focus on the **Transform** controls. As described previously, we want our animation to consist of movement, spinning, and scaling.

4. Click on the **Add a keyframe** buttons next to **Position, Rotation**, and **Scale**, as shown in the following screenshot:

We've now told FCPX that at this moment in time, we want to lock in these original values for these parameters. If it doesn't make sense yet, it will in a moment!

5. Reposition your playhead to the first frame of the clip. A neat way to do this without touching your mouse or trackpad is by hitting *Command + 2* on your keyboard, which is the **Go To Timeline** command. It makes your timeline the active pane within FCPX. Secondly, hit the up arrow to move your playhead to the first frame of the compound clip:

Now it's time to tell FCPX what we want the clip to look like at the very beginning.

6. In the Inspector, change the **Position** values to **-960,-540**. Your video will seem to shift to the lower-left corner and we'll only see a quarter of the original frame (which happens to be the whole image that was in the upper-right quadrant of the video wall):

7. Change **Rotation** to **-720** degrees. The video doesn't seem to change at all. This is because 720 degrees is two perfect spins

8. Lastly, change **Scale** to **0%**. The video will seemingly disappear, but is actually just infinitely tiny. You should still know something is there, as the red line indicating the motion path we made in step 6 should still be visible, as follows:

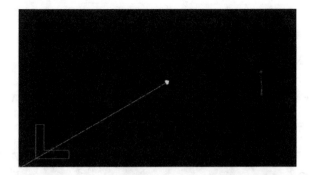

Your final **Transform** parameters should appear identical to the following screenshot:

Because we have already entered in keyframes at another point in time on the clip, FCPX knew to fill in keyframes at this point in time, as soon as we changed the values of the parameters.

9. Play your clip. The compound clip should now grow from the lower-left corner to the center while spinning twice:

There's more...

Moving an entire motion path

After you've created a motion path for your media to travel along, perhaps with many points, you may decide you wish you could reposition the entire path—not one keyframe at a time, but the whole shebang. This can be accomplished right in the Viewer with nothing more than a click-and-drag of the mouse paired with modifier keys:

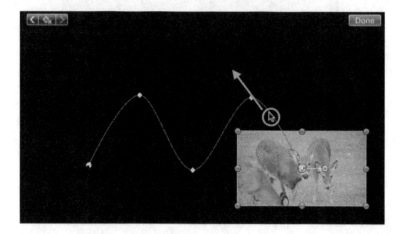

Simply hold down the *Option* and *Command* keys, and then click-and-drag directly on the path itself (indicated by the red lines). If you don't see red lines, make sure your clip is highlighted and the Transform tool is turned on.

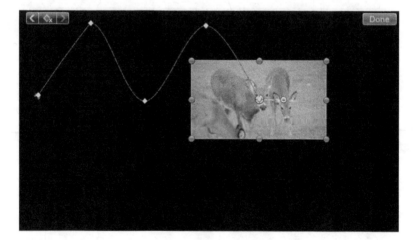

Changing keyframe timing in the timeline

You've completed your keyframing masterpiece, but perhaps the timing isn't quite right. Does the image spin a little too fast? Too slow? Maybe you don't want all the parameters to start and end exactly on the same frames. Or you want a particular animation to end on a beat in your soundtrack. You don't have to start your keyframing all over again. Keyframe retiming can be accomplished right in the timeline itself.

Getting ready

We're going to carry on with the animation we made in the last recipe, _Moving clips in sync with compound clips_.

How to do it...

1. Highlight the animated clip and choose **Clip | Show Video Animation** or hit _Command + V_. A large blue box appears above the clip. You may need to adjust your timeline height in order to see the entire thing. This window lets you see the location of keyframes for many properties of the clip including effects (if any have been applied), certain color corrections, transformations, crops, distorts, and opacity. You should see keyframes along the blue row labeled **Transform: All**. These represent the start and end points of the animation we created in the last exercise:

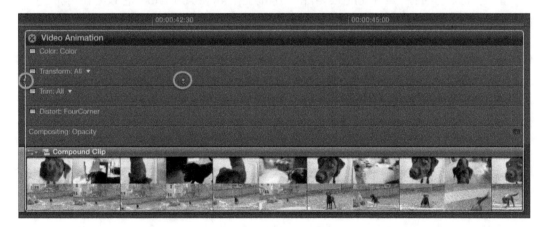

   Notice that there appear to be two keyframes stacked on top of one another. This indicates that there is more than one keyframe for multiple parameters at that point in time. This is why it says **All** next to **Transform**. Let's narrow down a bit.

2. Click on the triangle next to **Transform: All** and click on **Position**, as shown in the following screenshot:

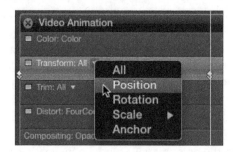

3. You will now see only one keyframe at each point in time, because we are only looking at the **Position** keyframes and no other Transform-related keyframes, as follows:

4. Click-and-drag the second keyframe to the left. As you do, a tool tip box will pop up showing you how far back in time you are moving the keyframe. By shortening the gap between the two keyframes, you are in turn speeding up the Position animation. Let go after you have dragged the keyframe about halfway between its original location and the first keyframe. You will also see a shadow in the keyframe's original location. This simply indicates that there are still some other keyframes at that location (in our case, **Rotation** and **Scale**).

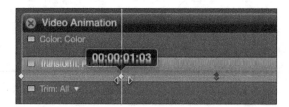

5. Play your animation back. Now the clip arrives at its final position in about half the time it did before while it continues to finish rotating and scaling at its original pace.

6. Click on the triangle next to **Transform: Position** and click on **Scale**. *Do not* select the **X** or **Y** subset, otherwise you run the risk of distorting your image! Just click on the word **Scale**, as shown in the following screenshot:

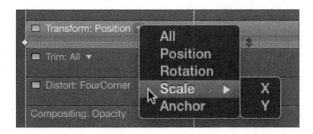

You will see stacked keyframes again, because technically the overall **Scale** parameter is made up of an x axis scale and y axis scale:

7. Drag the latter **Scale** keyframe stack to the right by about 1 second, as follows:

8. Play back your animation. If you have completed the steps correctly, you will now have a retimed animation that moves from the lower-left corner to the center in approximately 1 second, rotates twice over a period of 2 seconds, and scales from nothing to full size in 3 seconds.

Customizing motion paths with Bezier handles and modifying interpolation

We've kept our keyframing pretty simple up until this point. We've only used two keyframes per parameter, but the only limit to the number of parameter keyframes you can place on a clip is the number of frames in the clip! In this recipe, we'll create a motion path with three keyframes (still fairly simple), but we'll take it a step further by learning how to customize that path between the keyframes to create either a rounder shape to the path or straight, rigid lines.

Getting ready

This recipe assumes you are quite familiar with the Transform tool and basic keyframing, so make sure you've read the *Using the Transform tool* and *Making your image move by keyframing in the Viewer* recipes.

How to do it...

1. Highlight any clip in your timeline and turn on the Transform tool by clicking on the button underneath the Viewer, as shown in the following screenshot:

2. Using the onscreen controls, shrink the **Scale** parameter down to about **30%** and reposition it to be near the lower-left corner. No keyframes yet!

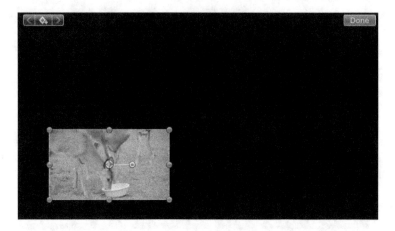

3. Move your playhead near the beginning of the clip, maybe a second or two after the beginning, as follows:

4. Now add a keyframe using the **Add a keyframe** button in the upper-left corner of the Viewer, as follows:

This button adds four (technically five) keyframes at this point in time, one for each of the **Transform** parameters (**Position, Rotation, Scale X and Y,** and **Anchor**). We are telling FCPX to lock in these values at this moment in time. Even if we're not animating every one of these parameters, it's usually ok to hit this button to save time. To verify, double-check the **Transform** properties in the Inspector. Your numbers will not likely match exactly, but they should be close:

5. Move your playhead about halfway through your clip.

6. In the Viewer, drag the clip up towards the top of the screen and near the center, as follows:

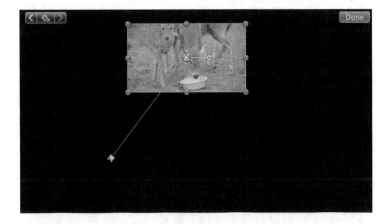

A motion path appears between the original and current locations.

7. Again, move the playhead forward, to be near the end of the clip.

8. In the Viewer, drag the clip again, this time towards the lower-right corner of the screen, as shown in the following screenshot:

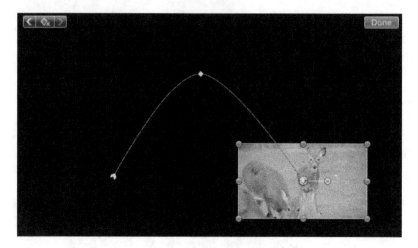

Our clip now moves in a near triangular shape with a slight curve to it.

9. Click directly on the second keyframe (that is, the peak of the triangular shape). A couple of things should happen. One, the clip jumps back to that position in time (your playhead should also move to the middle of the clip when you place this keyframe). Also, you should see two lines extending from the keyframe location with orange circles at both ends. These are your curve handles, formerly known as **Bezier handles**. (Although they overlap a bit, don't confuse the orange curve handles with the blue rotation handle near the center of the image):

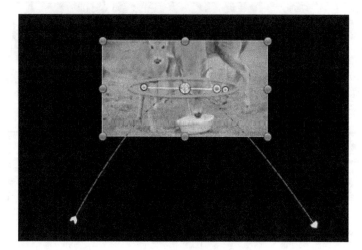

10. Click-and-drag on the orange curve handle on the left. Drag it all around in different directions to see what happens. As you drag, you are adjusting the curvature of the motion path. Dragging towards the left and right strictly affects curvature on the left of the keyframe, while dragging up and down influences the motion path on both sides of the keyframe. Drag outward (to the left-hasnd side) a bit till you have a larger curved path:

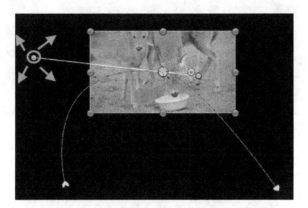

11. Click-and-drag the right curve handle. Try and create a similar curve to the one you have created on the left. Depending on where you drag the right handle to, it may impact the left handle, so it could take a little finessing on both sides before you get the shape that you want:

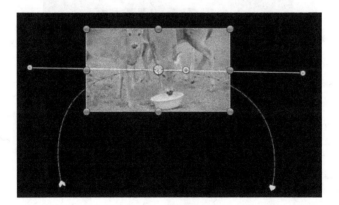

12. Play back your clip. Now the clip takes a larger, rounder trip from keyframe to keyframe.

But maybe, we decide we don't like the large curved path. In fact, we don't want any curve at all. We just want absolutely straight lines between each of our keyframes. Undoing these last two adjustments isn't the answer, however, as even the original paths had slight curves to them. We have to change the keyframe interpolation in order to get our straight lines.

13. Right-click directly on the second (middle) keyframe. A pop-up window shows you that the interpolation is set to **Smooth**:

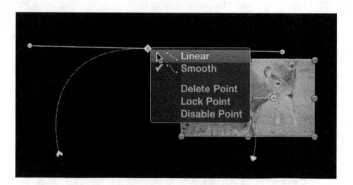

14. Click on **Linear**. Suddenly, your curved motion path turns into two perfectly straight lines! Also note that the curve handles disappear. The whole point of the **Linear** option is to create straight paths so that there is no curved line to manipulate, as follows:

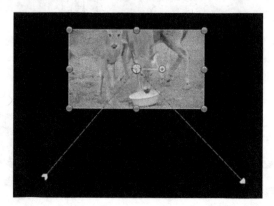

15. Play around with the interpolation of other keyframes and see what unique and creative paths you can create.

How it works...

When you change the interpolation (**Smooth** versus **Linear**) on a keyframe, it affects the motion path on both sides of the keyframe. Remember that only **Smooth** gives you curve handles to play with the curvature of the path.

9
Altering the Aesthetics of Your Image

In this chapter, we will cover:

- ▶ Stabilizing a shaky shot
- ▶ Automatically balancing color and/or matching color to another shot
- ▶ Manually color balancing with the Color Board
- ▶ Picking a color look or creating your own
- ▶ Fixing the exposure and adjusting the contrast with help from the Luma waveform monitor
- ▶ Adding secondary color corrections, part 1 – shape masks
- ▶ Adding secondary color corrections, part 2 – color masks
- ▶ Adding secondary color corrections, part 3 – combining color and shape masks
- ▶ Keeping only one color in your image
- ▶ Spotlighting an object or text

Introduction

We've spent the previous few chapters learning how to speed up your workflow, trim and re-edit clips, adding new visuals with text and generators, but we have barely touched the quality of your material itself. Does your image look any good? Does it look too good? Does the color and tone match the vibe and mood of your film?

There's a reason this chapter starts with the word altering and not improving. The goal isn't always about making an image better. Sometimes it's about making an image match either a vibe or another clip.

The next few recipes will take us through the basics of fixing basic image problems as well as learning how to use some of FCPX's color controls to not only improve upon an image, but to tweak it to make it unique and make it your own.

Stabilizing a shaky shot

Face it: We don't always have a tripod on hand when shooting, so inevitably, we're going to be shooting handheld at some point or another. Some of us are lucky enough to have rock solid muscle control and can keep a shot incredibly still, but for the rest of us, our arms start to shake and wobble after only a few minutes of holding a camera at eye level. How many of us have supported our camera-holding arm with the other when things get shaky? Yup, that's what we thought!

Getting ready

Look around your footage for a slightly shaky, handheld shot. We're sure it won't take long!

How to do it...

1. Add a clip to your timeline that requires stabilization. We can only fix stabilization on clips that have been added to a project, not unused clips just sitting in an event:

2. Highlight the clip in the timeline and open your Inspector (by pressing *Command + 4*)
3. Scroll down till you find the box for **Stabilization**.
4. Click the box next to **Stabilization** to turn it blue:

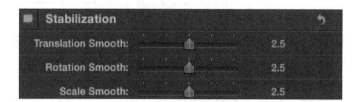

Notice in the Viewer that a label pops up over your video saying **Analyzing for dominant motion...**.

Analyzing for dominant motion...

What's happening is FCPX is beginning a background task that, depending on the length and bit rate (quality) of your clip, can take a while. Obviously, this varies depending on your processing power and length of the clip. FCPX is analyzing every frame of video closely to figure out the best way to stabilize the video. You can observe the progress of the task by clicking on the background tasks button in the dashboard (marked by the percentage circle slowing counting up) or by hitting *Command + 9*.

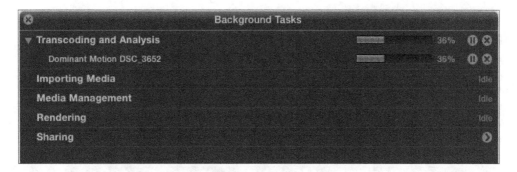

When the task is done, you'll notice that the video appears to have zoomed in a bit. This is often a required part of the stabilization process. In order to balance the footage, it usually must zoom in a bit to smooth any jerks or jostles of the camera; otherwise we'd see black edges around our frame edge.

5. In the Inspector, fiddle with the three stabilization parameters, **Translation Smooth**, **Rotation Smooth**, and **Scale Smooth**. If you feel your stabilized footage has zoomed in too far (which will happen with shakier shots), try dragging the **Translation Smooth** to the left a bit, but don't drag them all the way to the left or you're basically undoing your stabilization!

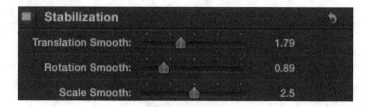

6. When you're happy with the look of your video, the clip will still have to be rendered to play back at full quality. Hit *Ctrl + R* to force the clip to render without having to wait for the background render process to begin.

How it works...

Similar to when we apply Optical Flow to slow motion clips, FCPX is running a complex algorithm on the clip, analyzing each and every frame, trying to identify camera shake, and balance for it by reframing the shot and zooming it in and out to compensate.

There's more...

Stabilization and fast action shots

Just like Optical Flow, there are certain scenarios where stabilization just won't cut it. If your camera jerks around a lot, whether it's because you were trying to keep up with a cheetah running across the savannah, or simply because you had too many Red Bulls the morning of the shoot and you couldn't keep your arm holding the camera still, stabilization can make these videos looks worse rather than better. Of course, if you try it out and don't like the end result, just click on the blue box next to **Stabilization** in the Inspector again to turn off the effect.

Automatically balancing color and/or match color to another shot

If you've never paid attention to that **white balance** (**WB**) setting in your camera, you've likely encountered outdoor footage that came out really blue or indoor footage that came out really yellow. These are two of the most common white balancing issues. In most editing programs, we usually define a white portion of the image, and then the program would color correct the image to the best of its ability from there.

In FCPX, Apple has decided to go for a more all-encompassing automatic approach called **color balancing**. When you activate color balance, FCPX magically tries to fix the color of an image with no input from the user. When you're in a time crunch, it's amazing to be able to just highlight 50 clips in a row, and boom, have FCPX improve the color balance of all the clips at once.

Of course, if you're a colorist, or an artiste, automatic color corrections are rarely going to make you happy. We'll be covering manual color correction a bit later in this chapter.

Another brand new feature FCPX has introduced is the **Match Color** feature. Perhaps you shot an event with two different cameras, which will inevitably leave you with two slightly different looking images, as it's virtually impossible to get the colors to match perfectly in the cameras beforehand. Match Color allows you to essentially sync up a clip's color to another clip of your choosing to help even out any jarring differences you might notice when cutting between the two cameras.

How to do it...

1. Find a clip in a project that seems to have a tint to it and highlight it. The most common occurrences of this are when your white balance settings in your camera were wrong, which often leads to bluish outdoor shots and yellowish indoor shots. In our example, we have a heavy yellow tint from an indoor shot:

2. In the toolbar, click on the magic wand button and choose **Balance Color** (by pressing *Command + Option + B*).

The clip is almost instantly balanced. In reality, sometimes the Balance Color tool goes a little overkill on clips that were heavily tinted. In our example, it certainly took away the yellow cast, but almost too much so, leaving a greenish-blue cast to the image. The sheets are light green, but now so is her face!

At the end of the day, it's your choice whether to keep this automatic correction or hit *Command + Z* to undo.

3. Find another clip in your timeline, preferably one whose color seems a bit off from how you remembered it when you captured it. Try and find another clip whose color is spot on that you can try and match the first clip with.

    The following first shot is an underexposed shot from a wedding reception lit by neon colors. This camera captured the color of the lights with a blue-green tint.

    This second shot was taken from another camera at the same reception. It captured the lights as a more solid green. We're matching the first shot to look more like this second shot:

4. Click on the image with the poorer color. In the toolbar, click on the magic wand icon and choose **Match Color** (*Command + Option + M*):

The **Match Color** interface pops up:

As the instructions tell us, we need to skim to a frame that we want to match.

5. In your timeline move your cursor over the appropriately colored clip to the exact frame you think has the ideal color balance and click on it:

The color match window displays a preview of what your first clip will look like. You can continue to click on different frames to get different results.

6. When you are happy with the end result, click on **Apply Match**. The initial clip's color is altered to closely resemble the second.

There's more...

Color Balance in the Event Browser

The Color Balance tool is one of the only visual alterations you can apply to a clip before it's even added to a project. To do so, just click on a clip in the event of your choice and choose the **Color Balance** option under the magic wand tool in the toolbar. The clip will be balanced and that balance will appear in every use of the clip from that point forward.

Change or turn off a color match

If hours have passed and suddenly you decide you are unhappy with the match you made on a clip, you have two options

If you simply want to match the color of a clip to a different clip, just repeat the Match Color process again: highlight the clip you want to improve, choose **Match Color**, and select a new frame on a different clip.

If you want to remove the match entirely and take the clip back to its original color, highlight the clip, open the Inspector and deselect the box next to **Match Color**.

Manually color balancing with the Color Board

Quick fixes like the Color Balance and Match Color tools are definitely handy tools fixes, but a computer is (usually) no match for a human eyeball. The phrase is 'beauty is in the eye of the beholder', not 'beauty is in the coding of the algorithm' (maybe someday, but not today).

For years, FCP editors have used the Three-Way Color Corrector to be able to enhance their images and colors by being able to control the color of the highlights, midtones, and shadows in an image. In FCPX, Apple has done away with the Three-Way Color Corrector, replacing it with the all-new **Color Board**, but the theory and methodology remains much the same.

Getting ready

Realistically, you can work with any clip you have for this exercise, but if you have one that has a slight tint that you want to try and remove, aim to use that one. We'll use one of the same clips as in the previous exercise, which has a very noticeable yellow tint:

How to do it...

1. Click and highlight the clip in your timeline and open the Inspector. Near the top of the Inspector are all the **Color** options. The boxes next to **Balance** and **Match Color** should be black, indicating that no automatic corrections have been applied to this clip. Below these is **Correction 1** as shown in the screenshot:

2. Click on the circle with the arrow pointing towards the right at the far right of the **Correction 1** parameter. You are brought to the Color Board:

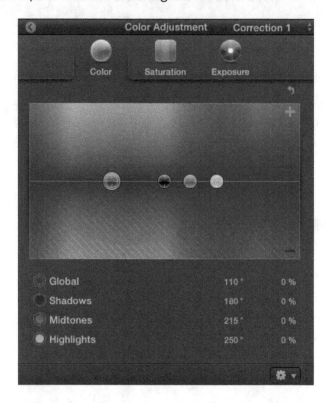

The Color Board contains four pucks. Going from left to right they are **Global**, **Shadows**, **Midtones**, and **Highlights**. The **Global** option is exactly what it sounds like, controlling the overall tint of the whole image. But often we want to be more precise than that, adjusting just the darker parts of our image (**Shadows**), the brighter parts of our image (**Highlights**), or right in between (**Midtones**).

The pucks can be dragged all around the color board, and although the top half and bottom half look like mirror images of each other, they don't act that way! Take note of the plus and minus signs in the top and bottom corners on the right, respectively. Dragging a puck into the upper half of the board adds a particular color to an image whereas dragging a puck towards the bottom half will subtract that color.

Rarely do you want to grab the **Global** slider and tint the whole image. That's like using a sledgehammer to put a nail through drywall. Skin tone often falls in the midtone range so let's try dragging the midtone puck to see what happens.

3. Click-and-drag the midtone puck into the lower half of the board, towards the same color that your image is tinted:

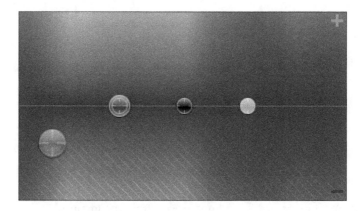

In our example, our image is tinted slightly yellow, so we'll drag the puck towards yellow:

The result is an image with less of a yellow tint because we are subtracting yellow from the midtones of the image. Be careful not to drag too far north or south as this may overcorrect the problem and leave you with another tint entirely!

Note that we could have dragged the puck towards the positive blue area of the board for a near identical result, but often it's easier to think of what color you want to remove or drain from an image rather than trying to figure out the opposite color you want/need to add. Read the *There's More...* section for more information.

The image still needs a bit of work. The brighter parts of our subject's face are still a bit reddish-orange.

4. If you need to, drag the **Highlights** puck towards the same vicinity as the **Midtones** puck:

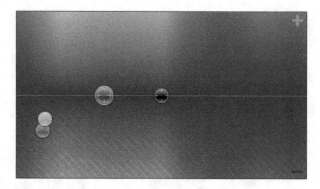

In our case it helped drain a bit more yellow from the image:

Our image certainly isn't perfect, but we had a pretty extreme tint beforehand, and it's a definite improvement over what we started with. If you're unhappy with your adjustment and want to start over, click on the reset arrow in the upper corner at the right of the Color Board. Just remember, if you shoot your video properly, you'll spend less time doing tedious stuff such as color correction and more time doing the fun stuff!

There's more...

I don't see the list of parameters in the Color Board

If you do not see the labels **Global**, **Shadows**, **Midtones**, and **Highlights** below the Color Board when you first brought it up, simply click-and-drag downward on an empty space in your toolbar. This will extend the height of the Color Board and reveal the labels.

What do those degrees and percentages mean?

We did our color correction by dragging around the pucks on the Color Board, but you may have noticed value parameters below the board changing as we did so. These are numeric values for the colors we chose.

The degrees values reflect the location of the color if we were using a color wheel. This is a bit goofy, as FCPX no longer contains an active color wheel, but if you want to see what one looks like, look no further than the Color Board's icon right above the board itself:

The percentages (ranging from **-100** % to **100** %) reflect how intense of a drain or tint we are applying respectively.

To truly appreciate how the board works, let's flip some values. In the previous image, we end up having a value of midtones of **34** degrees at **-42** % and a value of highlights of **37** degrees at **-28** %.

Think of a circle, which is made up of 360 degrees. The opposite value of 34 degrees would be 214 degrees (34+180), and the opposite of 37 degrees would be 217 degrees. Unsurprisingly, to flop the percentages, we just change the negative values to positive values.

If we make these changes, we should end up with a flopped board that looks like this:

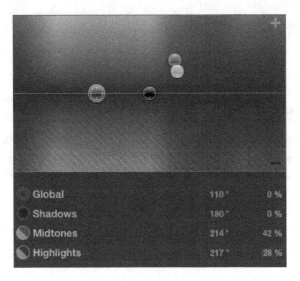

After flipping the values, take note of the most interesting tidbit—our image looks identical! Exactly opposite values will result in the same change to the image, giving you two different ways to work. If you're an old school editor coming from the era of the color wheel, you'll likely use the positive half of the board, as that is much akin to using the wheel, despite it being a different shape. If you are newer to editing and never used a color wheel, the lower half of the board might make more sense to you as it lets you simply tell FCPX which color you are trying to lessen or negate.

Picking a color look or creating your own

FCPX's Color Board isn't only for correcting an image. Sometimes you want to alter its color properties for artistic effect and ends. Take a look at movies like *Traffic*, *Sky Captain and The World of Tomorrow*, and *Pleasantville*, just to name a few. Each took color and made it part of the story in their own way, manipulating the mood and moment with a little color grading, as the artistic use of the process is often called.

FCPX offers 25 aesthetic-altering effects known as **Looks**, 20 color presets, and, to top it off, you can also make your own preset from the Color Board and save it for reuse down the line. In this exercise, we'll take a look at all three.

How to do it...

1. Open the **Effects Browser** and click on the **Looks** category. You'll find 25 different looks that can be applied to a clip:

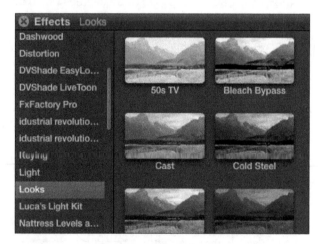

2. Click-and-drag the one called **Cast** to any one of your clips:

3. Position your playhead over the clip to see the results:

4. Make sure the clip is highlighted, and open the Inspector. Each **Look** effect has a few parameters available to adjust. In this example, **Amount** allows us to adjust the overall intensity of the effect, **Midtones** lets us pick a new color in that range, while **Protect Skin** attempts to lessen the tint on what it perceives to be skin tone:

5. Click on the **Cast** effect name in the Inspector and hit *Delete* to remove the effect, returning the clip to its original appearance.

6. Open the Color Board by hitting *Command + 6*. Notice the cogwheel drop-down menu in the bottom right side corner:

7. Click on it and choose **Moonlight**:

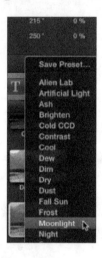

The Color Board's pucks move to all new, preset locations to achieve a new look for your image:

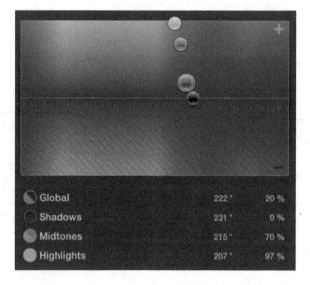

The resulting image shows a heavily blue-skewed tint as three of the four pucks have been pushed into positive blue territory:

8. Experiment with some of the other color presets.

9. When you're done, drag the color pucks around and try and come up with your own unique look to your video clip.

 Try not to pick something too dramatic or distracting—just aim to add a certain subtle mood to the shot, depending on the mood of your film.

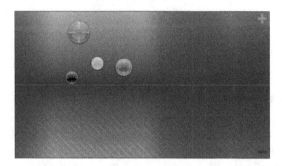

In our example, we've created a sickly-looking yellowish-green tint:

10. When you've achieved an aesthetic you're happy with, click on the cogwheel drop-down menu again and select **Save Preset...** .

11. In the dialog box that pops up, name your preset and click on **OK**:

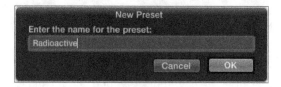

12. This color preset is added to the list of presets available to you in the Color Board window and can be used in every project from here on out:

There's more...

Color grading and media formats

The quality of your final color correction can often depend largely on your media format. Compressed video formats like H.264 don't have nearly the same amount of color information in each frame and pixel as less compressed (ProRes) or uncompressed formats (uncompressed HD or RAW formats) do. Regardless of whether you're working with a lower-end or higher-end format, you should ensure your timeline is playing back your original or optimized media while editing and not the proxy media. To double-check, go to **Final Cut Pro | Preferences** (*Command + ,*), click on the **Playback** tab and select **Use original or optimized media** under the **Playback** option.

Adding a color preset to multiple clips at once

After you've made a color preset, you may want to use it on more than one clip, perhaps your whole timeline! There are a couple ways you can achieve this:

First, you can simply highlight all the clips (possibly your whole timeline) that you want to apply a certain color preset to, and create a compound clip. Once packaged together, you can simply highlight the compound clip and add a color preset to the entire entity.

The other method would be to add a color preset to one clip, copy that clip with *Command +
C*, deselect the clip and highlight all the other clips you wish to add the preset to and choose
Edit | Paste Effects (*Command + Option + V*). This will paste all effects and color corrections
onto the highlighted clips.

Fixing the exposure and adjusting the contrast with help from the Luma waveform monitor

When correcting an image, not only do we want to make sure our colors appear as we saw
them with our own eyes, but we also need to ensure that the image is properly exposed, giving
us as full of a range of bright to dark as possible. Cameras do not have nearly the dynamic
range of light and color that the human eyeball does (yet), and so we must work to push our
darker and brighter areas of an image to create contrast. This can be tough to do relying on a
computer screen's portrayal of our media, but with the help of a video scope called the Luma
waveform monitor, which helps measure the brightness and contract of an image, this process
is made just a bit easier.

Getting ready

Find and highlight a clip in your timeline that you think is in need of some extra contrast or
exposure adjustment. If you are unsure, read along to learn how to understand and read
video scopes to spot clips in need of adjustments.

How to do it...

1. With the clip you want to adjust highlighted, make sure to park your playhead on a
   frame that represents the brightness (or lack thereof) or contrast of the image well.
   (You may want to optionally add a marker to this frame to be able to easily return to
   it later if need be). In our example, we have a shot of a couch full of colorful pillows
   used for a real estate promo video. The image is underexposed and the colors aren't
   coming through as they should be.

2. In the menu bar, select **Window | Show Video Scopes** (*Command + 7*). This brings up one of the video scopes. We want to see the waveform monitor and have it display the Luma values for the frame we are parked on.

3. Click on the **Settings** drop-down button and choose **Waveform** under **DISPLAY** and click on the **Settings** drop-down again and select **Luma** under **CHANNELS**:

The Luma waveform monitor appears:

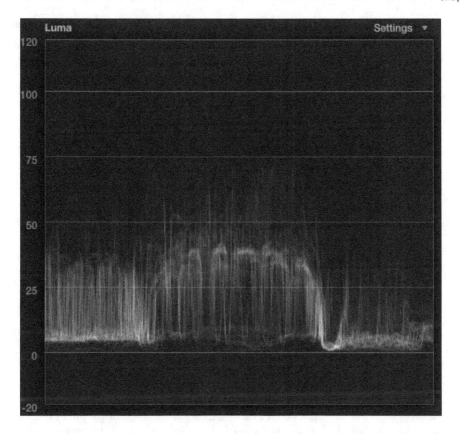

The Luma waveform monitor shows us the pixel brightness from left to right in an image. Looking at the previous image, we see a broad hump in the middle at around 40 to 45 percent with little strands or fingers reaching upward towards 75 percent. These are the whiter pixels in the image, seen in the center pillow. But there are virtually no pixels in the range of 75 to 100 percent in this image at all, meaning we have no highlights in the image, giving it a dark, flattened look. There's little contrast as the image as a whole is fairly dark. Many (but not all) images benefit from having a greater range of contrast with shadows hitting near zero percent and highlights touching close to 100 percent.

4. Hit *Command + 6* to open your Color Board, and then click on the **Exposure** tab at the top:

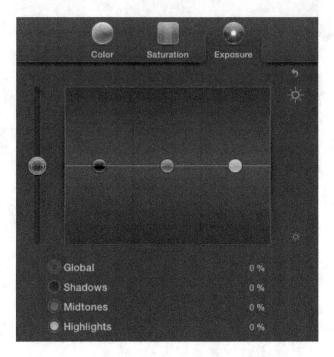

At this point, the top half of your FCPX interface may be getting a little tight for space with your event library, **Event Browser**, video scope, viewer, and Color Board open. Try closing the event library for the time being (*Command + Shift + 1*) and drag the divider between your **Event Browser** and the video scope pane to the left to shrink your event library as you're not currently using it.

If we only look at the image itself, we might mistakenly think we need to brighten up the darker pixels of the image. Doing so, however, would make us lose our blacks and shadows, and cause the image to have even less contrast! By looking at the Luma waveform, we see this image has almost no highlights, so we'll fix that issue first.

5. Drag the **Highlights** puck (the one on the far right up until the top edge of the highlights reach near 100 in the Luma waveform monitor. In our case, a good value ended up being 32 percent, however, this will differ with each and every image you ever correct:

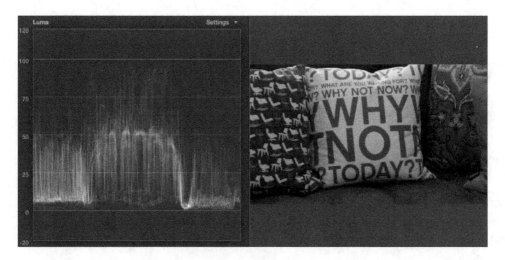

Our image has improved by giving it a greater contrast from the darkest to the brightest pixels. But looking closely at the Luma waveform we still see that most of the pixel density is centered around the 10 percent to 45 percent region. The problem is that we don't want to raise the values of our shadows for fear of losing our blacks, and we also don't want to raise our highlights anymore for fear of pushing them over 100 percent (a no-no in the broadcasting world—read the *There's more...*section). So what do we do?

6. Drag the **Midtones** slider up a bit until the concentration of pixels in the Luma waveform is centered a bit closer to 50 percent:

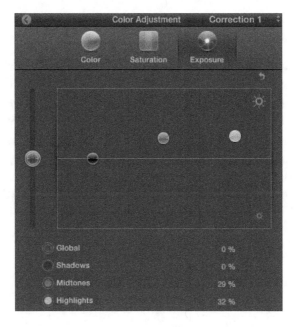

For our example, a value of 29 percent seemed to bring midtones of this image to a good place:

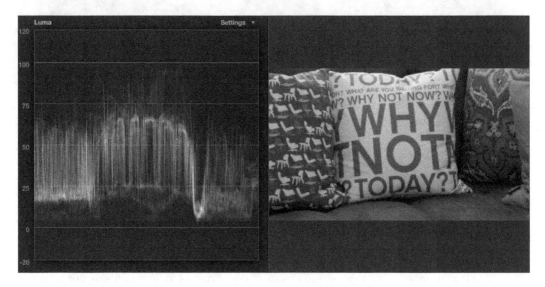

Our image is now significantly brightened compared to what we started with.

 A lot of this does come down to opinion and artistic license. Experiment with these sliders to get the look and feel that best fits your project.

There's more...

Meeting broadcast safe standards

If your project is eventually going to be broadcast on television, you need to ensure that your project meets certain guidelines, such as brightness levels. The Luma waveform should never reach 100, otherwise you run the risk of creating distortions (usually audio, oddly enough!) in your project.

FCPX offers the **Broadcast Safe** effect, found in the **Basics** video category. When applied, FCPX simply takes any highlights that are over 100 and brings them down to a safe level around 95 (you can watch this happen right in the Luma waveform as you apply the effect). There's one major catch, however, and it has to do with the order FCPX processes certain operations.

FCPX processes effects before color corrections. This means, if you color correct, and then apply the **Broadcast Safe** effect, it will have no useful impact on your clip. The workaround is yet another magical use of the ever-valuable Compound Clip tool. If you color-correct a clip, then convert it into a compound clip, and finally add the **Broadcast Safe** effect, the effect will work. It's a bit confusing, but by putting the clip inside a compound clip, we're forcing FCPX to process the color correction first. Because the shell of the compound clip isn't color corrected, we can easily apply the **Broadcast Safe** filter, and we're in business!

See also

If you've forgotten about compound clips and what they're all about, head back and read the *Grouping clips together as compound clips* recipe.

Adding secondary color corrections, part 1 – shape masks

So far, we've been learning about primary color corrections. These are corrections that affect the entire image. However, very often you only want to affect a certain range within an image, whether it's a certain range of colors or a certain physical area of the frame. Correcting or grading a limited selection within a clip is known as **secondary color correction**. FCPX's secondary color correction capabilities come in the form of color masks and shape masks.

A **shape mask** allows us to isolate a region of the frame and make adjustments to it. It is often used to make exposure adjustments on an interview subjects' face if they were poorly lit, for example.

A **color mask** allows us to isolate a color (or more likely a range of color) and perform adjustments on just that selection. We'll learn about both of these types of masks in the following two recipes.

Getting ready

See if you can find a clip with a human subject (sitting relatively still) that needs a bit of color correction or exposure adjustment.

How to do it...

1. Make sure your clip is highlighted and open the Inspector:

The focus of our clip, the man in the center, is poorly lit and the details of his face are hard to make out.

In the Inspector, to the right of **Correction 1** are two icons: **Add Color Mask** and **Add Shape Mask** (hover over each for the tool tip label to appear):

2. Click on the **Add Shape Mask** button. Two items appear on screen: a new label under **Correction 1** called **Shape Mask 1** and an on-screen control system appears on the clip in the Viewer:

The on-screen controls for the shape mask appear as two circles with green handles that allow you to stretch the shape of the circles. The inner circle is the inside of your mask. Any color adjustments we make will appear inside this circle. The outer circle is the feathered edge of the mask. You can control the size of the feather by dragging the outer circle's edge inward or outward.

You can also change the position of the shape mask by using the center puck and rotate it, if necessary, using the rotation handle extending off the center puck.

3. Drag the shape mask over your subject's face. Use the green resize handles to adjust the shape and size of the mask. Rotate the mask if necessary:

4. Press *Command + 6* to jump to our Color Board and click on the **Exposure** tab.

5. Drag the **Midtones** and **Highlights** sliders up a bit to increase the exposure of the image:

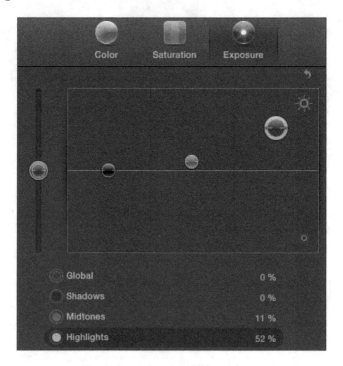

Notice that only the area inside the mask is being affected:

Be careful not to overdo it with the sliders. Otherwise, it'll look like a giant spotlight is on your subject!

6. When you think you are happy with the adjustment, deselect the clip in the timeline to make the on-screen control disappear.

There's more...

Keyframing the shape mask

One scenario you're likely to run into is that your subject doesn't sit/stand still. Or maybe the video was handheld so the subject is moving within the frame one way or the other. If your shape mask doesn't have much of a feathered edge and/or you made a dramatic change in color or exposure, this can create a rather jarring, visible halo if the subject moves out of the location of shape mask.

Luckily, you can keyframe the position, size, shape, and feathered edge of shape mask. Take note of the keyframe icon next to the **Shape Mask 1** label in the Inspector. If your subject moves within the frame, position, and size the mask correctly at the first frame of the clip using the on screen controls in the Viewer, then add a keyframe in the Inspector. Move your playhead a few frames ahead to where the subject has moved and reposition and/or resize the mask over the subject. FCPX will automatically enter another keyframe at that position time. Repeat the process as many times as you need to in order to reach the end of the clip.

See also

For a review on keyframing, read the *Changing the parameters of an effect over time with keyframes* recipe.

Keep reading to learn about the other kind of mask; a color mask!

Adding secondary color corrections, part 2 – color masks

In the previous exercise, we learned about the first of two forms of secondary color correction in FCPX, the shape mask. Shape masks allow us to define a region of the frame that we want to adjust in color, saturation, or exposure without altering the rest of the image.

Sometimes, however, you want to adjust a range of colors within an image, regardless of their location within the frame. Enter color masks!

Getting ready

Find an image that has an area in need of some color adjustment, but may be an area hard to define by a simple shape mask. In the example we'll use, we want to add a little more blue shade to the sky behind the Jefferson Memorial in Washington, D.C.

How to do it...

1. Make sure your clip is highlighted and open the Inspector.

The sky in this clip is woefully grey and we want to give it a bit of a blue tint.

In the Inspector, to the right of **Correction 1** are two icons: **Add Color Mask** and **Add Shape Mask** (hover over each for the tool tip label to appear):

2. Click on the **Add Color Mask** button. A new item appears under **Correction 1** called **Color Mask**. Next to the label is a black color chip:

3. Click on that black color chip and move your cursor over your clip in the Viewer. Your cursor turns into an eye dropper.

4. Read this whole step before trying this part out! Click and hold down on the area of the image containing the color range you want to adjust. While still holding down, drag slowly outward, away from where you clicked. FCPX will add to the surrounding colors to the selection. Do not drag very far or you'll select more colors than you want! You'll know if part of the image has been selected by the color mask if you see it in color while dragging; the unselected colors appear desaturated while dragging.

The only issue with our selection of color masks is that not only have we selected the sky, but FCPX has picked up on some of the water too, as it is reflecting the sky. Ignore this for now. We'll come back to this in the next recipe!

When you let go, the image seemingly returns to normal.

5. When you think you've selected the color range you like, let go of the mouse.

6. If you wish to add additional colors to the selection of color mask after you let go, hold the *Shift* key and repeat step 4. A plus sign appears over the eye dropper indicating you are adding color to the selection:

7. If you want to remove color from the selection, hold the *Option* key and repeat step 4, but click on the area you want to remove. A minus sign appears over the eye dropper indicating you are removing color from the selection.

8. Hit *Command + 6* to go to the Color Board and click on the **Color** tab if it is not already selected.

9. Make your color adjustment. This will obviously vary depending on your image. In our example, we are going to drag our **Highlights** and **Midtones** pucks towards the positive blue region a bit:

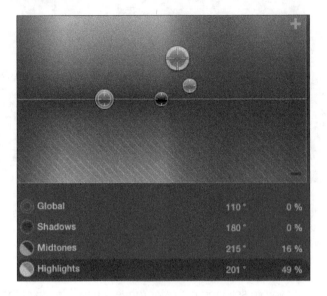

Only the area selected by the color mask will be affected by our adjustments:

Our sky looks nice and blue now, rather than steely grey. The problem is, our water has been tinted an unnatural blue as well.

See also

Refer to the *Adding secondary color corrections, part 3 – combining color and shape masks* recipe if you want to learn how to fix the problem we created with our color mask!

Adding secondary color corrections, part 3 – combining color and shape masks

In the previous chapter, we successfully isolated our gray sky with a color mask and made it a bit bluer. Unfortunately, we were a bit too successful—our color mask also picked up the similar gray color in the reflection in the water! We need to use the best of both worlds and add a shape mask to our color mask in order to keep our new blue sky while eliminating the radioactive looking water.

Getting ready

This recipe picks right up where the previous one left off, so if you haven't completed the previous exercise, do it now!

To make sure you're up to speed, make sure the clip with the color mask is highlighted in the timeline and that your Inspector is open:

How to do it...

1. In the Inspector, click on the **Add Shape Mask** button to the right of the **Correction 1**:

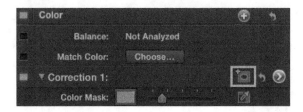

As soon as you add the shape mask, your image changes dramatically, seemingly for the worse. But look closely. Your color mask correction still exists, but only inside the shape mask.

2. Using the reposition puck, move the shape mask to the area of the image containing the color mask you want to keep. Stretch and resize the mask with the green handles to fit the mask appropriately:

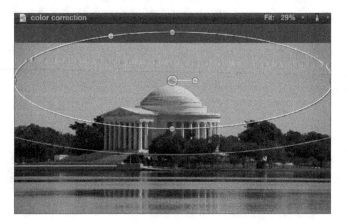

3. You can also convert the oval into more of a rounded rectangle shape by clicking and dragging on the sole gray handle on the inner mask circle:

Our sky is now blue, without tinting the water!

How it works...

You may ask, why couldn't we simply apply just a shape mask in the first place? It's a good question, and the explanation is rather simple. In our example, if we simply placed a shape mask where we did and then tried to tint the interior blue, it would've also severely and awkwardly tinted the Jefferson Memorial! Here's what it would've looked like:

It looks like someone dumped blue paint on the memorial and didn't even finish the job! By combining the two masks, we told FCPX to only adjust a certain color range within a certain physical range.

Keeping only one color in your image

Altering the color space of an image isn't always about correction. Sometimes we want to achieve some artistic end, whether it's to make a statement or simply draw viewers' attentions in a particular direction or manner. One simple way to do this is by the absence of color. Color in video is so commonplace these days, that desaturated (black and white) images tend to be far more dramatic or eye-catching despite not properly representing reality. Desaturating an image with the exception of single color—well, that's just crazy! Actually, it's not at all. Just take a look at modern classics like *Schindler's List*, *Pleasantville*, or even commercials for Gatorade to see effective uses of this technique.

Getting ready

If you haven't read the previous three recipes, it'd be a good idea to go check them out now!

Find a colorful clip in your repertoire to see this effect dramatically. Removing one color works best if that color is fairly consistent in the clip with little gradation, but your mileage may vary! In our clip, we're going to take this stuffed toy from an arts and crafts fair and only keep the orange of its body:

How to do It...

1. Highlight the clip in your timeline and open the Inspector.

2. Click the **Add Color Mask** button next to **Correction 1** in the **Color** box:

3. Move your cursor over the part of the image with the color you want to keep. Click and hold, dragging slowly away from the center of your click point to add more of the nearby range of colors to the selection. Let go when you've made your selection. You may not get all of it in the first go.

4. If necessary, hold down *Shift* and click-and-drag again on a different area containing the color you want to add the color to the selection.

It's OK if your color mask accidentally selects additional areas of the image containing that color. In our image, part of the background containing orange was also selected. We'll take care of that soon enough!

5. Press *Command + 6* to open the Color Board and click on the **Saturation** tab at the top.

6. Click on the **Outside Mask** button at the bottom of the pane:

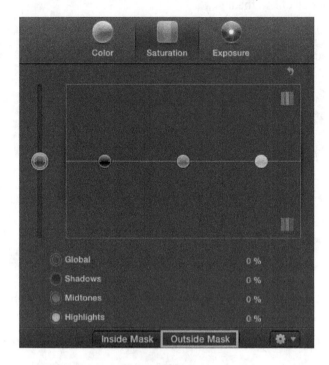

7. Drag the **Global** saturation slider on the left all the way to the bottom:

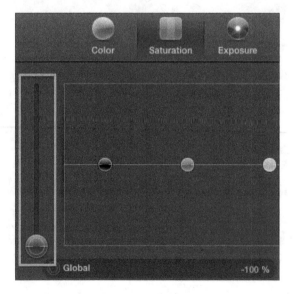

The image is entirely desaturated except for the selection from the color mask.

As we pointed out before and can easily see now, some of the orange in other parts of the image are still visible.

8. Return to the Inspector by clicking the back button found in the upper-left corner of the Color Board window:

9. Click the **Add Shape Mask** button in the **Color** parameter box:

The on-screen controls appear for the shape mask.

10. Adjust the position of the shape mask with the puck in the center and resize/reshape your mask by using the green handles on the circles:

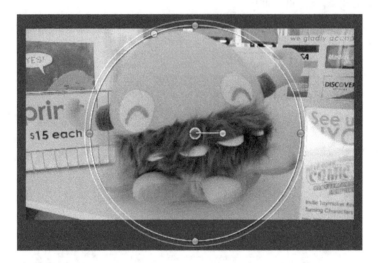

How It Works...

We had to apply both a color mask and a shape mask in order to ensure that we kept only the orange of the stuffed animal. However, don't forget that if you need to color adjust more than one physical areas of your frame instead of just one, you can always add multiple shape masks on top of a color mask to select multiple regions of a frame to adjust.

Spotlighting an object or text

Sometimes you need to draw attention to a very specific part of the frame whether it be highlighting text on a page, picking out a face in a crowd, or following a hard-to-see UFO in the sky. Color correction tools are not the first place most people would think to go to be able to accomplish any of these tasks, and while there is always more than one way to accomplish a goal in FCPX, here's one of the easiest.

Getting ready

In this example, we're going to use the color correction tools to highlight a paragraph of text on a document to draw attention to it:

xpires	Pub. 501, Exemptions, Standard Deduction, and Filing Information, for information.	Nonresid see Notic
olding		Instructic
	Tax credits. You can take projected tax credits into account in figuring your allowable number of	completir
ot claim	withholding allowances. Credits for child or	**Check y**
xceeds	dependent care expenses and the child tax credit	effect, us
ed	may be claimed using the **Personal Allowances**	having w
	Worksheet below. See Pub. 505 for information on	for 2012.
omplete	converting your other credits into withholding	exceed $
. The	allowances.	
	Nonwage income. If you have a large amount of	**Future d**
	nonwage income, such as interest or dividends,	on IRS.g
	consider making estimated tax payments using Form	*www.irs.g*
come,	1040-ES, Estimated Tax for Individuals. Otherwise, you	developn
	may owe additional tax. If you have pension or annuity	legislatioi
		on that p

Personal Allowances Worksheet (Keep for your records.)

else can claim you as a dependent . . . .

To import this document (which was originally a PDF) into FCPX, we opened it in Preview and converted it to a PNG file.

How to do it...

1. Highlight your clip and open the Inspector.

2. Click on the **Add Shape Mask** button in the **Color** panel:

Ignore the shape mask on-screen controls for the moment. Let's create the spotlight first.

3. Hit *Command + 6* to open the Color Board and click on the **Exposure** tab:

4. Click on the **Outside Mask** button at the bottom of the pane:

5. Drag either the **Highlight** or **Global** exposure slider down significantly. In our example, we dragged the **Global** slider to around -80 percent.

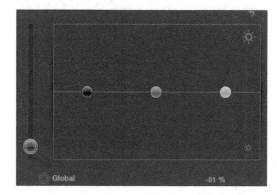

The image outside of the mask is darkened significantly:

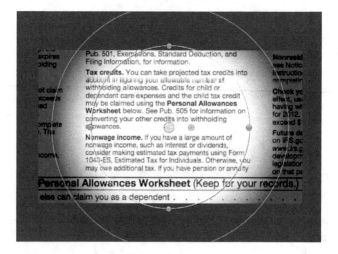

Now time to highlight the portion we want to spotlight.

6. In the viewer, resize and reposition the color mask around the object you want to highlight using the green resize handles and center position puck. Click-and-drag the outer circle inward to make the outer-feathered edge smaller in order to create a fairly defined line around your focus point. If you need to create a more rectangular shape, click-and-drag to the left on the sole transparent circle on the inner circle:

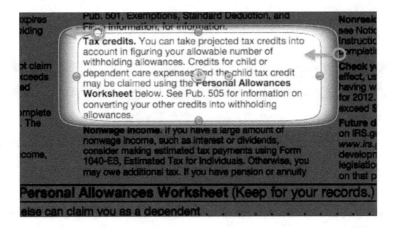

Now let's assume we need to make this spotlight move and change shape because we want to highlight a different portion of the frame later in the clip. In our example, we'll move the spotlight to highlight the next paragraph.

7. In the timelime, move your playhead to the frame of video where you want your spotlight to start changing/moving:

8. Click on the arrow pointing towards the left inside the circle in the upper-left corner of the Color Board to return to the Inspector:

9. Hover over the **Shape Mask 1** parameter and click on the **Add Keyframe** button that appears on the right:

10. Move your playhead forward in time to the frame where you want the spotlight movement to end:

11. If the on-screen controls for the shape mask have disappeared, click on the shape mask icon again in the Inspector.

12. In the Viewer, resize and reposition the shape mask to highlight the new region of the frame:

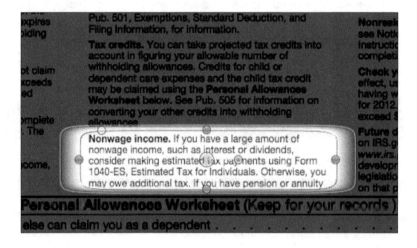

FCPX automatically adds the second keyframe for the shape mask.

13. Play back your clip to watch the spotlight move.

There's more...

Fade the spotlights in and out

You may want your document to start off evenly and normally lit and then have the highlight appear. If you've already created your shape mask, simply split the clip in two parts with the Blade tool and then reset the color corrections on the first chunk of the clip to return it to normal. Lastly, pop in a Cross Dissolve transition between the two and you'll create an easy fade between the normal image and the spotlighted version.

10
Getting Your Project Out of FCPX

In this chapter, we will cover:

- ▶ Exporting an archive-quality version of your film
- ▶ Exporting for Apple devices and computers
- ▶ Sharing your video on YouTube and other video sharing sites
- ▶ Burning a Blu-ray or DVD
- ▶ Roles, part 1 – labeling clips with Roles
- ▶ Roles, part 2 – exporting selected Roles
- ▶ Sharing large files over the web with Dropbox
- ▶ Sharing your project with other applications using XML
- ▶ Duplicating or moving projects from one drive to another
- ▶ Archiving a project for possible future editing

Introduction

Here we are, at the end of the road. Our project is perfect: the color is vibrant, the audio pristine, the actors compelling (if not, well, nothing you can do about that now...). So, how do we get out of here?

FCPX makes it easy to move on; you just need to ask yourself a question—where am I going? FCPX offers a large number of exporting options whether you want to take your video to YouTube, optical media, iPhone, iPad, AppleTV, the web, and many more.

This final chapter will take you through some of the more common scenarios found in the **Shared** menu of FCPX, as well as a few tips and tricks about how to share those large HD files over the web and how to archive projects in case you ever get asked by a client to re-edit a single transition two years down the line. Hey, it happens.

Exporting an archive-quality version of your film

Ready to take your film on the road to be projected larger than life on a 50-feet screen? Or simply want to make sure that you've always got the highest quality version of your film on a drive in case you need to make smaller versions in multiple formats? This recipe will show you how.

Getting ready

In just about every case in this chapter, the only part for getting ready is to have a project you're ready to export!

How to do it...

1. Select your project from the project library and choose **Share | Export Media** by pressing *Command + E*. The export media window appears:

2. From the **Export** drop-down menu, select **Video and Audio**, but take note that you can also select **Video Only** or **Audio Only** if desired. We will cover the other options in the *Roles, part 2 – exporting selected roles* recipe.

3. Under **Video codec**, there is a long list of options:

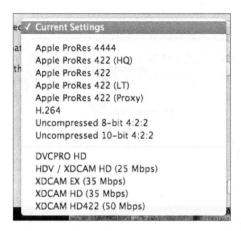

People argue which one of these options is best in certain scenarios. Just read a couple of video blogs and message boards. Some people argue over Citizen Kane versus Schindler's List, others argue over **ProRes 4444** versus **Uncompressed 10-bit 4:2:2**.

Our humble advice is as follows: Unless you are shooting with a camera that costs as much as a luxury car and shoots higher than normal HD video (1920 x 1080), you're very likely going to be OK choosing the **ProRes 422** option for an archival version of your movie. This is by no means the highest quality option available, however, you can't increase the quality level of the video you started with. If you shot your film on a DSLR (which usually shoots in the highly compressed H.264 video codec) and choose the **ProRes 4444** or **Uncompressed** options, it's like taking a glass of water and trying to fill a bath tub. You're going to create an unnecessarily large file with no useful gain.

If you're lucky enough to own a camera that has the words Red, Arri, or Phantom somewhere in the name, you're likely going to want to choose **ProRes 422 HQ** or **Uncompressed 10-bit 4:2:2**, but if you own one of those, you probably already know that!

Choose **ProRes 4444** if you're working with remarkably high quality footage and you need to maintain an alpha channel (that is transparency channel) in your footage.

The **H.264** option is a heavily compressed option, which will dramatically reduce your file size, but may not look quite as pristine as your original footage to the trained eye. Choose this option if you want a (mostly) high-quality option that is easier to share over the web (covered in the *Sharing large files over the web with Dropbox* recipe).

4. After selecting your codec, select whichever option you prefer from the **Open with** drop-down menu.

5. Click on **Next**, name your file, choose a place to save it, and click on **Save**.

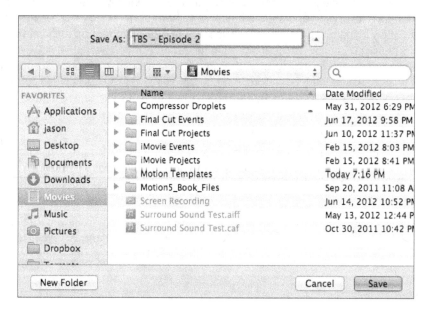

How it works...

Just know that when you export a version of your movie, part or all of it goes through what is often called a **generation loss**. The bits that make up your video are usually being converted from one codec (language) of video into another. Think of it as the modern version of hooking two VCRs up to one another to duplicate a tape. However, the good news is that as long as you are converting between two high quality codecs with the proper settings, any loss in quality is usually nearly imperceptible except to all but the most highly trained eyeballs.

There's more...

Need your video in other formats?

FCPX has limits as to what languages it can compress video into—mainly H.264, ProRes, and a few aging formats such as HDV and DVCPRO HD. If a client needs your film in a format not supported by export options of FCPX (such as Cinepak, DNxHD, WMV, among tons of others), then you might look into acquiring dedicated compression software such as Sorenson Squeeze (`www.sorensonmedia.com/video-encoding`) or Telestream Episode (`www.telestream.net/episode`). Both applications offer the ability to decode and encode a huge variety of video file formats with seemingly limitless quality settings.

Exporting for Apple devices and computers

You. Yeah, you, the one reading this book. You're obviously a Mac owner (or at least heavy Mac user). You're also a big Apple fan if you're using Final Cut Pro. We're going to guess you probably own an iPhone, iPad, iPod, or AppleTV (or some combination of all of the these devices). And if you're in the one percent that we were wrong about, you probably know about a million people who might want/need to view your video on one of the previously mentioned iDevices as well. Unsurprisingly, Apple has made it easy as (apple) pie (couldn't resist, sorry) to create versions of your movie for all the aforementioned iDevices.

But the **Apple Devices** menu found in FCPX's sharing options, is poorly labeled, or at least not completely labeled, as it is also about the easiest option to choose when you want to create a high-quality version of your movie that also looks great on a larger computer monitor and is a file size that's usually reasonable enough to send over the web (unlike those crazy-huge archival formats we talked about in the previous recipe!).

How to do it...

1. Select your project from the project library and then go to **Share | Apple Devices....**
    A window will pop up with a lot of options for creating Apple-friendly versions of your movie:

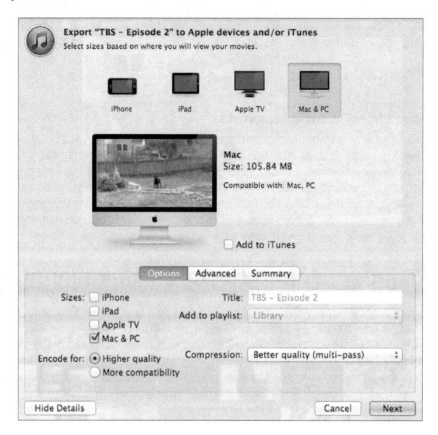

2. Place a checkmark in the box for each device you want to create a video for.

3. Make sure **Add to iTunes** is checked if you want to save a step by having FCPX immediately add the video to iTunes when it's done with creating the file (so that it can be synced to your iDevice at a later time). If you uncheck the box, the **Share** button will change into **Next** which, when clicked on, will prompt you for a location to save the file.

4. Next to **Encode for** select **Higher quality** if you're confident that you or your clients will be viewing these videos on more recent Apple devices. If you are unsure and want to play it safe, select **More compatibility**.

Both options will display what devices will be capable of playing your movie on the right of the window next to the **Compatible with** heading. For example, choosing the Apple TV option with **More compatibility** results in a file that is 1280 x 720 to ensure that it works on the previous second generation AppleTV as that generation was only capable of 720p output. Choosing **Higher quality**, however, results in a full 1920 x 1080 finished product as the third generation AppleTV is more powerful and is capable of displaying full 1080p content.

These sorts of tech specs change all the time from product generation to generation, so by the time you read this, the rules may have changed again! Always double-check the compatibility list in this window:

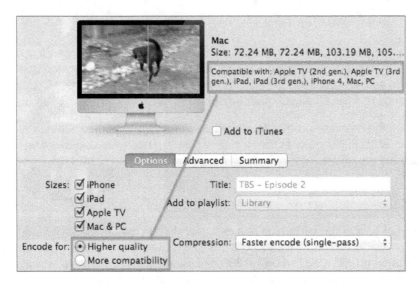

5. Next to **Compression**, select **Faster encode (single-pass)** to save on time or **Better quality (multi-pass)** if you want optimum quality and don't mind waiting for it. The dirty secret is that **Faster encode** looks great 95 percent of the time, but if your video has a lot of fast moving action or lots of dark scenes (horror film perhaps?), then you'll want to go with **Better quality**.

6. Click on the **Advanced** tab at the top. Here you have the option to change **Background Rendering** from **None** to **This Computer**. Choosing **This Computer** will push the task of creating the video(s) out to the **Share Monitor** application, allowing you to continue using FCPX if necessary:

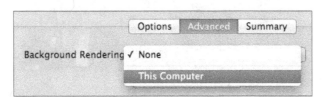

7. Click on the **Summary** tab. This will give you more detailed information about each of the files you're about to create:

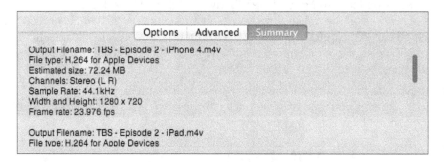

8. When you have made your selections, click on **Share** or **Next**, depending on whether or not you checkmarked the **Add to iTunes** button (mentioned in step 3). If you chose not to automatically add the files to iTunes, choose a name for your file(s) and a location to save. Finally, click on **Save**.

    When the process is complete, your files will be clearly labeled either in your movies' list in iTunes or at the location where you have saved, depending on the options you chose.

How it works...

No matter what option(s) you chose in this exercise, all the created videos are in the H.264 codec. The only difference from file to file is the quality level. This is determined partially by the **resolution** (that is 1920 x 1080, 1280 x 720, and so on) and partially by something called the **bit rate** or **data rate**. This is basically how many bits of information are thrown into each second of video. You can see a bit rate of a video in QuickTime Player by opening the Inspector window by pressing *Command + I*:

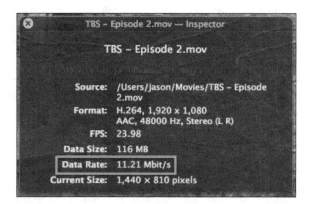

While that data rate in the previous screenshot may look like 11.21 megabytes per second, it's actually 11.21 megabits per second. There are eight megabits in a megabyte. Simple math (11.21 / 8) tells us that this video takes up about 1.4 megabytes for every second of video.

Sharing your video on YouTube and other video sharing sites

As the age of the physical distribution of media slowly crawls to its long, bitter end, video sharing sites have surged in popularity with none more omnipresent in our everyday lives than YouTube.

FCPX has kindly built YouTube uploading directly into the application, along with other sites with video sharing such as Vimeo (more trendy, chic younger sibling of YouTube), CNN, and, of course, Facebook.

This exercise will focus on uploading a project to YouTube, but the uploading process for the other sites is very similar.

How to do it...

1. Select a finished project that you are ready to share with the world and select **Share | YouTube**. A dialog box will appear:

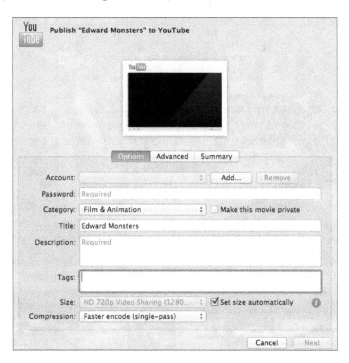

2. Click the **Add...** button next to **Account**, enter your user name in the resulting box, and click on **Done**:

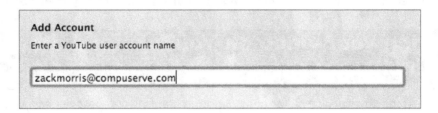

3. Enter your password.

4. Pick a category for your video from the drop-down list:

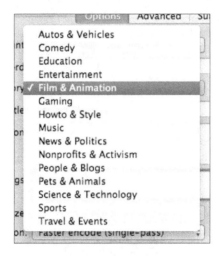

5. Check the box **Make this movie private** if you wish to hide your video on YouTube. If you do, the video will not show up in any YouTube searches and will only be accessible to you when you are logged into your own YouTube account.

6. Enter a title for your video.

7. Fill in the **Description** box. This is required.

8. Add **Tags** to your film. These are words or phrases, separated by commas, that can help people search for your video on YouTube. If you made a hip-hop music video with a Nikon D7000, you might enter **hip hop, music video, Nikon**, and **D7000**.

9. If you want the highest possible quality video uploaded to YouTube, keep **Set size automatically** checkmarked. If you want to purposely upload a version with a lower resolution, uncheck the box and select a size from the drop-down menu:

10. Next to **Compression**, select **Faster encode (single-pass)** to save on time or **Better quality (multi-pass)** if you want optimum quality and don't mind waiting for it. As mentioned in the previous exercise, the secret is that **Faster encode** looks great most of the time, but if your video has a lot of fast moving action or lots of dark scenes, then you'll want to go with **Better quality**.

11. Click on the **Advanced** tab at the top. Here you have the option to change **Background Rendering** from **None** to **This Computer**. Choosing **This Computer** will push the task of creating the video and uploading it out to the Share Monitor application, allowing you to continue using FCPX if necessary.

12. Click on **Next**, which brings up the YouTube **Terms of Service** screen. Read this carefully! (Yeah, right, who reads these things?).

13. Click on **Publish**.

How it works...

Once you click on **Publish**, a two-step process begins. First, your movie file is created at the quality level you selected, and then the file is uploaded.

Once complete, you can easily find a link and/or share the video. Select the project in your project library (do not open the project) and open your Inspector by pressing *Command + 4*. Click on the **Sharing** tab at the top and then click on the tiny triangle next to the **Published to YouTube** listing:

There's more...

Your video is still on your computer

After FCPX uploads your video to YouTube, it secretly keeps a copy of the generated video file it created on your computer, but not in the most obvious location.

In **Finder**, open the **Final Cut Projects** folder on the drive your project is stored on (this will either be in the **Movies** folder of your booted drive or the root level of your external drive). Open the folder with the title of your project and inside you will find a folder titled **Shared Items**. Inside is the hidden video file!

Burning a Blu-ray or DVD

While Apple is slowly but surely cutting the cord on optical media from its computer lineup, plenty of existing Macs still have DVD burners and plenty of clients out there still have a want for their projects on optical discs. Macs never have, and likely never will, come with pre-installed with a Blu-ray burner, so if you have the need for burning to Blu-ray, you'll need to pick up an external one or get advanced and install an internal one. They can be purchased relatively inexpensively these days.

Additionally, while DVD Studio Pro and iDVD have been axed from the Apple software lineup, FCPX provides limited disc burning capabilities. It does the job, but don't expect to make any fancy menu screens. This is pretty quick and simple work.

How to do it...

1. Open the project you want to burn and choose **Share** | **Blu-ray** or **Share** | **DVD**. The menu screens are almost identical, with a few differences we'll point out in the following two screenshots:

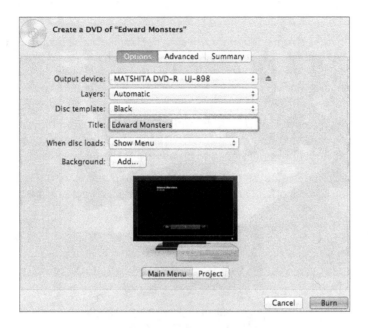

2. Select your appropriate **Output Device**. This is usually set to your internal SuperDrive, but if you own an external SuperDrive or purchased a Blu-ray burner, make the selection here.

There is an option for **Hard Drive**. This will make a disc image of your DVD or Blu-ray disc in the event that you don't have access to a burner at the moment. This way, you can take the image file that gets created to another Mac with a burner and use Disk Utility to burn the actual disc.

3. In most cases, leave **Layers** to **Automatic**. FCPX will detect what type of blank media you stick in your Mac. You would choose **Dual-Layer** if you needed to create a disc image that would eventually need to be burned to a dual-layer disc.

4. Pick a disc template for the disc's menu as shown in the following screenshot. The Blu-ray options offers five templates, while the DVD options offers only two.

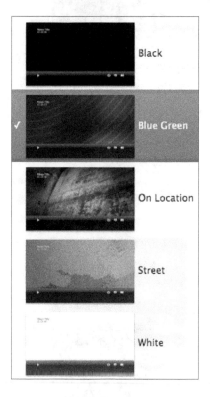

5. Enter a title for your disc in the **Title** box. This will show up on the main menu.

6. Choose **Show Menu** or **Play Movie** from the **When disc loads** drop-down to determine what happens when the disc is fired up in a player. The Blu-ray options give an additional option to add a **Loop** button on the menu screen.

7. The **Background** option allows you to override the template options by putting an image in the background.

8. The Blu-ray options additionally let you add a **Logo** graphic, which will be applied to the upper-right corner of the menu and a **Title** graphic, which will be applied to the center of the menu. A tiny preview is displayed at the bottom of the Blu-ray options screen:

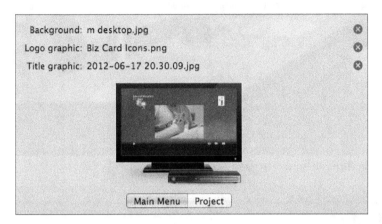

9. Click on the **Advanced** tab at the top. Here you have the option to change **Background Rendering** from **None** to **This Computer**. Choosing **This Computer** and hitting **Burn** will push the task of creating the disc out to the Share Monitor application, allowing you to continue using FCPX if necessary.

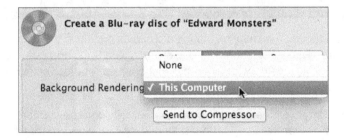

Click the **Send to Compressor** button if you want to send the project to Compressor, if you need the additional compression tools found in that application. Some of the features of Compressor are covered in the appendix of this book.

10. Click on the **Summary** tab. This simply displays the details and settings of the output. Don't be confused when it says two output files will be created. The end result that you will be left with is either a finished optical disc or a single disc image in a location of your choosing.

> 2 output files will be created.
>
> Output Filename: Edward Monsters.ac3
> File type: Dolby Digital Professional
> Estimated size: 8.2 MB
> Channels: Stereo (L R)
> Sample Rate: 48kHz
>
>
> Output Filename: Edward Monsters.264
> File type: H.264 for Blu-ray
> Estimated size: 1.28 GB
> Width and Height: 1280 x 720
> Frame rate: 29.97 fps

11. Click on **Burn** when you are ready to burn your disc.

See also

Read this book's appendix, *Working with Motion and Compressor*, for a number of recipes on how to use Compressor and scenarios in which you may want to send a project to the application.

Roles, part 1 – labeling clips with Roles

In a large-scale production, you may be editing a complex project with a primary storyline, b-roll, titles, subtitles, narration, sound effects, music, room tone, and more. Each of these acts as a role in your movie. And with larger productions, sometimes you're not ultimately in charge of all of these roles.

For example, you may have created a project with manually created subtitles and you need to be able to export a clean version, without subtitles, of your video so that someone else in another country can take the movie file and add their own subtitles. With the **Rules** feature in FCPX, we can easily pick and choose which elements or roles we want to export.

What's even better is that FCPX does most of the work for us. We don't have to go and tag every single clip with a role. FCPX puts generic roles on every clip automatically (that is video, titles, dialogue, music, and so on). But it's up to us if we need to further break these roles down into further categories like subtitles, sound effects, narration, and so on.

Getting ready

In this exercise, we're going to learn how to view a project's preset roles as well as make our own role for subtitles. Your project will likely vary widely from our example. You may not need to export a version of your project with/without subtitles, for example, but you may need to export a version of your movie with no music bed or no sound effects. Either way, after reading this exercise, you will have the skills necessary to handle a variety of scenarios.

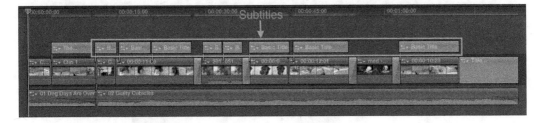

How to do it...

1. Click on the **Timeline Index** button in the bottom left of your screen, or hit *Command + Shift + 2*. The **Timeline Index** appears.

2. Click on the **Roles** button if it is not already selected. A list of all the preset roles FCPX has created appears.

In our project, we see that FCPX has labeled some elements as **Video**, **Titles**, **Dialogue**, and **Music**. Some of this is quite obvious. All video clips are labeled with the **Video** role. The **Dialogue** role is any audio that is a part of the video clips. The green audio clips in our example are **Music** roles. And, unsurprisingly, any and all purple title clips are labeled with the **Titles** role.

And therein lies our problem. In our example, the very first title clip and the very last title clip are indeed titles for our project.

However, all the title clips in between are actually Spanish subtitles. We want to be able to export a version of a video without those subtitles:

 Simply choosing the Disable command (by pressing *V*) does not impact your exported project in any way.

3. Choose **Modify | Edit Roles...**. The **Role Editor** window appears:

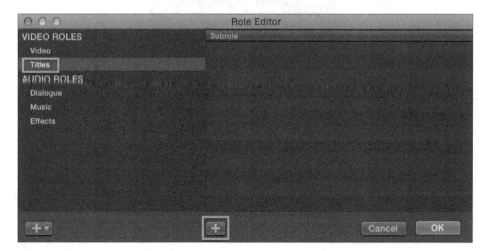

4. Click on **Titles** under **VIDEO ROLES**.

5. Click the **+** button at the bottom of the **Subrole** list.

6. Type in `Spanish Subs` in the textbox that appears:

7. Click on **OK**.

8. In your timeline, highlight every clip that you consider to be a subtitle:

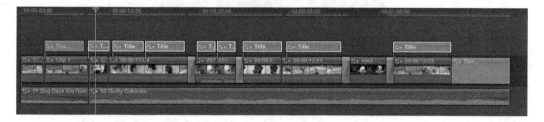

9. Choose **Modify | Assign Roles | Spanish Subs**:

A couple of things will happen. Your subtitle roles may change in size in the timeline. This will not impact your output (more on this in the *There's more...* section). Also, in your **Timeline Index**, you will see two subheadings appear under the **Titles** role; **Spanish Subs**, and **Other Titles**.

Read the next exercise to learn how to export a video without the subtitles.

What are those checkboxes and icons in the Timeline Index?

You may have noticed a couple of extra options in the **Timeline Index**, namely checkboxes and another icon to the right of the Role names.

Unchecking a checkbox will disable all clips of a particular role. You'll see them turn gray. It works just like the Disable command, but saves you from having to manually highlight all clips of a particular nature. Want to instantly mute all music? Just uncheck the **Music** role checkbox. This does not impact exporting in any way. You have to read the next recipe to learn how to disable a role for exporting!

The icon to the right is simply a quick way to minimize all clips of a particular role. If you click on the minimize icon next to **Music** (turning it blue), all music roles will be minimized. This simply allows you to customize the look of your timeline to an even further extent than the normal clip appearance window allows.

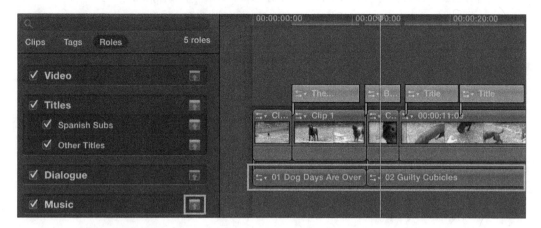

See also

Make sure to read the next recipe to learn how to use these skills to selectively choose which elements/roles get exported from FCPX.

Roles, part 2 – exporting selected Roles

Now that we've learned how to identify roles and create our own if necessary, let's learn how to pick and choose what roles will be used when we export a final version of your project.

Getting ready

We're going to carry on from the previous exercise. As your project will be very different, just make sure you've read the previous recipe and have defined your roles and subroles as necessary.

How to do it...

1. With your project open or selected in the Project browser, choose **Share | Export Media** (by pressing *Command + E*). The export dialog box appears:

2. Select the appropriate **Video codec** option from the drop-down menu, depending on what quality level you are aiming for (this is covered in depth in the *Exporting an archive-quality version of your film* recipe).

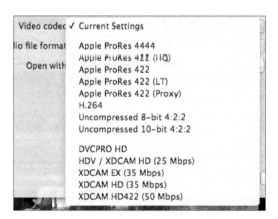

3. Click on the **Export** drop-down menu and select **Roles as Multitrack QuickTime Movie**. A new tab appears above the options simply called **Roles**:

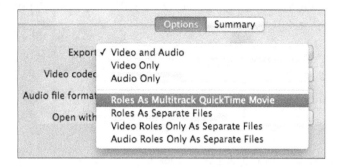

4. Click on the **Roles** tab. A new assortment of options appears which allow you to select which roles you wish to export.

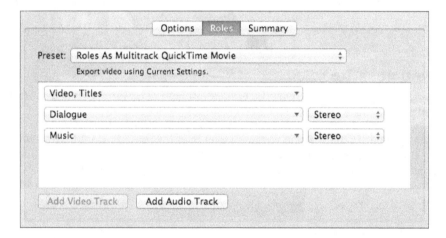

In our example, the first drop-down shows both **Video** and **Titles** listed. Well, we know that we don't want to export the **Spanish Subs** subrole that we created in the previous recipe.

Click on the drop-down that reads **Video, Titles**, (or whatever role may contain the subrole you want to deactivate). We see a list of the subroles within the **Titles** role:

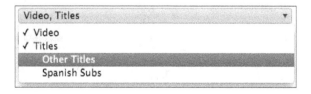

5. Click on **Other Titles** to select just that subrole. These are the remaining titles that were not labeled as **Spanish Subs**.

6. Click on the drop-down menu again to confirm that the **Spanish Subs** subrole does not have a checkmark next to it.

7. Click on **Next**. The Save dialog box appears.

8. Enter a name for your video, select a save location, and click on **Save**. FCPX begins the compression process and will spit out a QuickTime movie file with just the roles you chose.

There's more...

Deactivating entire roles

In this exercise, we selectively turned off a subrole, which exists within a role. But what if we just wanted to deactivate an entire role, such as **Music**, in its entirety?

In the **Roles** tab in the Export Media window, hover over the role you want to remove from the export. A – (minus) sign button will appear to the right of it. Click on the button and the role will disappear. Follow through with the rest of the Export process and that's it!

See also

If you don't know what the best option is for the **Video Codec** settings, read the *Exporting an archive-quality version of your film* recipe.

Sharing large files over the web with Dropbox

YouTube and other video sharing sites make it easy to share your video with an audience as large or as small as you like, but these sites are really set up for streaming your content rather than easily allowing downloads. While there are some workarounds or exceptions, sometimes you simply want to be able to shoot someone a link to your video so they press a button and voilà, your file just starts downloading to their computer.

E-mail is not a realistic option as most e-mail services have strict file size limits for attachments, usually between five to 25 MB, and you will often need to send a file that is many times that size!

The easiest solutions today are the various cloud storage services out there. We'll take a look at Dropbox, but there are additional options out there such as Google Drive, Amazon S3, box.net, SugarSync, and many, many more.

Getting ready

First off, you need to understand that you are unlikely to be able to send an uncompressed, archival quality version of your video over the web. If you chose ProRes 422 or above, or one of the Uncompressed formats talked about in the *Exporting an archive-quality version of your film* recipe, you'd be better off shipping a hard drive to your client/end viewer than trying to share it online. The files are almost always going to be too large to be practical. So if you're going to attempt this, your best bet is to make an H.264 file via either **Share | Apple Devices** menu (and selecting the **Mac and PC** option) or from **Share | Export Media** (and selecting **H.264** from the **Video codec** drop-down menu).

To complete this exercise, you'll need to download and install Dropbox from `www.dropbox. com`. It is a free cloud-based storage solution that gives you 2GB of free storage space (although you can purchase more or earn free additional space by completing certain tasks such as tweeting about the service, inviting other users, and so on).

Once you've downloaded and installed Dropbox, you will have a new folder in your home folder simply called **Dropbox** (during installation you may have selected a different location for your Dropbox folder, but for the purposes of this exercise, we'll assume the default location).

How to do it...

1. Navigate to your **Dropbox** folder and open it. Anything placed inside this folder is uploaded to the servers of Dropbox. The local copy remains as well. If you move something from inside the folder to outside of the folder, it will be removed from the servers of Dropbox. By default, the files you place in Dropbox are only accessible to you (but we'll get to sharing in a moment).

    You can also create your own folders within the **Dropbox** folder.

2. Right-click in the empty space of the **Dropbox** folder and select **New Folder**. Call it My Oscar Winners or something along those lines:

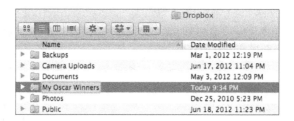

3. In a new **Finder** window (*Command + N*), navigate to the folder containing the video file you wish to share.

4. Drag the file to the **My Oscar Winners** folder. If the file was in the same drive as your **Dropbox** folder, it will move the file out of the original folder and into the **My Oscar Winners** folder. If the video file was in a different drive, it will copy it into the folder. If you want to copy a file from a folder in the same drive to **Dropbox**, hold the *Option* key while dragging and then let go of the mouse/trackpad first. This will force your Mac to duplicate the file into **Dropbox**, leaving the file in its original location as well.

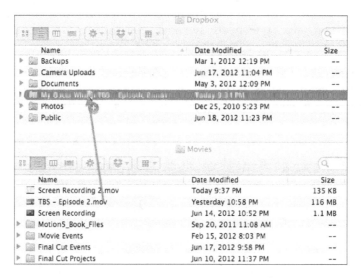

5. Look up at the menu bar at the top of the screen and click on the animated Dropbox icon. The small pop-up window will tell you how long it will take to upload the file. Although it isn't required, it's best to wait for this to finish before moving onto sharing the file in step 6.

6. When the file has finished uploading (easily indicated by the **Dropbox** icon going still and solid again), right-click on your video file and select **Dropbox | Get Link**.

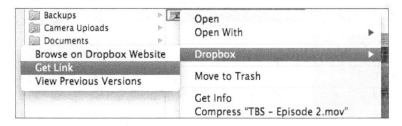

This will open up a browser window to a page offering up a direct download to your file:

7. Highlight and copy (*Command + C*) the web address from the address bar of the browser.

8. Open your e-mail application or web service and paste (*Command + V*) the link into an e-mail. The recipient of the e-mail will now have one-click access to download the file.

There's more...

Removing links

When you choose the **Get Link** command with Dropbox, a permanent link is created for that file that lives on forever. If your recipient wanted to, they could forward on the address to others to share, which you may not want. Luckily, you can kill links whenever you want. Visit the address www.dropbox.com/links and log in if necessary. The links page lists every file in your Dropbox that you've created a link for. Just click on the **Remove** button to the right of any file to destroy the link and return the file to the privacy of the rest of your Dropbox files.

Sharing your project with other applications using XML

While FCPX is a one-stop shop for just about every aspect of post-production (editing, audio sweetening, basic motion graphics, color correction, compressing, and so on), there are situations where you'll want to be able to share a work-in-progress with another application. Enter **Extensible Markup Language** (**XML**), also known as a rosetta stone format, that allows cross-platform interoperability.

A common use for this with FCPX is exporting a project to DaVinci Resolve, a high-end color grading application. While FCPX has some great color correction tools, they have their limits, whereas Resolve is an application that lives and breathes nothing but color grading and correction. Let's see how to create an XML project file in FCPX and then share it with another program, in this case Resolve.

Getting ready

If you don't own DaVinci Resolve, they make a free version called DaVinci Resolve Lite, which, to be honest, has almost as many features as the paid-for version. Download it at `www.blackmagic-design.com/products/davinciresolve`. This exercise was completed with version 8.0 of the software. If you are using a new release, the process of importing an FCPX may have changed.

How to do it...

1. If you have a project open, return to the project library by hitting *Command + 0*.

2. Select the project you want to share.
3. Select **File | Export XML...** .
4. In the resulting dialog box, pick a name and location for your XML file, and then click on **Save**.

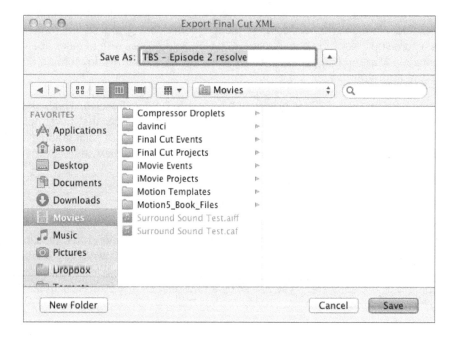

5. Quit or hide Final Cut Pro X.
6. Open DaVinci Resolve.

7. Double-click on your user. If you are just starting with Resolve, you may not have created one, which is fine. Just select the **admin** user:

The main Resolve interface appears.

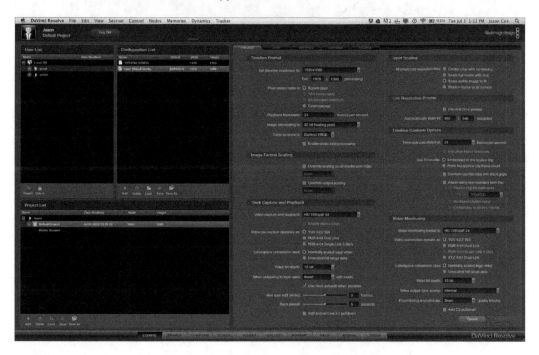

8. Click on the **CONFORM** tab at the bottom of the application interface:

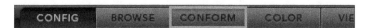

The interface changes to the **CONFORM** interface.

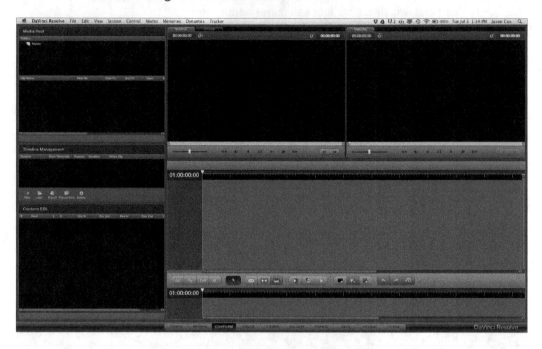

9. Click on the **Load** button on the left of the screen:

10. Find and choose your FCPX XML file and click on **Ok.** The Load XML window appears:

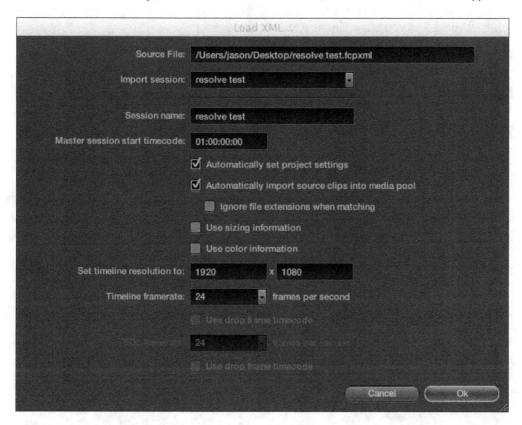

11. Click on **Ok**. If asked, find the path to your files. As they may be in multiple events, simply select the largest encompassing folder, which is likely to be your **Final Cut Events** folder as shown in the following screenshot:

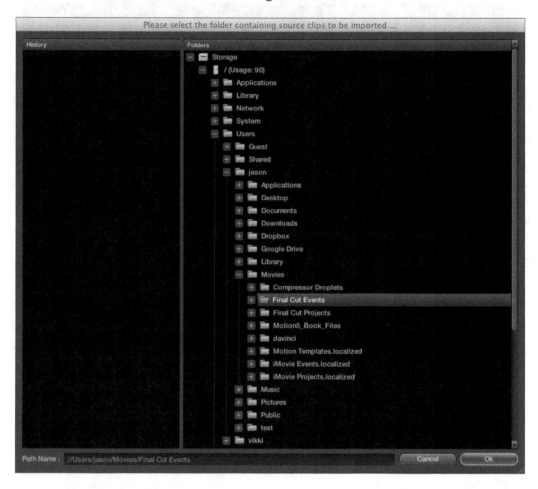

Your project has now been loaded into Resolve!

Duplicating or moving projects from one drive to another

You may or may not have completed work on a project yet, but there are a number of scenarios where you need to duplicate projects and events, sometimes to the same drive, sometimes to another. Whether it's creating multiple cuts/versions of a project or a need to move a project from your computer to an external drive to save space or take the project to another computer, all this can be accomplished from one window in FCPX.

Getting ready

If you're hoping to move a project from one hard drive to another, go ahead and plug that drive in now.

How to do it...

1. If you have a project open, return to the Project Library by hitting *Command + 0* or by clicking on the **Project Library** button in the bottom-left corner of the screen.

2. Highlight the project you want to move.

3. Choose **File | Duplicate** (*Command + D*). The **Duplicate Project** window appears:

There are three options here and a common scenario for each. Read the following three points all the way through, before picking which one is right for you.

   i. **Duplicate Project Only**: Select this option if you simply want to make a duplicate of the project file. You will most likely choose this option if you have completed a rough cut of your project and want to make a lot of other changes, but also have the prior version to fall back on, in case anything goes awry or you are unhappy with your new cut.

You have the option to change the **Location** of the project to a different drive, but when only duplicating a project, you are most likely going to keep it on the same drive the project currently resides on, as it's not moving or duplicating any media, just the project file.

ii. **Duplicate Project and Referenced Events**: You are most likely to choose this option if you are part-way through editing a project, but want to continue working on it from a different drive or computer.

Let's paint a common scenario: You've been working on a TV spot with all the media on your local hard drive. It's not totally complete, but it's getting there. Now you need to bring the project and media in on an external hard drive to the client's office so they can see it on their own computers with FCPX. Choosing **Duplicate Project and Referenced Events** does two things. One is that it moves the project file to the drive of your choice (you will likely change this option to an external or alternate drive from the current location). Another thing is that it copies every single referenced event to the drive of your choice as well. For example, if you used only one clip from an event that had 50 clips in it, the entire event will be copied to the drive. If you used clips from four different events, all the clips from all four events will be copied. This has both pros and cons. On one hand it's good because it guarantees you'll be able to continue to pull media from any of the referenced events if necessary, but remember that it'll take longer to copy and will eat up potentially a lot of hard drive space.

iii. **Duplicate Project + Used Clips Only**: The third option is most likely to be used if you are confident you are done with a project for good, but want to keep around the bare essential materials, in case you ever need to make some minor edits one day.

Again, this command does two actions: one, it moves the project file to the drive of your choice (you will likely change this option to an external drive). The second action is a bit different, however. It will pull just the media you used from all their original events and create an entirely new event on the chosen drive. This saves a lot of space and only copies the necessary elements. However, keep in mind that if you need to make any major changes down the road, this option is the most limiting, as it will leave behind any of your unused material.

When you select this option, you are given the ability to name the newly created event.

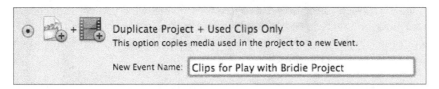

4. Choose to uncheck or keep checked the box next to **Include Render Files**.

    Every time an orange bar appears in your timeline, render files need to be created in order for your project to play back smoothly. These render files are convenient, but often eat up a lot of hard drive space. If you are archiving a project that you may never edit again, it usually makes sense to uncheck the box and leave the render files behind. The worst-case scenario is that the unrendered elements of your project may simply need to be rerendered if you ever open the project again.

    If you are mid-project, however, and have a complex timeline with a lot of completed rendering, it may make sense to keep the render files so you don't have to rerender anything once you open the project from the new drive.

5. When you've made the appropriate selections, click on **OK**. If you want, you can monitor the copying process in the **Background Tasks** window by hitting *Command + 9*. If you're just copying a project, this usually only takes seconds (or minutes with render files). But if you're copying whole events with hours of footage, go play a few rounds of *Words with Friends*.

Archiving a project for possible future editing

George Lucas supposedly once said, "A movie is never finished, only abandoned." Of course, legend has it Leonardo Da Vinci once said, "Art is never finished, only abandoned." So apparently quotes are never finished, only modified and reused. But the point is this: you truly may never feel as though your film is 100 percent complete. Or, if you do, your client may not feel that way. So even after you've exported a final cut of your film in ProRes and H.264, you might want to consider keeping around all your hard work just in case one day you have the urge or need to tweak one last transition.

The annoying part is that your finished event and project seem to stay visible in FCPX forever and ever, even if you aren't going to touch them ever again. To make matters worse, a build-up of events and projects can actually slow down FCPX's boot time! So let's hide the elements that are not needed now from FCPX's wandering eyes.

How to do it...

1. Quit Final Cut Pro X.

2. Navigate to your **Final Cut Events** and **Final Cut Projects** folder that contains the events and/or projects you want to prevent from showing up in FCPX. This might be your user's Movies folder or the root level of an external drive.

3. Switch to the list view of the **Finder** window by hitting *Command + 2* or hitting the list view button in the toolbar. This will make the next couple of steps much easier.

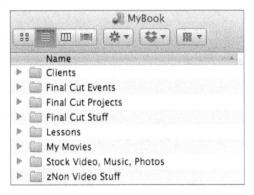

4. Create two new folders (*Command + Shift + N*), one titled `Archived Events` and one called `Archived Projects`.

5. Click on the disclosure triangles next to the **Final Cut Events** and **Final Cut Projects** folders to display their contents:

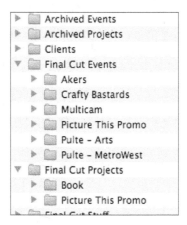

6. Drag any event folders from the **Final Cut Events** folder that you no longer wish to see in FCPX into the **Archived Events** folder:

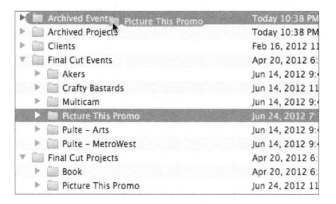

7. Drag any project folders from the **Final Cut Projects** folder that you no longer wish to see in FCPX into the **Archived Projects** folder.

    When you reopen FCPX, the moved events and projects will not appear, as FCPX only looks for them in those very specifically named folders.

    If you ever wish to bring back those events or projects, simply quit FCPX again, and move the folders back to their original location. FCPX will display them again the next time you launch!

There's more...

Deleting an event or project entirely

If you decide that you never want to look at a project or event ever again, of course you can always delete them. Simply right-click on any event or project and select **Move Event to Trash** or **Move Project to Trash**.

Conclusion

There are more exporting options than we got to cover here in this chapter. The share menu also contains options for creating image sequences, still frames, and streaming files. And for expanded exporting capabilities, consider purchasing Compressor, a companion application covered in the appendix of this book.

Have you learned every bell and whistle available inside of FCPX? Not even close! OK, well maybe close, but there's far more to learn than can be covered in even a book having 400+ pages. For the few areas we couldn't cover in depth, we hopefully provided you with enough hints and nudges in the right direction that you can explore and fill in the details.

There are tons of ways to get out of FCPX and they all begin with a simple existentialist question—where am I going? It's a question that shouldn't simply be asked at the end of the production process, but from the moment you begin. Asking yourself where you are going will help dictate many of the creative decisions one must make in the editing process, whether it be choice of sound effects, song selection, color aesthetics, or picking the right take for a piece of dialogue. While this chapter focused on the more literal interpretation of the question to help decide how to export a project, never forget to ask yourself this question all along the way.

So... where are you going?

Working with Motion and Compressor

In this appendix, we will cover:

- ► Getting acquainted with the Motion interface
- ► Enhancing title templates with Motion
- ► Creating a custom lower third
- ► Publishing a template to FCPX
- ► Publishing parameters to a template
- ► Getting acquainted with the Compressor interface
- ► Adding chapter markers in Compressor
- ► Burning a Blu-ray or DVD with chapter markers
- ► Creating your own compression preset
- ► Creating a droplet based on a preset

Introduction

When Apple released Final Cut Pro X, they let a few apps fall by the wayside, namely DVD Studio Pro, Color, and Soundtrack Pro. Once part of the entire Final Cut Studio suite, these apps were cut from the lineup to the chagrin of many long-time users, despite many (but not all) of their features being integrated into FCPX itself. Two applications that luckily survived the chopping block were Motion and Compressor.

Motion is high-end motion graphics software from Apple that gives users advanced compositing tools as well as the ability to create fantastic animated type and manipulate objects in a 3D space. Priced at $49.99 on the Mac App Store, this is one of the greatest priced software deals of all time, and that's not an exaggeration.

Compressor is compression (duh) software from Apple, allowing users to convert batches of videos into a wide variety of formats with a large palette of tinkering options to make sure you attain the exact level of quality and file size you want.

These two applications function perfectly fine on their own and are not required along with FCPX, but if you really want to harness the full capabilities of FCPX, these are fantastic extras to consider acquiring. This chapter will show just a tiny sample of what Motion and Compressor are capable of in conjunction with FCPX.

Getting acquainted with the Motion interface

Motion is an application that is incredibly deep and rich in features. Teaching its ins and outs in a chapter, let alone a whole book, is nearly impossible, but we can get your feet wet and teach you enough to make you dangerous (in a positive and creative way!). For users of past versions of Motion, the interface hasn't received quite the intense overhaul as FCPX did, but has still gotten a bit of a face lift. Let's take a look at the Motion interface before we tackle any real exercises.

Getting ready

If you haven't purchased Motion, open up the Mac App Store application and purchase it for $49.99.

How to do it...

1. Open Motion. Like FCPX, it's a big app, so it takes a few moments to get cranking. You'll be brought to the **Project Browser** window, which lets you pick from a variety of types of projects as well as presets:

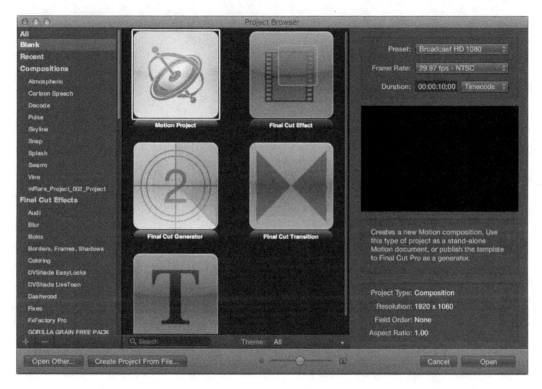

2. Make sure the **Motion Project** icon is highlighted. The presets on the right are fine for now, but if you know you want to incorporate a Motion project into an FCPX project later on, your best bet is to try and pick the preset and frame rate that matches your FCPX project.

3. Click on **Open**. The entire empty Motion interface comes into view. There are four major components to the Motion interface, in addition to a toolbar much like the one found in FCPX. Each section is highlighted in the following screenshot. (If your interface doesn't look like this screenshot, select **Window | Revert to Original Layout**.)

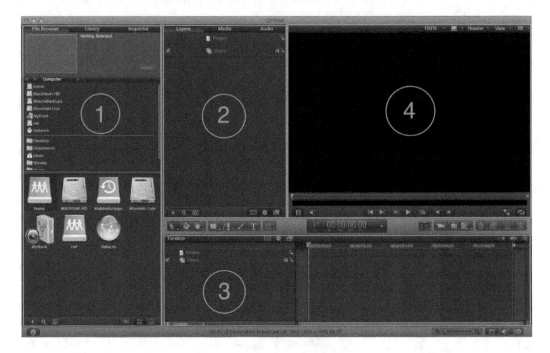

i. Section 1: This window pane consists of three major tabs, the **File Browser** (*Command + 1*), **Library** (*Command + 2*), and **Inspector** (*Command + 3*).

Bringing media into Motion differs greatly from how it is done in FCPX. Instead of having to go through an Import process, users merely have to navigate in the **File Browser** to the folder on their computer containing the media they want to use. You can then drag media right into a project, bypassing any sort of so-called importing. As convenient as this sounds, just be careful with your media management as moving or renaming items could cause Motion to lose track of them.

The **Library** tab contains virtually all of Motion's bells and whistles. While FCPX has titles, transitions, and effects, Motion has its own set of tools such as behaviors (think of preset magical keyframing techniques), replicators, particle emitters, and more.

Lastly, the **Inspector** tab is pretty much exactly the same as it is in FCPX, but be prepared to (usually) face a far greater number of parameters to tweak!

  ii. Section 2: This window pane consists of three tabs as well: **Layers** (*Command + 4*), **Media** (*Command + 5*), and **Audio** (*Command + 6*).

    The **Layers** tab will display the list of all the objects (the term Motion is used for basically all elements—pictures, clips, text, and so on) currently being used in your project. Often objects are put into groups to consolidate the view as complex motion graphic project usually have dozens upon dozens of objects to them.

    The **Media** tab shows a list of all possible media readily available for a project. It is most similar to the Event Browser in FCPX. Clips can be dragged into this window without having to be added directly to a project first.

    The **Audio** tab functions fairly similarly to the **Media** tab, but for audio only. It also gives some basic controls over the audio properties.

  iii. Section 3: This window pane is the timeline of Motion. Most of the time is spent in the standard timeline view (*Command + 7*), although you can also hide and show timelines strictly for keyframes (*Command + 8*) and audio (*Command + 9*) .

  iv. Section 4: This window is the Viewer and has the same function as the Viewer in FCPX. The one thing to be careful about with this Viewer window is the Zoom level. When starting a new project, it always defaults to 100 percent, which is not what you usually want as your will unlikely be able to fit all the pixels within the Viewer at full size.

4. Click on the **Viewer Scale** button above the Viewer and choose **Fit to Window**. You can also do this with *Shift + Z*, identical to the command in FCPX:

Enhancing title templates with Motion

FCPX comes with dozens of text templates built right in. As we learned about in *Chapter 7, Titles, Transitions, and Generators,* many of these templates have a number of parameters and qualities that can be tweaked, but all of them have their limits. Motion will help us take those limits and make them nearly limitless.

Getting ready

Although not absolutely essential, it's a good idea to read the previous *Getting acquainted with Motion's interface* recipe, if you are new to the program.

How to do it...

1. In FCPX, open your Titles browser and browse to the **Bumper/Opener** category:

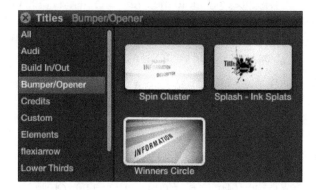

2. Edit the title **Winners Circle** into your timeline (if it is the first clip you are placing in a timeline and are prompted to choose **Video Properties**, simply accept the defaults by clicking on **OK**. If you know you have specific settings in mind, feel free to adjust the settings here.)

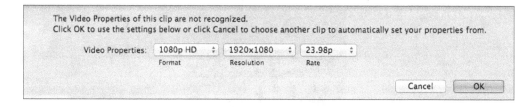

3. Click on the clip in the timeline, open the Inspector (*Command + 4*), and click on the **Title** tab at the top. As you can see, the only available parameters to tweak are the lines of text in the text animation:

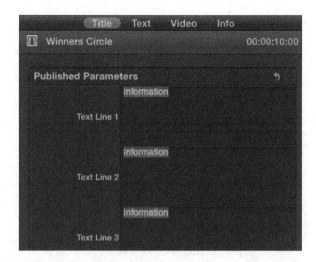

4. We can hop over to the **Text** tab to change the basic and style font attributes, but we don't have any options to customize the background of the title, for example. Let's say we like the sunrays, but we wish they were green and white instead of orange and white.

5. Right-click on the original **Winners Circle** title clip in the Titles browser (not your timeline) and choose **Open a copy in Motion**:

Motion will launch and after a few moments, you will see the interface of the program appear:

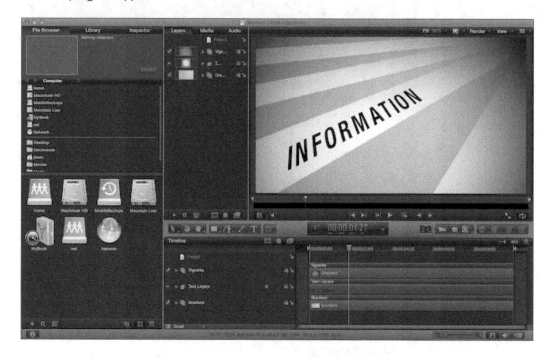

Virtually every title, transition, and effect in FCPX was originally built in Motion. When we send a copy of one of these items to Motion, we get to modify the actual project file! Don't get overwhelmed by what you see here. We are going to make one simple modification without having to understand Motion's entire interface!

6. In the bottom portion of the window, we have the **Timeline** pane. This is the timeline in Motion, although it obviously looks a bit different than the timeline in FCPX. Because motion graphic projects can be very complex and made of dozens or sometimes hundreds of objects, these objects are usually organized into groups.

Click on the disclosure triangle next to the word **Gradient** to see what's inside the group called **Gradient**:

We see one object called **Gradient**. This is the object we want to modify to change the orange sunrays.

7. Click on the **Gradient** object to highlight it:

8. In the upper-left corner of the screen, click on the tab labeled **Inspector**. This is a much more in-depth version of the similarly titled tab in FCPX:

In the list of parameters, we see the Gradient editor, currently with a rather orange setting.

9. Click on the orange color tag on the bottom right of the Gradient editor to select it:

10. Click on the disclosure triangle next to the **Color** parameter, located just below the Gradient editor. A color palette will appear, allowing you to select from a wide range of colors. As you do so, you will get an instant update about the color change in Viewer in Motion.

11. Move your cursor towards some hue of green and click on it to select it:

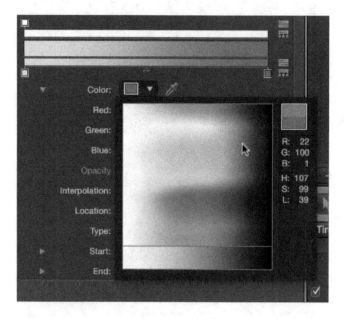

Your Viewer updates immediately with the new color selection:

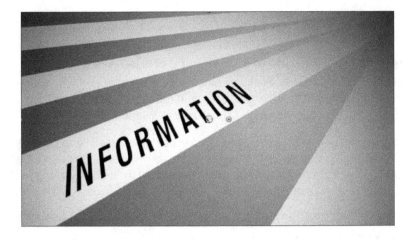

12. Choose **File | Save** (by pressing *Command + S*) and return to Final Cut Pro X.

13. If it is closed, reopen your Titles browser and re-select the **Bumper/Opener** category. You will now see a new title clip called **Winners Circle Copy** with the green sunrays:

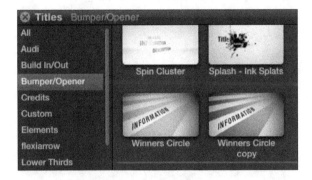

14. Use the title clip as you would any other in any project from now on.

How it works...

Almost all of FCPX's titles, transitions, and effects were made with Motion, and if you have purchased Motion, Apple essentially let's you play with copies of the original project files to tweak each one to look exactly the way you want. Of course, we took one very simple example here, but far more sophisticated changes can be made—if you know the ins and outs of Motion.

There's more...

Changing the title clip name in the Titles browser

Unfortunately, FCPX automatically gives any modified title the original name with the word **Copy** after it. Luckily, this can be changed, but not in the most obvious way. Let's say we wanted to change our new title, **Winners Circle Copy** to **Winners Circle – Green**.

Close FCPX. Open a **Finder** window and go to your user's Home folder. From there, go to **Movies | Motion Templates | Titles | Bumper/Opener**. Inside you will see a folder called **Winners Circle copy**. Rename that folder **Winners Circle – Green** and inside that folder, rename the Motion project file the exact same thing (make sure you keep the .moti on the end):

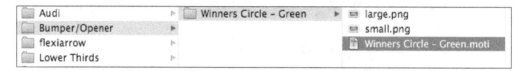

When you re-open FCPX, you should see the newly named title:

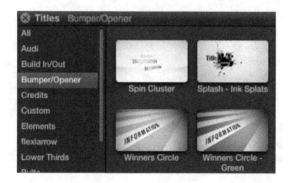

Creating a custom Lower Third

FCPX has plenty of great built-in templates for Lower Thirds, but for higher-end projects and clients, you might need or want to create something a little more original and less recognizable. The relationship between Motion and FCPX makes this easy and even a bit fun. We'll design a simple Lower Third with a few elements in this recipe, and then show how to get the title to appear directly in FCPX as a reusable, editable template.

How to do it...

1. Open Motion.

2. From the **Template Chooser** window, click on the **Final Cut Title** icon. If you like, modify the options in the upper-right corner to fit your needs. We'll keep them as is.

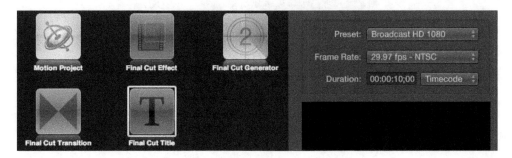

3. Click on **Open**. We are brought to the Motion interface with a few items already in the timeline. These are merely placeholders:

In fact, in the timeline we see what looks like a title box of some sort, but we don't see it in the Viewer. This is because the Viewer is set to **100%** scale and we are not actually seeing the entire frame.

4. Click on the Viewer scale button above the Viewer and set it to **Fit In Window**:

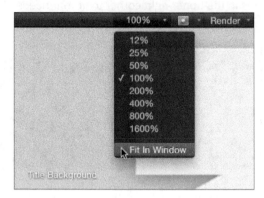

Now we can see the entire frame as well as the placeholder textbox.

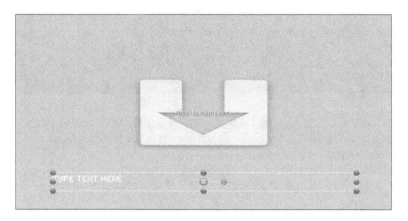

5. Double-click on the textbox (where it says **TYPE TEXT HERE**). Write in **FIRST LAST**, hit *Return*, and type **DESCRIPTION**:

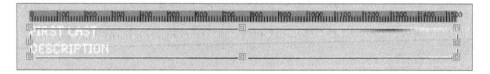

6. Double-click on the word **DESCRIPTION** and hit *Command + 3* to open the Inspector. A long list of parameters will appear on the left of the screen. We could spend all day in here, but we'll keep it simple.

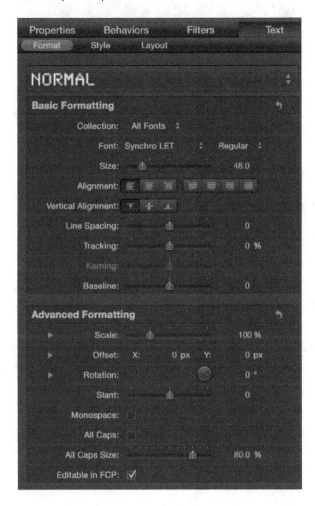

7. Pick a new font and size of your choice. We chose Strenuous at size **70**.

8. Click the **Style** tab and choose a new color for the **Face** parameter. We chose bright green.

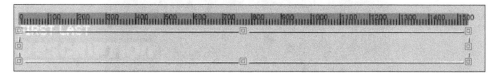

9. Back in the Viewer, highlight the entire **FIRST LAST** text line and make changes of your choosing to the text in the Inspector. We chose the Misadventures font at size **80** in a bright blue color.

10. Hit *Escape* to exit the text edit mode. The textbox itself should still be highlighted.

11. In the Inspector, click on the **Right Alignment** button to right side align the textbox:

The textbox will immediately align to the right:

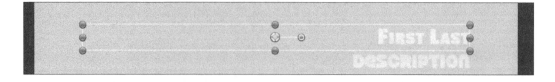

12. Click-and-drag the textbox anywhere you want on the screen. We'll drag it up a bit to make sure it fits within a title safe area for broadcast.

13. Hit *R* to turn on the Rectangle tool:

14. Click-and-drag in your Viewer to create a rectangle shape that stretches across the lower third of your screen. Do not be worried that it covers up your text. We'll fix that shortly.

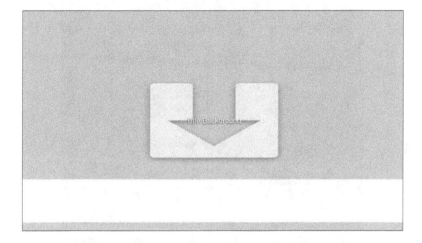

15. Choose **Object | Send Backward** (or hit *Command + [*). The white rectangle should now be below the text:

Let's enhance the look of this Lower Third just a bit more by adding some transparency and a bit of movement by having the text animate in.

16. In the Inspector, drop the **Opacity** down to **50%**.

17. Click once on the **TYPE TEXT HERE** object in the timeline to highlight it.

18. Hit *Command + 2* to bring up your **Library** tab.

19. Click on **Behaviors** in the left side list and then **Text Sequence** in the right side list. More folders will appear underneath:

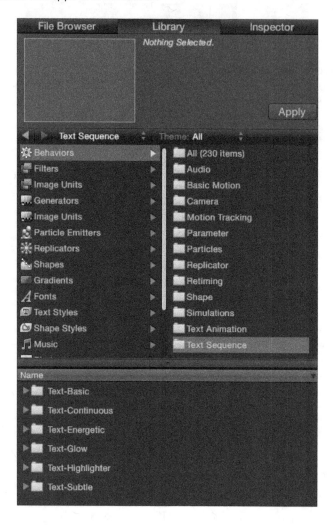

20. Click on the disclosure triangle next to the folder **Text-Energetic**.

21. Highlight **Blast In**, watch the preview in the upper part of the window, and click on the **Apply** button:

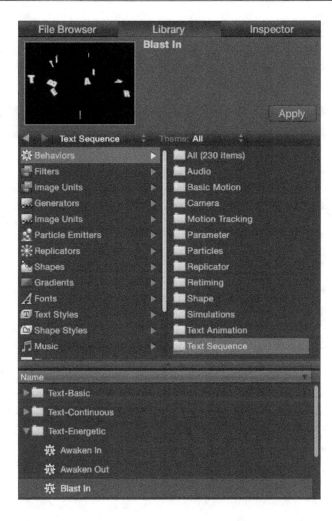

22. Click on the play button underneath the Viewer to play your newly added text animation.

23. Read the next recipe to learn how to properly save this title as a title template accessible right in FCPX!

There's more...

The Title Background box

As you may have noticed, we ignored the grey **Title Background** placeholder in this exercise. While you can drop in an image to see how your title may appear on top of a particular clip or image, you can also simply choose to ignore its existence and it will not show up once we access the title template in FCPX.

See also

The next recipe is sort of a must, as it explains the proper steps on how to save this new lower third so it appears in your Titles browser in FCPX.

Publishing a template to FCPX

In the previous recipe, we've created our custom lower third, one that we plan to reuse many times in future projects, perhaps for a video series we are creating. While we could export a video file of this title, the problem is that it would lock in the actual words we have now (**FIRST LAST** and **DESCRIPTION**), so that's obviously a no-go. Instead we will publish this project as a template to FCPX so it shows up in our Titles browser so we can reuse it forever and change the text on a case-by-case scenario.

Getting ready

We're picking up right where we left off in the previous recipe.

How to do it...

1. Go to **File | Save**. (by pressing *Command + S*). The window that pops up is not a traditional save window. This is because when we first started the project from the **Template Chooser**, we chose a very specific type of file, a Final Cut title. So Motion is immediately trying to save this directly as an FCPX title template.

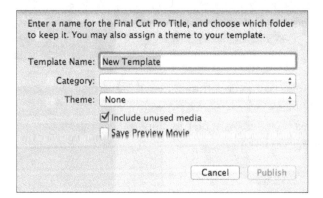

2. Give the template a name. We'll call it `Blue Green Lower 3rd`.
3. Under **Category**, select **New Category...** and type `My Lower Thirds` and click on **Create**.
4. Leave **Theme** to **None** for now.

5. Put a checkmark next to **Save Preview Movie**:

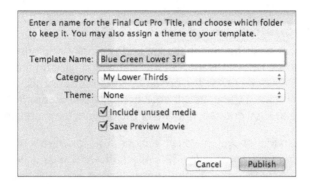

6. Click on **Publish**. Motion takes a moment to process its task.

7. Quit Motion and open up FCPX.

8. Open your Titles browser and click on the new **My Lower Thirds** category. You will see your **Blue Green Lower 3rd** appear:

9. Click-and-drag the title on top of any clip you like, most likely, a speaker shot.

10. Make sure the title clip is highlighted in the timeline and double-click on the text to edit it and replace the placeholder text.

In our example, these default colors are a pretty awful choice for this shot. Don't forget you can adjust font color in the Inspector under the **Text** tab.

There's more...

Modifying your custom template

If you decide somewhere down the line that you need to modify your original template, there are multiple ways to do so. One of the easiest ways is to right-click on the title template in the Titles browser in FCPX and choose the option **Open in Motion**. This will open the original project file and let you make any changes. It does not say **Open a copy in Motion** like before because this is a template you created, not one of the original templates that came with FCPX.

After making changes in Motion, you have two options. You can save it normally to immediately update your title template in FCPX. Alternatively, you can choose **Save As**, which will take you through the template publishing process again. You might want to do this if you wanted to keep the original text template and have a second, slightly altered template.

For example, with the lower third we created, perhaps we wanted a second version with a logo. We could open the original template in Motion, drop in a logo, choose **File | Save As**, and name the new **Blue Green Lower 3rd Logo** template. When you returned to FCPX, you'd have both versions of the lower third to select from!

See also

Read the next recipe to learn how to make it even easier to modify elements of your new lower third without having to go back to Motion!

Publishing parameters to a template

In the previous exercise, we mentioned how easy it was to go back and re-edit a template by sending it back to Motion, making your changes, and simply clicking on **Save**. You can also choose **Save As** to create a second template with your alterations, leaving the first untouched. But the former option can be time-consuming and the second can create clutter! What other possible alternative is there?

What if we could publish certain parameters of our lower third from Motion to FCPX so we didn't have to hop back and forth between the two programs at all?

In this exercise, we'll go back to our **Blue Green Lower 3rd** project file and publish a parameter for the white banner box behind the text, so we can change its color to whatever we want in FCPX!

Getting ready

This exercise assumes you've created the lower third from the previous two exercises.

How to do it...

1. In FCPX, find the **Blue Green Lower 3rd** title in the Titles browser.

2. Right-click on it and choose **Open in Motion**:

The original project is loaded into Motion.

3. In the **Layers** tab or the timeline, click on the **Rectangle** object to highlight it:

4. Press *Command + 3* to open the **Inspector** tab.

5. Hover your mouse over the **Fill Color** parameter and notice a disclosure triangle appear on the far right side. This is the **Animation** menu.

6. Click on it and choose **Publish**:

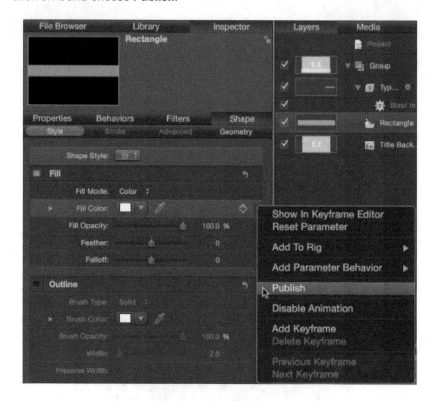

What we have done here is tell Motion to send this editable parameter along for the ride, when the template is published to FCPX (or in this case, when the template is updated for FCPX).

But before saving it, we're going to make one more tweak to make sure this parameter is properly labeled.

7. Back in the **Layers** tab or **Timeline**, click on the object at the top labeled **Project**. This lets us see and modify properties for the overall project in the **Inspector**:

8. Back in the **Inspector**, click on the **Project** tab and then on the **Publishing** tab below it, if these are not already selected. You should see the label **Published Parameters**, with the **Fill Color** parameter below it:

9. Double-click on the words **Fill Color** and type Banner Color followed by *Return*:

This step is totally optional as we are unlikely to get confused as we are only publishing one parameter. But as you may be beginning to realize, you can publish tons and tons of parameters, and it can be a very good idea to rename them to avoid confusion in more complicated projects.

10. Hit *Command + S* to save and return to FCPX.

11. In the Titles browser, find the **Blue Green Lower 3rd** title and add it to a new clip.

12. Highlight it, open your Inspector, and click on the **Title** tab. Your published **Banner Color** parameter will be visible.

13. Click on the disclosure triangle or on the color chip to pick a color of your choice. The background banner will update accordingly. You can now reuse this title clip over and over and choose a different color for the banner background every time.

There's more...

Replacing existing titles in the timeline with modified ones

Perhaps you've already laid down a bunch of titles in your timeline and decide afterwards that you want to make a slight change to the title. You do not have to go and delete every title and start over. Simply follow the steps in the previous couple of exercises to make any of the changes you want in Motion. When you save and return to FCPX, take the updated title clip from the Titles browser and drag-and-drop it right on top of the original title clip in the timeline. You will be given a list of replacement options. You might need to make a judgment call here depending on what sort of change you made, but generally choosing **Replace from Start** is the safest option. FCPX should keep whatever text you had typed into the original title clip while also showing whatever aesthetic changes were made to the new one, so there's no need to retype everything!

Getting acquainted with the Compressor interface

Compressor is built for one task—compressing. Obviously, there's a bit more to it than that with enough compression variables to make your eyes roll into the back of your head, but let's get a good peek at the body before getting under the hood.

Getting ready

If you haven't purchased Compressor, open up your Mac App Store application and purchase it for $49.99.

How to do it...

1. In FCPX, open a project that you are 100 percent satisfied with and is ready for completion.

2. Choose **Share | Send to Compressor** to open Compressor. The interface is split up into five major areas, each highlighted in the following diagram. (If your screen doesn't look similar to the one in the following screenshot, choose **Window | Layouts** and then pick the **Standard** setting with a resolution closest to the resolution of your monitor.)

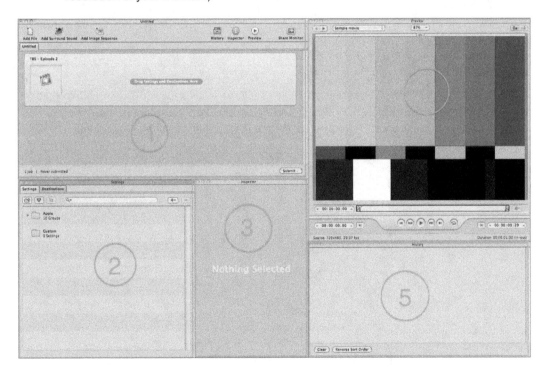

   i.   Section 1: This is your **Batch** window. It contains a list of jobs. In the previous image, the one item labeled **TBS – Episode 2** is the job. In this case, the job at hand is the project we just sent over from FCPX. Compressor can operate totally independently from FCPX, allowing users to drag-and-drop any video files from **Finder** right into this part of the interface to create jobs, but for these exercises we'll create the job based upon our work in FCPX.

    ii. Section 2: This is the **Settings** window. Here is where we can browse all the presets in Compressor, including ones we'll make ourselves in a later exercise. When you find a setting you want to use, simply drag-and-drop it on top of the job in the batch window. You can also click on the **Destinations** tab to select a destination for a job.

    iii. Section 3: This is the **Inspector** window. Although it is very different from Inspector windows in both FCPX and Motion, the concept remains the same. This window allows you to finely tune the details of your compression settings for a job. When you first send a project to Compressor, it will likely display **Nothing Selected**.

3.   Click on the one job in the batch window:

The **Inspector** window now displays some options and information about the job you've highlighted. We'll go over these in a bit more detail in later exercises:

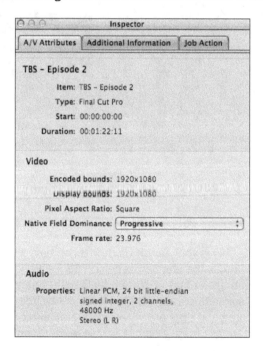

i. Section 4: This is the **Preview** window. It functions similarly to the Viewers in FCPX and Motion. As we highlighted a job in the batch window, the preview now displays our FCPX project. The Preview window will let us add chapter markers (which we will do in the next recipe) and preview how our video will look using different presets.

ii. Section 5: This is the **History** window. It displays a log of all exports for a particular batch. This can be handy in large projects where you may want to re-export a particular job with slightly different settings.

Adding chapter markers in Compressor

While burning projects to DVDs and Blu-rays is slowly but surely becoming a thing of the past, there are still plenty of situations that necessitate burning a movie to optical media. The good news is that FCPX has the ability to burn such discs built right into the software. The bad news is that there are no controls to add chapter markers, and so a project must be sent to Compressor in order to make them. Once you've done so, you can burn your disc directly in Compressor, chapter markers, and so on.

Getting ready

Simply open a project of yours that is 100 percent complete and ready to burn.

How to do it...

1. In FCPX, choose **Share | Send to Compressor**. Compressor opens.

2. Click on the job in the batch window that you just sent over from FCPX:

Over in the preview window, your video will appear. Take note of the playhead indicated by the green triangle at the beginning of the scrubber area:

3. Click-and-drag the playhead to the right to the location where you want your second chapter to begin. By default, the first chapter always begins at the beginning of your movie so there is no need to place a marker there.

4. Click on the marker pop-up box to the right of the scrubber area and choose **Add marker**, or simply hit *M* on your keyboard. A marker will be placed at your playhead's location:

5. Repeat the process as many times as necessary: move the playhead forward and hit *M*.

Your chapter markers are all set. Read the next recipe to learn how to choose the right settings to burn your movie to a Blu-ray or DVD disc.

There's more...

Chapter markers and third party software

If you're planning to burn a disc using third party software such as Adobe Encore, don't bother with this exercise! Adobe Encore has its own chapter marker creation process, so you would just add your chapter markers within that program after importing your video file. Roxio Toast can read chapter markers of Compressor, but with varying degrees of success, so it's also better to create your markers directly in the software you plan to use to burn your disc.

Chapter markers without Compressor

If you really need to add chapter markers to a project but you don't want to shell out $50 on Compressor, check out a program called Metadata Hootenanny. It may have a wacky name, but it's a great, free utility to add chapter markers to any QuickTime movie file. With it, you would export a standard QuickTime movie file out of FCPX (read the *Chapter 10, Getting Your Project Out of FCPX*) and drag it into Metadata Hootenanny to add chapter markers. From there, you could take the QuickTime file into iDVD and DVD Studio Pro and the chapter markers will carry over.

Burning a Blu-ray or DVD with chapter markers

Our video has been exported to Compressor and the chapter markers have been set in place. The last piece of the puzzle is learning how to tell Compressor to take our FCPX timeline and burn it to a disc of our choosing—DVD or Blu-ray.

Getting ready

No factory-issued Mac comes with a Blu-ray drive of any sort. You can get them installed with a bit of hassle, or, much easier, you can buy yourself an external unit for about $100. Either way, you've got to get your hands on one!

As for burning DVDs, Apple is slowly cutting the SuperDrive from their computer lineup, so if you don't have one, you can buy their external SuperDrive for $80 at any Apple Store or online. Most third party drives work as well, but the Apple one sure is tiny and pretty!

How to do it...

1. If you haven't done so already, open your project in FCPX and choose **Share | Send to Compressor**. If you're picking up from where we left off in the previous recipe, ignore this step!

2. In the **Settings** window, click on the disclosure triangle next to the folder labeled **Apple**. More folders appear inside:

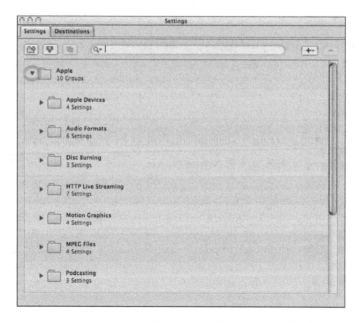

3. Drag the entire **Disc Burning** folder up into your batch window and drop it on top of your job (in the following screenshot, we dropped it on top of **TBS – Episode 2**):

Three lines, called **targets** in Compressor, appear on our job. The one labeled **Dolby Digital Professional** is the compression setting for our audio. The **H.264 for Blu-ray** is, unsurprisingly, the compression setting for Blu-ray video and the **MPEG-2 for DVD** is for burning to DVD.

 Most of the time, video and audio are merged into one target, but the world of DVDs and Blu-rays works a bit different than normal digital movie files on computers.

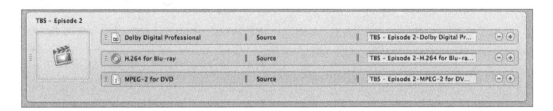

In reality, you're probably burning to just Blu-ray or DVD, but not both. So let's get rid of the extraneous option. In our case, we want to burn a Blu-ray disc, so we'll delete the DVD option.

4. Click on **MPEG-2 for DVD** and hit *Delete*. The target disappears:

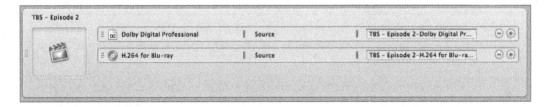

5. Click on the **Destinations** tab in the **Settings** window and then on the disclosure triangle next to the **Apple** folder:

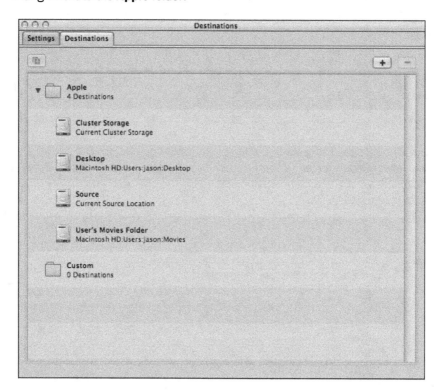

6. Drag the **Desktop** destination onto each of the two targets:

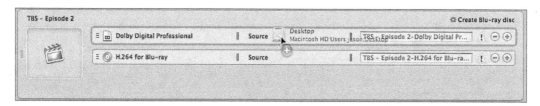

This tells Compressor where to create the two files. You can pick a different location, but we used the **Desktop** for ease.

7. Click somewhere in the empty space of the job to ensure it's highlighted. You'll know you've successfully highlighted the entire job if the whole item in the batch window turns blue-gray:

8. In the **Inspector**, click on the **Job Action** tab and choose **Create Blu-ray Disc** from the drop-down menu (or **Create DVD** if that's what you're choosing to burn). A series of preferences will appear:

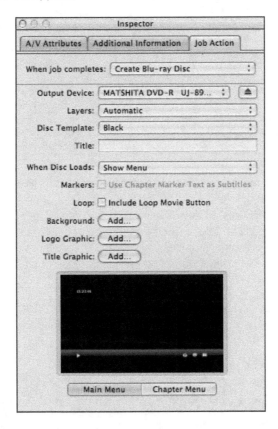

9. If you have a Blu-ray burner, make sure it is selected in the **Output Device** drop-down menu. If you do not have a Blu-ray burner, you can choose the **Hard Drive (Blu-ray)** option to create a disc image file that can be taken to another computer with a Blu-ray burner to burn at a later time.

10. Select a **Disc Template** from the drop-down menu and choose from the rest of the rather self-explanatory options.

11. When you are done selecting your disc burning options, click on **Submit** in the lower-right corner of the batch window. Click on **Submit** again in the second dialog box that pops up (more on that in the *More Info* section):

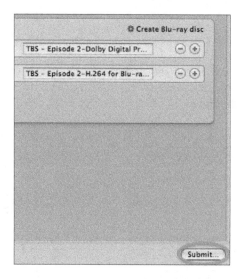

Compressor begins the task of compressing the video for Blu-ray and when it is done, it will prompt you to insert a blank disc if you have not done so already. If you choose the **Hard Drive (Blu-ray)** option, it will create the disc image. Once you submit the batch, this process can take a wildly varied time depending on the length of your movie and your computer's processing power. Compressor will do its best to give you an estimated wait time, but it's rarely accurate, so don't hold your breath!

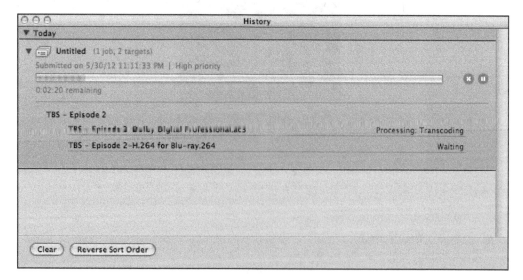

Why did we click on Submit twice?

This exercise glossed over what the dialog box was all about after clicking on **Submit** the first time in step 9. The **Name** field lets us optionally name the batch in case we're going to be submitting many batches for compression and we want to easily keep tabs on all of them. The **Cluster** option is well beyond the scope of this book, but has to do with distributed processing, that is, the ability to split the batch up into chunks that will be processed on multiple networked machines to speed up the workflow. Finally, the **Priority** option let's us set a priority level for the batch (that is how much processing power it will throw at the batch):

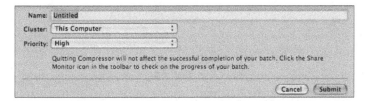

Creating your own Compression preset

Compressor comes with more than 40 compression presets for the most common scenarios, but sometimes 40 just isn't enough! Compressor lets you custom design your own preset if you have special circumstances for how you need to compress or convert a video.

1. Open Compressor. When a window pops up asking you to **Choose a template for your batch**, click on **Cancel** as the whole point of this exercise is to start from scratch!

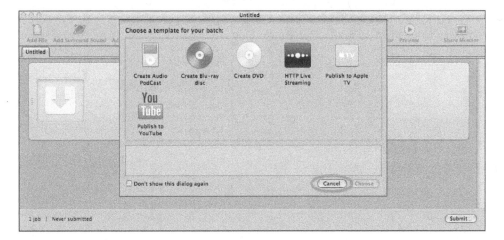

2. In the **Settings** window search box, type `image`. Only two options appear, **Open EXR Image Sequence** and **TIFF Image Sequence**:

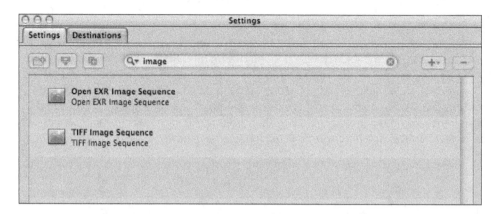

Well, let's say what we actually want is a JPEG image sequence at 50 percent scale of our source material. At first, it doesn't appear to be an option.

3. Click on the close button on the right of the search box to cancel out the search and return all of the options:

4. Click on the **+** button drop-down menu to the right of the search box and choose **Image Sequence**:

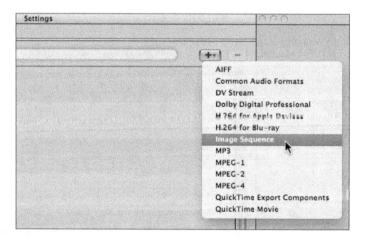

A new preset appears in the **Custom** folder under the **Settings** tab:

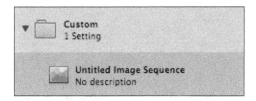

5. In the **Inspector**, rename the preset **JPEG Image Sequence 50%**. You can optionally put in a description.

6. In the **Image Type** drop-down menu, choose **JPEG**:

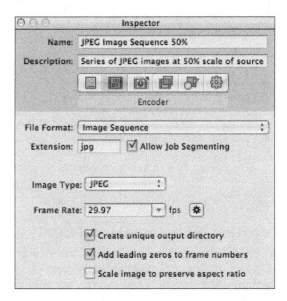

7. To ensure the smoothest, cleanest still images, click on the cogwheel button to the right of **Frame Rate**. This will export the appropriate number of images per second, no matter the frame rate of your source material.

8. Click on the **Geometry** button in the Inspector window:

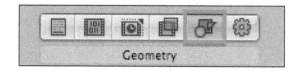

9. In the **Frame Size** drop-down menu, select **50% of source**:

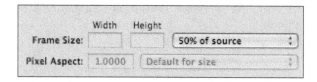

10. Click on the **Save** button at the bottom.

How it works...

Now that we have created a custom preset, it will always appear in the **Settings** tab and be available for any project we send over from FCPX or for any video file at all that we drag into Compressor.

There's more...

Quick access to custom built presets in FCPX

If you have a project in FCPX that you want to be able apply this new preset to, you don't have to even open Compressor to do so! After creating the preset, open a project in FCPX and go to **Share | Export Using Compressor Settings**. A new window will appear that lets you choose from any of Compressor's presets, including your new custom-made one!

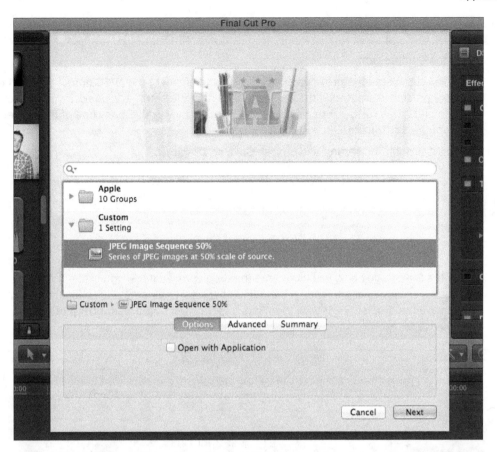

Creating a droplet based on a preset

Apple is all about efficiency, and that is very clearly exemplified with the invention of droplets. In Compressor, we can make droplets out of any preset (built by Apple or ourselves). A **droplet** is a user-created, mini application that can be saved to any folder on our computer. Then, in **Finder**, all you have to do is drop a video file of your choice on top of the **Droplet** icon and voila! It will create a new video file based upon the compression settings of the droplet—Compressor never even opens!

Getting ready

We'll carry on from the last exercise, although you can start from scratch.

How to do it...

1. Open Compressor.

2. If you completed the previous exercise, find and highlight the **JPEG Image Sequence 50%** preset we created in the **Settings** tab within the settings window. If you did not complete the previous exercise, you may choose and highlight any one of the presets from the **Settings** tab.

   Right-click on the setting and choose **Save as Droplet...**:

3. In the **Save** dialog box, you can name the droplet to whatever you like, although it usually makes sense to keep it the same as the setting name. Pick a location where to save the droplet. We'll save them in a folder called **Compressor Droplets** in our **Movies** folder:

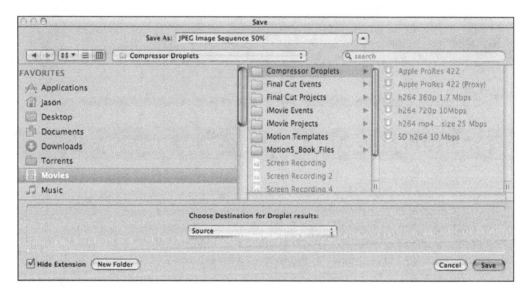

4. Quit Compressor (by pressing *Command + Q*).

5. In **Finder**, navigate to where you saved your new droplet.

6. In a second **Finder** window (easily created by either double-clicking on Macintosh HD or by hitting *Command + N*), navigate to a folder that contains a video file you want to compress to the droplets' settings:

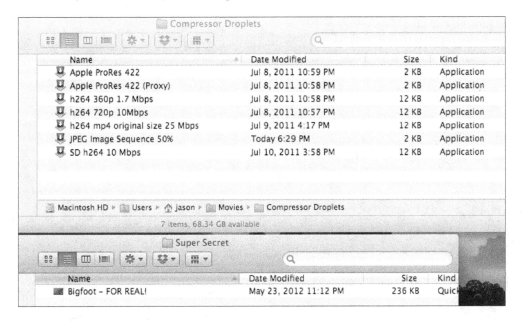

7. Drag-and-drop the video file on top of the droplet:

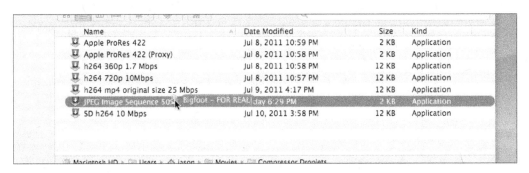

An application simply titled **Droplet** opens and a window appears. Here we can adjust a couple of last-minute options:

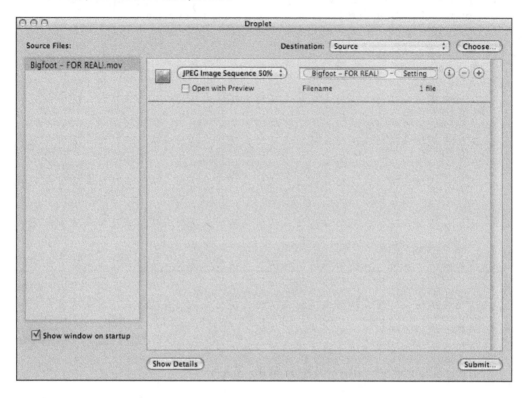

8. The default **Destination** is set to **Source** (meaning the location of the source media) but you can change this if you like.

    Most interesting to note, however, is the **+** button which lets us add additional presets to our video. For example, if we wanted to, not only could we create our JPEG image sequence, we could hit the **+** button and tell the Droplet to upload a version to YouTube as well!

9. Click on **Submit**. When the additional menu pops up, click on **Submit** again (there's more info on this window in the previous recipe).

   The compression process begins. The file appears almost immediately, but may take a while to fully finish compressing, depending on the preset. An image sequence generally does not take very long to create. Check out the *There's more...* section on how to observe the progress of the droplet.

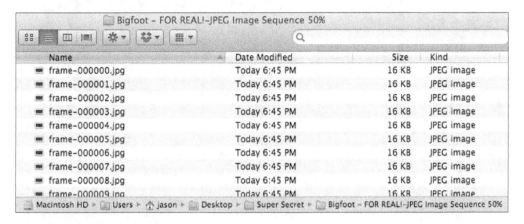

There's more...

Checking progress of a droplet

Unfortunately, after clicking on **Submit** within a droplet, the window just disappears and you're left to guess how long the process will take. However, there is a slightly hidden application that let's you view the progress of the droplet.

Open Compressor and in the batch window, click on the button that says **Share Monitor**:

This small application displays a progress list of all batches sent off for compression whether it was from inside Compressor or from a droplet:

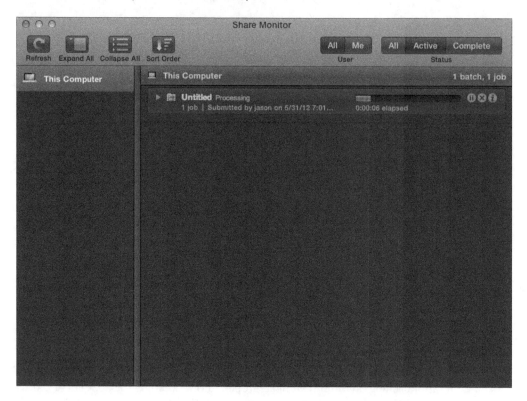

The application is normally hard to find because it is stored inside the Compressor application. The trick here is to add this application to your dock so you can access it easily at any time. After opening it once, right-click on the icon in the dock and choose **Options | Keep in Dock**. Now the application will always be in your dock for easy access!

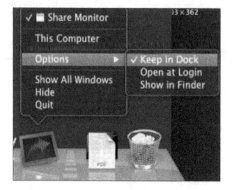

Index

Symbols

7toX 26

A

actor 49
Add a keyframe button 278, 289
Add button 348
Add Color Mask button 328
Add Keyframe button 336
Add Rule pop-up menu 50
Add Shape Mask button 331
Add to iTunes 344
Advanced tab 345, 353
Aged Film effect 178, 179
AJAX
  URL 55
alpha 186
Amount slider 170
Analyze and Fix command 41
Anchor parameter 261
Append button 70
Apple devices
  exporting for 343-346
Apple Store
  URL 52
Apply button 398
Apply Match 300
Archived Projects folder 378
archive-quality version
  of film, exporting 340-343
artist 42
audio
  and video trimming separately,
      with J cut 112, 113
  and video trimming separately,
      with L cut 112, 113
  bad audio, replacing with cleaner
      recording 151-153
  edit, changing 114
  or video, editing 73
audio and video
  relinking, after detaching 168
  unlinking 166, 167
Audio (Cmd+6) tab 385
Audio (Cmd+9) tab 385
audio effects
  from logic 171
Audio Inspector tab 160, 165
audio meters 142-145
Audio tab 145, 152, 385
audition
  about 120-122
  Duplicate as Audition (Option + Y) 123
  multiple shots or takes 120-122
  with connected clips 122
auto audio enhancements
  using 169-171

B

Background Noise Removal 170
Background option 353
Backgrounds category 196
backtimed three-point edit 108
bad audio
  replacing, with cleaner recording 151-153
basic attributes 224
Batch window, compressor interface 407
beat
  editing in 123-125

Bezier handles
motion paths, customizing 287-292
bin 42
bit rate 346
Black Magic Design
URL 55
Black & White effect 177, 180
blade tool
blade without 86
b-roll, adding 85
used, for splicing clips 83-85
blend modes 233
Bloom transition 209
Blue Microphones
URL 173
Blu-Ray
burning 350-354
burning, with chapter markers 412-416
blurs
animating, with keyframes 192
Broadcast Safe effect 316, 317
broadcast safe monitor 55-57
Bumper/Opener category 386

C

camera archive 9
Camera Import window 9
Cast effect 307
channel
turning off 164
chapter markers
and third party software 411
Blu-ray, burning 412-416
DVD, burning 412-416
submit, hitting twice 417
without compressor 411
cleaner recording
bad audio, replacing with 151-153
clips
adding, on compound clip creation 241
adding, to secondary storyline 111, 112
appending, to storyline 70-72
backtiming, in timeline 126
connected clips, auditioning with 122
connected clips, creating 77, 78
connected clips, repositioning 79

cropping 263-267
deleting, and magnetic timeline 77
deleting, magnetic timeline used 77
gap clips, creating 101-103
grouping together, as compound clip 114-117
inserting, to storyline 70-72
labeling, with roles 354-358
length, adjusting 148
moving in sync, with compound
clips 280-283
multiple clips, volume changing at once 145
names, batch changing 60-63
overwriting, to storyline 70-72
panning, Ken Burns effect used 267-270
playing, backwards 250
rearranging 77, 78
replacing 79-81
segment, removing with range select tool 86
silent start 153
splicing, with blade tool 83-85
transitions, adding 206-209
trimming 263-267
volume, raising by more than 12 dB 145
zooming, Ken Burns effect used 267-270
clips, FCPX
keywords, adding 42-44
keywords, applying 45
keywords, removing 45
marking, as favorites 45-49
marking, as rejected 46-49
rejected clips 49
ClipWrap
about 11
URL 10
Cluster option 417
color
and shape mask, combining 325-327
color balancing
about 297, 300
manually, with color board 301-304
color board
Color Balance, manual 301-304
color look
picking 306-310
color mask
about 317-322
Add Color Mask button 322

color preset
  adding, to multiple clips 310
color samples
  picking, throughout clip 201
Command + - 106, 145
Command + = 106
Command + 4 294
Command + D 214
Command + E 340
Command Editor window 40
Command key 31, 151
Command + Option + B 297
Command + Option + M 299
Command + T 207
Command + Z 298
compound clip
  clips, adding on creation 241
  clips, grouping together as 114-117
  clips, moving in sync 280-283
  effects, applying to 117
  transforming 117
compression preset
  creating 417
  creating, steps for 417-419
compressor
  about 406
  Batch window 407
  History window 409-411
  Inspector window 408
  Preview window 409
  Settings window 408
CONFORM interface 370
connected clips
  about 15
  creating 77, 78
  markers, placing on 120
  repositioning 79
contrast
  adjusting, Luma waveform
    monitor used 311-316
Copy Files to Final Cut Events folder 31
countdowns
  creating 214-216
Counting generator 215
countries
  creating 214-216
Create Archive button 9

Create optimized media option 11
credit sequence
  creating, steps for 227-230
  extra lines, adding 231
Crop button 263, 265
crowd keyword 42
Ctrl + R 296
custom animated title
  creating, steps for 234-236

D

data
  importing, from tape-based camera 19, 20
data rate 346
decibels (dB) 143
Delete key 86
Dialogue role 355
Digital single-lens reflex. *See* **DSLR**
Dropbox
  about 363
  large files, sharing over web 363-366
  links, removing 366
  URL 363
droplets
  creating, preset based 421-425
  progress, checking 425, 426
DSLR 12
DSLR video
  importing 12
ducking your audio 145
Duplicate as Audition (Option + Y) 123
Duplicate Project and Referenced Events 375
Duplicate Project Only 374
DVD
  burning 350-354
  burning, with chapter markers 412-416

E

Earthquake transition 207
Echoes parameter 212
edges button
  flowing hair, fine-tuning 201, 202
effect
  about 175
  adding 176-178
  applying, to multiple clips 178

copying, into multiple clips 194, 195
downloading 186-189
installing 186-189
order, changing for different results 179
parameters, animating with
    keyframes 179-181
parameters, changing 176-178
pasting, into multiple clips 194, 195
Effects browser 176, 306
Effects browser section, FCPX 40
event
deleting, entirely 379
Event Browser section, FCPX
about 39
customizing 57-59
Event Library section, FCPX
about 39, 57
customizing 57, 58, 59
Events browser 177
Export drop-down menu 341
exposures
fixing, Luma waveform monitor used 311-316
Extensible Markup Language. *See* **XML**
exterior 49

F

face
blurring out 190-192
Face parameter 396
FCP7
about 29, 75
importing 26-29
FCPX
about 38
Effects browser section 40
Event Browser section 39
Event Library section 39
auto audio enhancements, using 169-171
effect 176
sound effects 154-157
template, publishing for 400, 401
Inspector section 39
keyboard, customizing 40
opening 38
Timeline section 40
Toolbar section 40
Viewer section 39

files
large files sharing over web, with Dropbox
    363-366
Fill Color parameter 405
film
archive-quality version, exporting 340-343
filmstrip view
list view 60
Filter pop-up menu 49
Filter window 50
Final Cut Pro 7 projects. *See* **FCP7**
Final Cut Pro 7 Tool. *See* **FCP7**
Final Cut Projects folder 378
Final Cut Pro X. *See* **FCPX**
Format parameter 216
Framing parameter 221
Fred 52
freeze frames
making 244-249
FXFactory 190

G

gap clips
about 101
creating, steps for 101-103
inserting, at beginning 111
GarageBand
music, importing from 14, 15
generation loss 343
Get Link command 366
GIFs
advantages 186
Global option 302
Global saturation slider 330
Global slider 302, 334
Gradient 388

H

H4n model
URL 151
H.264
transcoding 13
H.264 option 342
Hard Drive 352
Hard Drive (Blu-ray) option 415
HDMI adapter 160

Hide Sound Browser button 14
Highlights 302
History window, compressor
  interface 409-411
Hum Removal 171

I

image
  blending, with surrounding 202
  desaturating, with single color 328
  moving, by keyframing in viewer 277-279
  multiple images, selecting at once 18
  not importing, in Apple photo software 18
  wanted parts cutting, mask
    effect used 202-204
iMovie events
  importing 26
iMovie projects
  importing 24-26
Import All 7
Import button 8
Import Files window 12
Import from Camera icon 6
Import from Camera window 6, 9, 12, 13
importing
  about 5, 6
  data, from tape-based camera 19, 20
  FCP7 26-29
  from, tapeless video camera 6-8
  iMovie events 26
  iMovie projects 24-26
  layered Photoshop files 21-24
  M2T files 10, 11
  M2TS files 10, 11
  MTS files 10, 11
Import options screen 8
Import Selected 7
Insert button 71
inspector
  transitions parameters, adding 210-213
Inspector (Cmd+3) tab 384
Inspector section, FCPX 39
Inspector tab 384
Inspector window, compressor
  interface 64, 408
In Spread slider 236

instant replay
  displaying 254
  displaying, steps for 254-256
  part of clip, replaying 256
  part of clip, rewinding 256
  title clip, adding for added effect 256
interpolation
  modifying 292
interview 49
In Unit Size parameter 236
iTunes
  music, importing from 14, 15

J

J cut 112
Job Action tab 415

K

KB Covers company
  URL 42
Ken Burns effect
  and video 271
  slowing down 270
  speeding up 270
  used, for panning over photo 267-270
  used, for zooming over photo 267-270
keyboard
  marker to marker, jumping from 120
keyboard, FCPX
  customizing 40, 42
  shortcuts 45
Key Detail box 40, 41
Keyer effect
  about 196
  improving, steps for 197-201
keyframes
  about 148-150, 159
  adding 182
  animating with 157-159
  audio keyframes, deleting on clip 160
  blurs, animating 192
  effect parameters, animating with 179-181
  image, to move in viewer 277-279
  timing, changing in timeline 285-287
  used, for lowering background
    sound 148-150

keyframes (Cmd+8) tab 385
keyframing
  in surround panner 164
  shape mask 321
Keyword Editor button 42
keywords, FCPX
  adding, to clips 42, 44
  applying, to clips 45
  removing, from clips 45

L

layered Photoshop files
  importing 21-24
Layers (Cmd+4) tab 385
Layers tab 385
L cut 112
Library tab 384
Linear option 292
links, Dropbox
  removing 366
list view
  versus filmstrip view 60
Load button 370
logo
  adding, to video 182-185
  blurring out 190-192
  graphic 353
Long Shot (LS) 221
Look effect 307
low-frequency effects (LFE) 143
Ls channel 162
Luma Keyer effect 182
Luma waveform monitor
  about 311
  used, for adjusting contrast 311-316
  used, for fixing exposure 311 316

M

M2T files
  importing 10, 11
M2TS
  importing 10, 11
magnetic timeline
  about 74-77
  used, for deleting clips 77

Make Muticam Clip window 134
markers
  about 118, 119
  placing, on connected clips 120
  to marker jumping from, with keyboard 120
marker timing
  adjusting 126
mask effect
  used, to cut wanted parts of image 202-204
Mask Position parameter 192
Match Color feature
  about 297-300
  changing 300
  turning off 300
media
  optimized media 32
  organized media, working with 31, 32
  proxy media 32
Media (Cmd+5) tab 385
media files
  relinking 33
  relinking, steps for 33-35
media limit 89
Media tab 385
Medium Shot (MS) 221
metadata
  changing, steps for 60, 62, 63
Metadata Hootenanny 411
Midtones 302
M key 124
More compatibility results 345
motion
  about 382
  Audio (Cmd+6).tab 385
  audio (Cmd+9) tab 385
  File Browser (Cmd+1) tab 384
  Inspector (Cmd+3) tab 384
  keyframes (Cmd+8) tab 385
  Layers (Cmd+4) tab 385
  Library (Cmd+2) tab 384
  Media (Cmd+5) tab 385
  opening 383, 384
  path, customizing with Bezier 288-292
  path, customizing with Bezier handles 287
  standard timeline view (Cmd+7) tab 385
  title templates, enhancing with 385-391

motion path
  moving 284
Motion Project icon 383
Motion Templates folder 190
Move Playhead Position command 181
MTS
  importing 10, 11
multicam edit
  about 131-134
  effects, adding 139
  fine-tuning 137, 138
multiple clips
  color preset, adding 310
  effect, applying 178
  effect, copying into 194, 195
  effect, pasting into 194, 195
music
  importing, from GarageBand 14, 15
  importing, from iTunes 14, 15
  lowering during speakers 146, 147
  lowering, during speakers 145
Music roles 355

N

Naming Presets window 63
New Compound Clip 168
New Multicam Clip window 131

O

object
  spotlighting 333-336
online clips
  relinking 35, 36
Open in Timeline option 96
Optical Flow 296
Optical Flow algorithm 249
Option symbol 41
Option + W 111
Outside Mask button 330

P

Pan Amount slider 157
Pan Mode option 158
pan modes 164

parameters
  publishing, to template 402-405
photo
  panning, Ken Burns effect used 267-270
  zooming, Ken Burns effect used 267-270
placeholder clip
  inserting, steps for 220-223
Playback option 310
playhead
  precision, checking 73, 74
PNGs
  advantages 186
Position parameter 261
position tool 77
precision editor
  about 127-130
  rolling in 130
preset
  based, droplets creating 421-425
Preview window, compressor interface 409
primary storyline 109-111
Priority option 417
project
  archiving, for future editing 376-378
  deleting, entirely 379
  duplicating, from one drive
    to another 373-376
  moving, from one drive to another 373-376
  sharing with other applications, XML used
    367-372
Project Browser window 383
Project Library button 239, 374
ProRes 422 HQ option 341
ProRes 422 option 341
ProRes 4444 option 341
PROVANTAGE company
  URL 42
proxy clips
  editing, efficiently 64-67
PSDs
  advantages 186

Q

Q button 107

R

range selection tool
  clip segment, removing 86
  speed, changing for 249, 250
R channel 163
Record Audio window 172
Relink Files window 34
relinking
  in timeline 36
  media files 33-35
  online clips 35, 36
Replace and add to Audition command 83
Replace command 82
Replace from End 82
Replace from Start 81
Retime button 245
Retime pop-up menu button 247, 256
reusable show intro
  creating, steps for 237-240
ripple tool
  about 86-89
  clip, trimming 90
  in or out point, highlighting 90
  rippling, ways 90
Role Editor window 356
roles
  clips, labeling with 354-358
  entire roles, deactivating 362
  exporting 359-362
rolling tool
  about 91-93
  and multicam edits 94
  keyboard used 94
  timed project 94
  using, for timing issues 126
rosetta stone *See* **XML**
Rs channel 162
RT Face Obscure Effect 187, 192

S

Save Preset 310
scale parameter 288
SD video 275
secondary color correction 317

secondary storyline
  clips, adding to 111, 112
second computer displays
  about 52-55
  options 55
Send to Compressor button 353
Settings button 135
Settings drop-down button 312
Settings window, compressor interface 408
Shadows 302
shaky shot
  stabilizing, steps for 294-296
shape mask
  about 317, 321
  Add Shape Mask button 318
  and color, combining 325-327
  dragging 319
  keyframing 321
Shape Mask 1 parameter 336
Share Monitor application 345
Show Sound Browser button 14
slide tool
  about 95-99
  keyboard used 100
slip tool
  about 94-99
  keyboard used 100
Smart Collection
  creating, steps for 50, 51
  metadata surface, scratching 52
software iSkySoft
  URL 11
Sorenson Squeeze
  URL 11, 343
sound animating
  in surround panner 164
sound effects
  downloading 157
sound panning 154
speakers
  music, lowering 145-147
sped-up video
  rendering 250
speed
  changing, for range selection tool 249, 250
speed changes
  making 244-249

speed ramps
creating 251
creating, steps for 251-253
split edit 112
stabilizing
shaky shot 294-296
standard definition. *See* **SD video**
standard timeline view (Cmd+7) tab 385
still images
importing 16
importing, steps for 17, 18
storyline
and transitions 111
clips, appending to 70-72
clips, inserting to 70-72
clips, overwriting to 70-72
gap clip, inserting 111
more clips, adding to secondary storyline
111, 112
secondary storylines, editing in 73
style attributes 224
subwoofer. *See* **low-frequency effects (LFE)**
Summary tab 354
surround panner
keyframing in 164
sound animating in 164
surround sound space
working in 160-163
Synchronize Clips (Command + Option + G)
152
synchronized clip 152
sync point 134

T

Tags button 118
tape-based camera
data, importing from 19, 20
tapeless video camera 6-8
Telestream Episode
URL 11, 343
template
custom template, modifying 402
parameters, publishing to 402-405
publishing, for FCPX 400, 401
text
spotlighting 333-336

text style template
creating, steps for 223-226
preset, deleting 227
three-point edit
backtiming 108
creating, steps for 106-108
errors 108
inserting 108
overwriting 108
Three-Way Color Corrector 301
through edit 84
timecode
about 217
adding, steps for 218, 219
location, changing 220
timeline
clip, backtiming in 126
keyframe timing, changing 285-287
transitions parameters, adding 210-213
Timeline Index
checkbox, unchecking 358
Music role checkbox 358, 359
Timeline pane 388
Timeline section, FCPX 40
Title Background placeholder 399
Titles role 355
title templates
custom lower third, creating 392-399
enhancing, with motion 385-391
to do items 118, 119
Toolbar section, FCPX 40
Transform button 23
Transform parameters
resetting 262
Transform properties 289
Transform tool
about 257
button 258
using, steps for 257-261
transitions
about 205
adding, to clips 206-209
and media limits 209, 210
duration, changing 214
parameters, adding in inspector 210-213
parameters, adding in timeline 210-213
parameters, adding in viewer 210-213

Translation Smooth 296
trim tool
  media limit 89
  ripple tool 86-89
  rolling tool 91-93
  slide tool 95-99
  slip tool 95-99

U

Uncompressed option 341
unwanted audio channels
  removing 165
Use audio for synchronization checked 135

V

video
  and audio trimming separately,
     with J cut 112, 113
  and audio trimming separately,
     with L cut 112, 113
  in other formats 343
  logo, adding 182-185
  on computer 350
  or audio, editing 73
  Quadrant math, for standard
     definition video 275
  sharing, on sites 347, 348, 349
  sharing, on YouTube 347-349
  watermark, adding 182-185
Video codec drop-down menu 363
video-in-text effect
  creating, steps for 231, 232
Video Quality option 249
Video tab 178
video wall
  50% scale 275
  creating 271
  creating, steps for 272-274

viewer
  image, moving by keyframing 277-279
  transitions parameters, adding 210-213
Viewer Scale button 385
Viewer section, FCPX 39
View parameter 201
voice
  disguising 193, 194
Voice category 193
voiceover
  auditioning 173
  microphones 173
  recording, steps for 171, 172

W

watermark
  adding, to video 182-185
WB 296
web
  large files sharing, Dropbox used 363-366
white balance. *See* WB

X

XA10 keywords 51
XML
  used, for sharing project with other
     applications 367-372
Xto7 30

Y

YouTube
  video, sharing 347-349

Z

Zoom H1 model
  URL 151

About Packt Publishing

Packt, pronounced 'packed', published its first book "*Mastering phpMyAdmin for Effective MySQL Management*" in April 2004 and subsequently continued to specialize in publishing highly focused books on specific technologies and solutions.

Our books and publications share the experiences of your fellow IT professionals in adapting and customizing today's systems, applications, and frameworks. Our solution based books give you the knowledge and power to customize the software and technologies you're using to get the job done. Packt books are more specific and less general than the IT books you have seen in the past. Our unique business model allows us to bring you more focused information, giving you more of what you need to know, and less of what you don't.

Packt is a modern, yet unique publishing company, which focuses on producing quality, cutting-edge books for communities of developers, administrators, and newbies alike. For more information, please visit our website: www.packtpub.com.

Writing for Packt

We welcome all inquiries from people who are interested in authoring. Book proposals should be sent to author@packtpub.com. If your book idea is still at an early stage and you would like to discuss it first before writing a formal book proposal, contact us; one of our commissioning editors will get in touch with you.

We're not just looking for published authors; if you have strong technical skills but no writing experience, our experienced editors can help you develop a writing career, or simply get some additional reward for your expertise.

Cinema 4D R13 Cookbook

ISBN: 978-1-84969-186-4   Paperback: 514 pages

Elevate your art to the fourth dimension with Cinema 4D

1. Master all the important aspects of Cinema 4D

2. Learn how real-world knowledge of cameras and lighting translates onto a 3D canvas

3. Learn Advanced features like Mograph, Xpresso, and Dynamics.

4. Become an advanced Cinema 4D user with concise and effective recipes

Sony Vegas Pro 11 Beginner's Guide

ISBN: 978-1-84969-170-3   Paperback: 264 pages

Edit videos with style and ease using Vegas Pro

1. Edit slick, professional videos of all kinds with Sony Vegas Pro

2. Learn audio and video editing from scratch

3. Speed up your editing workflow

4. A practical beginner's guide with a fast-paced but friendly and engaging approach towards video editing

Please check **www.PacktPub.com** for information on our titles

Mastering Adobe Captivate 6

ISBN: 978-1-84969-244-1   Paperback: 476 pages

Create Professional ScORM-compliant eLearning content with Adobe Captivate

1. Step by step tutorial to build three projects including a demonstration, a simulation and a random SCORM-compliant quiz featuring all possible question slides.

2. Enhance your projects by adding interactivity, animations, sound and more

3. Publish your project in a wide variety of formats enabling virtually any desktop and mobile devices to play your e-learning content

4. Deploy your e-Learning content on a SCORM or AICC-compliant LMS

Adobe Edge Quickstart Guide

ISBN: 978-1-84969-330-1   Paperback: 136 pages

Quickly produce engaging motion and rich interactivity with Adobe Edge Preview 4 and above

1. Learn to use Adobe's newest application to create engaging motion and rich interactivity

2. Familiarize yourself with the Edge interface and unleash your creativity through standard HTML, CSS, and JavaScript

3. Add motion and interactivity to your websites using Web standards

4. A quickstart guide for creating engaging content with Adobe Edge

Please check **www.PacktPub.com** for information on our titles

www.ingramcontent.com/pod-product-compliance
Lightning Source LLC
LaVergne TN
LVHW062300060326
832902LV00013B/1985